W9-COU-912

The MAILBOX
IDEA MAGAZINE FOR TEACHERS®

2006–2007 YEARBOOK

The Education Center, Inc.
Greensboro, North Carolina

The Mailbox® 2006–2007 Kindergarten–Grade 1 Yearbook

Managing Editor, *The Mailbox* Magazine: Amy Erickson

Editorial Team: Becky S. Andrews, Kimberley Bruck, Diane Badden, Sharon Murphy, Karen A. Brudnak, Hope Rodgers, Dorothy C. McKinney

Production Team: Lori Z. Henry, Margaret Freed (COVER ARTIST), Pam Crane, Rebecca Saunders, Chris Curry, Sarah Foreman, Theresa Lewis Goode, Greg D. Rieves, Eliseo De Jesus Santos II, Barry Slate, Donna K. Teal, Zane Williard, Kitty Campbell, Tazmen Carlisle, Kathy Coop, Marsha Heim, Lynette Dickerson, Mark Rainey

ISBN10 1-56234-814-0
ISBN13 978-156234-814-4
ISSN 1088-5528

Printed in the United States of America.

The Education Center, Inc.
P.O. Box 9753
Greensboro, NC 27429-0753

Look for *The Mailbox® 2007–2008 Kindergarten–Grade 1 Yearbook* in the summer of 2008. The Education Center, Inc., is the publisher of *The Mailbox®, Teacher's Helper®, The Mailbox® BOOKBAG®,* and *Learning®* magazines, as well as other fine products. Look for these wherever quality teacher materials are sold, call 1-800-714-7991, or visit www.themailbox.com.

Contents

Math Units

Science and Social Studies Units

Teacher Resource Units

Thematic Units

Index

ARTS & CRAFTS

Arts & Crafts

The Best Bus!

Follow up a review of bus safety rules with this simple project. In advance, set out shallow containers of black and gray paint. To make one project, round the corners of a 9" x 12" sheet of yellow construction paper. Glue the resulting bus shape in the center of a 9" x 12" sheet of construction paper. Next, dip one end of a large empty thread spool in the black paint. Then make two paint prints to resemble wheels. To make windows, dip a 1" x 2" sponge in the gray paint and make several prints on the bus as shown.

After the paint dries, fold a 1" x 2" yellow construction paper strip in half. Glue one end to the bus as shown, leaving the other end free. Then place a red adhesive dot on each side of the free end. Finally, use a black marker to personalize the project as desired.

Janet Boyce, Cokato, MN

Sunny Windsock

This sunflower decoration leaves no doubt that fall is in the air!

Materials for one windsock:
9" x 12" sheet of brown construction paper
12-inch-long green and yellow crepe paper
   streamers
3 yellow cupcake liners
green construction paper scraps
cotton swab
brown paint in a shallow container
green marker
tape
glue
stapler
string

Steps:
1. Horizontally position the sheet of construction paper and then tape the crepe paper streamers along the bottom edge of it.
2. Turn the paper over. Draw three flower stems.
3. Glue a cupcake liner at the top of each stem.
4. Tear leaf shapes from green construction paper and glue them to the stems.
5. Dip the cotton swab into the brown paint. Make prints on the cupcake liners as shown, reloading the paint as necessary. Allow the paint to dry.
6. Roll the paper into a cylinder shape with the streamers to the inside. Staple the overlapping edges together.
7. To make a hanger, tape a length of string to the inside of the cylinder on opposite sides.

Janet Boyce

Did You Know?
Some sunflowers grow more than 11 feet tall!

Apple Pal

A bushel of these projects makes a great hallway display for open house.

Materials for one apple:
8" x 8" construction paper apple
two 1" x 9" construction paper strips (arms)
two 1" x 12" construction paper strips (legs)
brown construction paper (stem)
construction paper scraps (shoes)
two 3" x 4" green construction paper rectangles
2" x 6" yellow construction paper rectangle
crayons
glue
scissors

Steps:
1. Draw a face on the apple.
2. Accordion-fold the two shorter strips of paper. Glue them to the apple to resemble arms.
3. Accordion-fold the two remaining strips of paper. Glue them to the apple to resemble legs.
4. Cut a stem from construction paper and glue it in place.
5. Fold the two green rectangles in half lengthwise. Cut along each fold to make a leaf. Glue the leaves to the apple.
6. Cut two shoes from construction paper and glue them in place.
7. Cut one end of the yellow rectangle to resemble a pencil tip. Color both ends of the pencil, write your name on it, and then glue it to the project as shown.

Lisa Buchholz, Abraham Lincoln School, Glen Ellyn, IL

Terrific Teddy

With this torn-paper technique, no two bears are alike!

Materials for one bear:
6" x 9" brown construction paper rectangle (body)
five-inch brown construction paper square (head)
two 3" x 6" brown construction paper rectangles (arms)
four 3" x 4" brown construction paper rectangles (legs and feet)
brown construction paper scraps (ears)
colorful construction paper scraps (bow tie)
glue
markers, including black

Steps:
1. Tear the edges of the 6" x 9" rectangle (body), five-inch square (head), and the two long rectangles (arms).
2. Glue the head and arms to the body.
3. Tear the edges of the four 3" x 4" rectangles. Glue them to the project to resemble legs and feet.
4. Tear two ear shapes from construction paper scraps. Glue them in place.
5. Draw a face and add marker details to the paws and ears as shown.
6. Cut a bow tie from construction paper and add desired marker details. Glue the bow tie to the bear.

Laurie Birt, Belinder Elementary, Prairie Village, KS

7

Arts & Crafts

Autumn Colors

Bring the beauty of fall foliage indoors with this colorful wreath. To prepare, thin a shallow container of liquid starch with a small amount of water. For each student, cut the center from a white paper plate.

To make one wreath, place a prepared paper plate on a sheet of waxed paper or another nonstick surface. Then tear small pieces of fall-colored tissue paper. Use a paintbrush and the liquid starch mixture to adhere the tissue paper to the plate. Cover the front of the plate completely, overlapping the tissue paper and allowing it to extend a little beyond the edges of the plate. Let the plate dry overnight. After the plate is dry, twist a six-inch pipe cleaner to make a hanger. Use masking tape to secure the hanger to the back of the wreath. For decoration, glue on a jute bow and fray the ends or glue on a ribbon bow.

adapted from an idea by Janet Boyce
Cokato, MN

Firefighters' Friend

Have students make this cute headband during Fire Prevention Week.

Materials for one headband:
red construction paper copy of the hat pattern on page 17
yellow construction paper copy of the badge pattern on page 17
9" x 12" sheet of white paper
black paint in a shallow container
3" x 24" white construction paper strip (or a white sentence strip)
scissors
glue
tape

Steps:
1. To make two ears, trace your shoes on a sheet of white paper. Cut out the tracings.
2. Use the paint to make black thumbprints on the ears and on the white construction paper strip. Allow the paint to dry.
3. Cut out the hat and badge. Glue the badge to the hat.
4. Glue the hat and ears to the strip as shown.
5. Size the strip to fit your head and tape the ends in place.

Janet Boyce

Did You Know?
When Dalmatians are born, they are all white and have no spots.

Adorable Owl

To make this simple project, round the corners of a six-inch brown construction paper square and a 6" x 9" brown construction paper rectangle. Glue the shapes together, as shown, to resemble an owl's head and body. To make two eyes, cut two yellow circles and color a black circle in the center of each one. To make a beak, fold a small piece of orange paper in half and then cut a triangle along the fold. Glue the beak and eyes in place. Next, cut a 6" x 9" rectangle in half diagonally. Carefully tear the cut edges to achieve a feathered effect. Glue the resulting wings to the owl. Cut two feet from construction paper and then glue them in place. Tear small pieces of brown and gray paper, and glue them to the owl's body. If desired, glue two triangles to the head to create a horned owl.

For a fine-feathered display, post a paper tree on a hallway wall and decorate it with a flock of owls.

Johanna Litts, North Central Elementary, Hermansville, MI

Turkey Time

Post several of these gobblers on a bulletin board to create a three-dimensional holiday display.

Materials for one turkey:
brown construction paper copy of the turkey head and neck pattern on page 17
construction paper circle in each of these sizes: 4½", 6", 7½", 8½"
yellow, red, and brown construction paper scraps
scissors
glue
black marker

Steps:
1. Fringe-cut the edges of the circles.
2. Cut out the turkey head and neck. Draw two eyes on the head.
3. To make a beak, fold a yellow rectangle in half and then cut a triangle along the fold. Cut a wattle from red paper. Glue the beak and wattle to the head.
4. Glue the center of the 7½-inch circle to the 8½-inch circle, keeping the edges free. In the same manner, glue on the six-inch circle and then the 4½-inch circle.
5. Glue the head (not the neck) of the turkey to the smallest circle. Tuck the end of the neck under the second smallest circle, as shown, and then glue it in place.
6. Cut two legs from brown paper. Glue them to the back of the project.

Karen Adams Stone, West Elementary, Goodland, KS

Arts & Crafts

Dancing Snowpal

Welcome winter with this cool mobile!

Materials for one snowpal:
2 white circles of each of these sizes: 4", 5", 7"
various colors of paper scraps, including orange, brown, and black
scissors
glue
black marker
tape
24" length of string

Steps:

1. Cut out two triangles (noses) from orange construction paper. Glue each triangle on a four-inch white circle. Add marker details to complete each face.
2. Place a seven-inch circle on a work surface and tape one end of the string to it.
3. Position a five-inch circle above the taped circle. Then tape the string to it as shown.
4. Place a four-inch circle facedown above the five-inch taped circle. (Be sure that the face is oriented correctly.) Tape the string to the circle.
5. Cut two arms and two boots from construction paper. Glue them to the snowpal.
6. Glue each remaining circle to the matching taped circle, keeping the faces to the outside. Press the edges of the circles together.
7. Decorate both middle circles as desired.
8. Tie the free end of the string to make a hanger.

Johanna Litts, North Central Elementary, Hermansville, MI

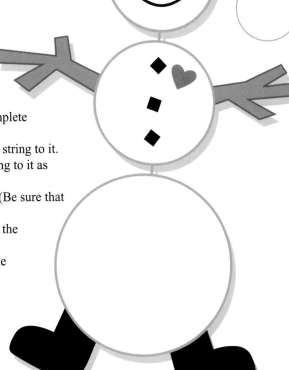

Bountiful Branches

To make this unique tree, paint one nine-inch uncoated paper plate green. After the paint dries, cut the plate into four different pie-shaped pieces. Make short cuts in the fluted edge of each piece, cutting from the outer edge toward the point.

Next, glue the largest piece of the plate near the bottom of a sheet of construction paper with its point at the top. Glue the next largest piece above it, slightly overlapping the two pieces as shown. Glue on the remaining two pieces in a similar manner. Gently spread apart the fluted edges of the plate where they were cut. Then cut a tree trunk from brown construction paper and glue it in place. Finally, decorate the tree with chosen arts-and-crafts materials, such as sequins, glitter, and paper shapes.

Janet Boyce, Cokato, MN

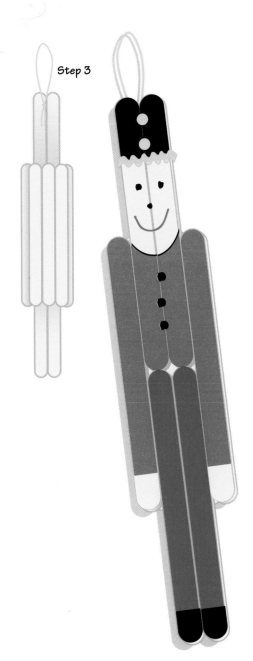

Step 3

Toy Soldier

This cute holiday ornament stands at attention!

Materials for one soldier:
9 craft sticks (not jumbo craft sticks)
waxed paper
glue
black, red, and blue permanent markers
hole puncher
scrap of yellow construction paper
narrow gold rickrack
string (or gold cord)

Steps:
1. Place two craft sticks side by side on a piece of waxed paper. Position two other craft sticks directly below them.
2. Place one craft stick on each side of the grouped sticks so that the tops of them are about halfway down the first two sticks.
3. To secure the sticks, glue three craft sticks on top of the grouped sticks as shown. (This side of the project will be the back.) Allow the glue to dry.
4. On the front of the ornament, illustrate a face and a uniform similar to the one shown.
5. Hole-punch two yellow circles. Glue the circles and a small piece of rickrack to the hat as shown.
6. Color the back of the ornament red. Use a generous amount of glue to secure a loop of string for a hanger.

Lori Medlock, Alimacani Elementary, Jacksonville, FL

"Hand-Some" Kinara

Add this simple project to your Kwanzaa celebration. To prepare, set out shallow containers of red, black, green, yellow, and brown paint. Also set out paper towels or wet wipes for easy cleanup. To make one project, make the following paint prints as shown:
   three red candles: index, middle, and ring fingers
   one black candle: index finger
   three green candles: index, middle, and ring fingers
   yellow flames: fingertip
   brown kinara: palm and fingers, excluding thumb
After the paint dries, glue the paper to a slightly larger piece of construction paper to frame it. Or glue it to the front of a construction paper Kwanzaa card.

Lisa Crystal
Bret Harte Elementary
Burbank, CA

Arts & Crafts

Heart Art

Drops of diluted food coloring give this project the look of tie-dye. In advance, set out containers of food coloring that you have diluted with water. Place an eyedropper beside each container. To make one project, place a paper towel on a piece of waxed paper or another nonstick surface. Use the eyedroppers to squeeze drops of food coloring all over the paper towel. Then allow the paper towel to dry. To make a frame, fold a sheet of paper in half. Draw half of a large heart on the fold, as shown, and cut it out. Then unfold the paper and discard the solid heart. If desired, draw a decorative border around the frame opening. Glue the frame to the paper towel and then trim any excess paper towel.

Janet Boyce
Cokato, MN

Great for Giving

No doubt your students would love to present this Valentine's Day wreath to their families! To prepare, make a supply of hearts in various colors and sizes. (For easy preparation, use a die-cutter to make large hearts and a heart paper punch to make small hearts.) For each student, cut out the center of a white paper plate. To make a wreath, place a prepared plate upside down on a newspaper-covered surface. Sponge-paint the plate a chosen color. Allow the paint to dry. Then glue the hearts on the wreath as desired. After the glue dries, punch two holes at the top of the wreath. Thread a length of ribbon through the holes and then tie the ribbon into a bow. Attach a loop of string to the back of the project to create a hanger.

Melissa Merritt
East End Elementary
Humboldt, TN

Woolly Lamb

To prepare this adorable project, tape a piece of bubble wrap to a disposable cup, as shown, with the textured side outward. Also, set out a shallow container of white paint. To make a lamb, place a 9" x 12" sheet of gray paper and a 5" x 6" piece of gray paper on a newspaper-covered surface. Dip the bubble-wrap into the paint and then make prints all over the gray paper, reloading the paint as needed. Allow the paint to dry.

Next, trim the large paper to make a body and the small paper to make the woolly top of a lamb's head. Cut a tail from the scraps. Then cut a head similar to the one shown from a five-inch gray construction paper square. Also, cut one ear and four legs from gray construction paper. Glue the pieces together as shown. Then draw a face and color the lamb's hooves.

St. Patrick's Day Pal

Decorate a March bulletin board with several of these wee projects.

Materials for one leprechaun:
6" skin-tone construction paper square
5" x 6" green construction paper rectangle
1½" x 8" green construction paper strip
1" x 6" yellow construction paper strip
scissors
crayons
glue
shredded orange paper
pencil with an unused eraser
green paint in a shallow container
glitter (optional)

Steps:
1. To make a head, round the corners of one side of the skin-tone paper. Draw a face, orange hair, and an orange beard as shown.
2. Glue the shredded paper to the beard.
3. Round one short side of the green rectangle to make the top of a hat. Glue the hat to the head.
4. Glue the green paper strip to the hat to make a brim.
5. Dip the pencil eraser into the paint. Make clusters of prints on the yellow paper to resemble shamrocks. Allow the paint to dry.
6. Draw stems on the shamrocks. If desired, glue glitter to the yellow strip for decoration.
7. Glue the yellow strip above the hat brim.

Janet Boyce
Cokato, MN

Arts & Crafts

Vs by the Bunch

V is for vase, violet, and vinegar! Cut out a supply of *v*'s from violet tissue paper and make a 4" x 6" tagboard vase for students to use as a tracer. Also, set out a shallow container of vinegar.

To make one project, trace the vase on violet paper and then cut out the tracing. Add desired crayon decorations to the vase. Then glue it at the bottom of a vertical 12" x 18" sheet of white paper. Next, draw leafy stems similar to the ones shown. Arrange several tissue paper *v*'s on the stems as desired. Then use a cotton swab to dab vinegar on the letters until they are saturated. After the letters dry, discard them. (The letters will lift slightly as they dry.) **For an easier version,** glue violet construction paper *v*'s to the stems instead of applying vinegar to tissue paper letters.

Bernette V. Alegre
Olive Branch Elementary
Portsmouth, VA

Bluebird Buddies

For easy management, work with small groups of students to complete this springtime project. In advance, draw a 4" x 6" rectangle. On each long side of the rectangle, draw a 1½-inch line one inch from each short side as shown. Copy the rectangle on white construction paper to make a class supply.

To begin the project, illustrate the blank side of the rectangle to resemble a brick wall and then cut on the lines. With adult assistance, fold and crease the resulting flaps, keeping the coloring to the outside, and then staple the flaps together as shown. To make a bird, glue two one-inch blue pom-poms in a stack on the wall. Fold a small piece of yellow paper in half and cut a triangle on the fold. Glue the resulting beak and a construction paper tail to the bird. Then dip the end of a paintbrush in black paint and make two dot eyes. Make another bluebird in the same manner. **For an easier version,** instead of making a wall, color a small paper plate green and glue shredded paper to it to make a nest.

Lisa Harris
Westernport Elementary
Westernport, MD

Sweet Bunny

To make this Easter scene, fringe-cut one long side of a 4½" x 12" strip of green paper. Glue it to a horizontal 9" x 12" sheet of blue paper, keeping the fringed edge free. Next, trace your shoe on a piece of white paper. Cut out the tracing and draw a bunny face on it as shown. Cut two bunny ears from white paper and color the inner portions pink. Roll the tip of each ear around a pencil. After you glue the ears to the bunny, glue the bunny to the grass and glue a cotton ball to the bunny to resemble a tail.

To complete the scene, fringe-cut one long side of a 2" x 9" strip of green paper. Glue the strip along the bottom of the project, keeping the fringed edge free. Then add details such as torn-paper clouds and flowers made with crumpled pieces of tissue paper.

Sue Lewis Lein
Wauwatosa, WI

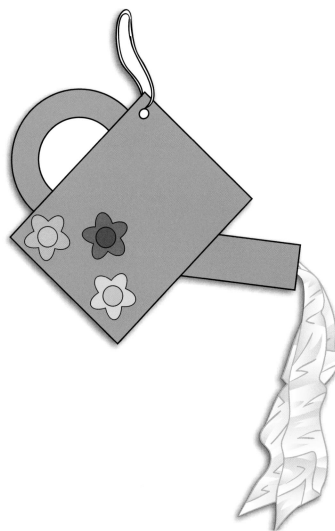

Watering Can Wonder

When you suspend this eye-catching mobile, it will look as though water is pouring from its spout!

Materials for one watering can:

two 6" x 8" construction paper rectangles   crayons
3" x 6" construction paper rectangle   glue
two 2" x 6" construction paper rectangles   scissors
2 strips of iridescent cellophane   masking tape
flower cutouts   hole puncher
   string

Directions:

1. Add crayon details to the flowers if desired. Glue the flowers to the two large rectangles for decoration.
2. Cut a handle from the 3" x 6" rectangle. Glue it to the blank side of one large rectangle.
3. Glue one 2" x 6" rectangle to the blank side of the same large rectangle to make a spout. Tape one end of each cellophane strip to the top of the spout. Glue another 2" x 6" strip to the taped spout, aligning the edges.
4. Glue the two large rectangles together, flower sides out.
5. Hole-punch the watering can as shown and thread a length of string through the hole to make a hanger.

adapted from an idea by Linda Oesterle
Eggert Road Elementary
Orchard Park, NY

Arts & Crafts

Winged Wonder

Create a three-dimensional display with several of these butterflies! To prepare, make two copies of the butterfly pattern on page 18. Cut out one pattern along the bold outline. Cut out the inner wing on the other pattern for students to use as a tracer; then discard the rest of that pattern. For each student, fold a 9" x 12" sheet of construction paper in half. Trace the intact butterfly pattern on the fold and then cut out the tracing. Set out colorful tissue paper rectangles and a container of liquid starch thinned with water.

To make one butterfly, trace the inner wing four times on a sheet of white construction paper. Use a paintbrush and the liquid starch mixture to adhere tissue paper to the wings. Let the wings dry for several hours and then cut them out. Next, color the body on the front and back of a folded butterfly. Then unfold the butterfly and glue the inner wings to both sides of it as shown. Glue two narrow strips of black paper to the head to make antennae. Glue the body and head closed to complete the project.

Maureen Glennon
Faller Elementary
Ridgecrest, CA

Simply a Bee!

Geometric shapes make this insect project a snap! To begin, draw a face on a four-inch yellow circle. Glue two narrow black rectangles to the back of the head to make antennae. Next, color black stripes on a six-inch circle. Then glue the head to the striped circle as shown. Glue a black triangle to the bottom of the project. To make wings, cut two 2½" x 5" ovals from waxed paper and then glue them to the back of the project.

Debra R. Paez
Graham Elementary
Austin, TX

Firefighter Badge and Hat Patterns
Use with "Firefighters' Friend" on page 8.

Turkey Head and Neck Pattern
Use with "Turkey Time" on page 9.

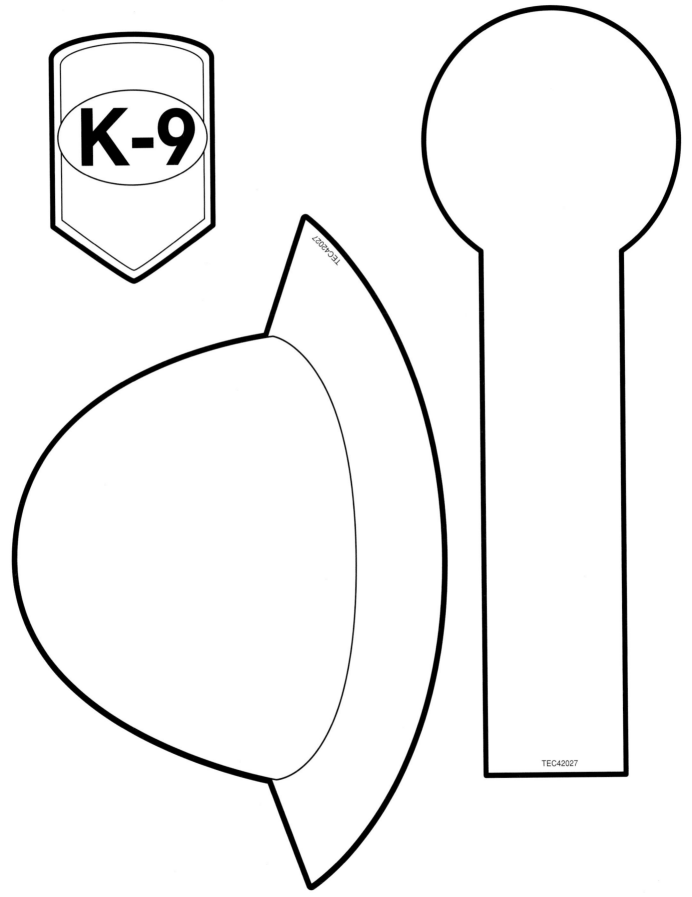

K-9

TEC42027

TEC42027

Butterfly Pattern

Use with "Winged Wonder" on page 16.

TEC42031

Shell Pattern

Use with "From Plain to Perfect" on page 226 and "Moving On" and "Seaworthy Neighborhood" on page 227.

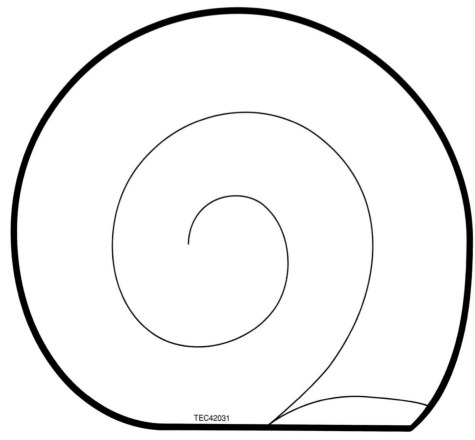

TEC42031

BUILDING MATH SKILLS

Building Math Skills

Deck of Sums

Beginning addition

Success is guaranteed when students use playing cards to model math problems! Remove the face cards from a deck of cards. Mask any extra symbols so that the total number of symbols on each card matches the numeral. To create and solve a problem, ask two students to each take one card at random. Have them say an addition problem with their numbers and then count the symbols on the cards to determine the sum.

For a whole-class activity, give one card to each student. Then have the youngsters walk around the room as you play some music. After a few moments, stop the music. Instruct each student to pair up with a nearby classmate. Have the students in each twosome create and solve a problem as described above. **For an easier version,** use only cards with the numbers 2 through 5.

Patrice Bryson
Hawk Ridge Elementary
Charlotte, NC

Shapes Everywhere

Geometry

To introduce this booklet project, encourage students to look for shapes at home and at school. After discussing their observations, give each youngster a copy of the booklet pages on page 26. Have each student illustrate each shape to resemble a chosen object. Help her complete the sentences to match her illustrations. Then instruct her to cut out her pages and stack them between two 4" x 5" construction paper rectangles. After you staple the stack at the top, ask her to title the booklet as desired and sign her name.

Tammy Lutz
George E. Greene Elementary
Bad Axe, MI

"Hand-y" Comparisons

Number sense

Since no materials are needed for this class activity, it's a perfect choice when you have just a few minutes. Pair students. (If there is an odd number of students, plan to participate.) Next, have each student stand facing his partner with his hands behind his back. Then lead the class in saying, "One, two, three, show me!" At this signal, each student holds up one or more fingers on one hand. The students in each twosome softly use the word *more* or *equal* to compare the number of fingers each of them is holding up. Then they put their hands behind their backs to show that they are ready for another comparison. **For more advanced students,** have them use both hands and compare numbers up to ten.

Nancy Aquino
Steele School
Baldwin, NY

Five is more than three.

Building Math Skills

Seeing Fives
Number sense

Use yes-or-no questions to promote skip-counting. Here's how! Make a two-column poster titled as shown and with nearly as many rows as you have students. Color the rows in groups of five, beginning at the top. (Leave any extra rows blank.) Then display the poster within student reach, keeping the sides free.

To begin, pose a yes-or-no question to students. Then have each youngster indicate her response by clipping a clothespin to the first empty row in the appropriate column. Next, ask students to tell how many clothespins are in each column and to explain how they determined the totals. As appropriate, guide students to realize how the groups of five can help them determine the totals quickly.

Allison Pratt
Onalaska Kindergarten
Onalaska, WI

Hopping Ahead
Addition

This number line idea makes adding bunches of fun! Have each student color and cut out a copy of the carrot number line and a rabbit pattern on page 27. Instruct him to glue together the number line as shown and to fold back the tabs on his rabbit. Next, invite a student to roll a die. Have each youngster stand his rabbit on the corresponding point on his number line. To determine the number that students will add, ask a student to roll the die again. Then, as you lead students in the song below, substitute the appropriate numbers and have youngsters move their rabbits as indicated. Afterward, write the corresponding number sentence on the board.

(sung to the tune of "Little Bunny Foo Foo")

Little bunny rabbit,
Hopping during math time.
Starting on the number [3],
Then counting on [two] more.

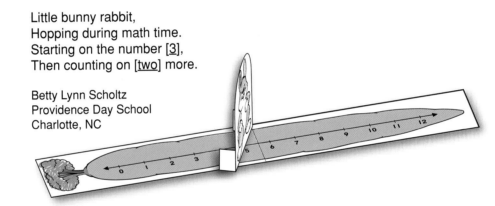

Betty Lynn Scholtz
Providence Day School
Charlotte, NC

Guess Who!
Ordinal numbers

For this math mystery, make five copies of the apple card on page 27. Color one apple green and four apples red. To begin, ask five students to stand side by side at the front of the classroom and put their hands behind their backs. Put an apple card in each standing student's hands without revealing the apples. Next, say, "Apple, apple, who has the green apple?" Have a seated student use an ordinal number to describe the student he thinks has the apple. Then instruct the corresponding youngster to show her apple. If it is green, have her trade places with the youngster who made the guess. If it is not green, have students continue guessing as described. **For more advanced students,** use more red apples.

Angie Kutzer
Garrett Elementary
Mebane, NC

The fourth person has it!

Do you like chocolate milk?

Yes	No

Building Math Skills

Check the Clock!

Telling time

This kid-pleasing activity encourages students to read the clock throughout the school day. On the board, list in chronological order several times to the hour (or half hour). Write your name beside the last time and a different student's name beside each of the other times. When it is the first listed time, place a small stuffed toy at the corresponding student's workspace. Explain that the youngster is responsible for delivering the toy to the next listed person at the designated time. When that child receives the toy, encourage him to pass the toy to the next person at the appropriate time, and so on. Repeat the activity if necessary to give each youngster a turn with the toy.

Sheila Criqui-Kelley
Lebo Elementary
Lebo, KS

At the Bakery

Beginning subtraction

A catchy chant and simple manipulatives make this idea a treat! To prepare, have each child make five round construction paper cookies with sprinkles on them. Instruct her to glue a copy of the chant card on page 28 to a white paper lunch bag (bakery bag). Then have her stand her bag open and place her cookies beside it.

To play one round, lead students in the chant, prompting each child to put one cookie in her bag during the last line. Then have students tell how many cookies they have left. Continue with additional rounds until students "purchase" all of the cookies. **For more advanced students,** have youngsters cut out more cookies. Instruct them to "purchase" more than one cookie during each round and write each corresponding subtraction sentence.

Cookies

[Five] yummy cookies at the bakery shop,
Round and sweet with sprinkles on top.
A child came in with some money in her hand.
She bought [one] cookie(s), and away she ran.

Shelly Man
Bais Rachel School
Brooklyn, NY

Bear Facts

Addition and subtraction

Who better to help students explore fact families than the well-known family of the three bears? Program a copy of the bear cards on page 28 with the numbers in a chosen fact family so that the largest number is on Papa Bear, the second largest number is on Mama Bear, and the smallest number is on Baby Bear. Instruct each student to lightly color a copy of the programmed cards. Then have him cut out the cards and a copy of the symbol cards (page 28). Next, guide students to form addition and subtraction facts with their cards and write the number sentences on provided paper. Guide students to notice that the largest number in a fact family is the last number in an addition fact and the first number in a subtraction fact.

Amy DePew
Frazer Elementary
Canton, OH

$3 + 2 = 5$
$2 + 3 = 5$
$5 - 2 = 3$
$5 - 3 = 2$

Building Math Skills

"Tree-mendous" Shapes

Geometry

This song activity can be adapted to review any shapes. Post a large tree. Cut from construction paper one red rhombus, two blue circles, and the shapes listed below for the third through the fifth days. Place the shapes near the tree. To begin, lead youngsters in singing the first verse. Then ask a student to attach the corresponding shape to the tree. Continue in the same manner with the remaining verses and shapes. After students are familiar with the song and shapes, have each youngster draw a large tree. Then sing the song with students, allowing time after each verse for each child to draw the appropriate shape(s) on his tree.

Hilda Fields
Georgetown Elementary
Savannah, GA

(sung to the tune of "The 12 Days of Christmas")

On the first day of math class, my
     teacher gave to me
A red rhombus for my shape tree.

On the second day of math class, my
     teacher gave to me
Two blue circles
And a red rhombus for my shape tree.

Use the phrases below to continue with verses 3–5, repeating each previous line in descending order.
Third day: three yellow hexagons
Fourth day: four green triangles
Fifth day: five orange squares

Three in a Row

Coins

For this version of tic-tac-toe, pair students. Give each twosome a copy of the tic-tac-toe grids on page 29 and markers of two different colors. Assign each player a symbol (X or O). To play one round, Player 1 names the coin in a chosen grid space. If she is correct, she labels the space with her symbol. If she is incorrect, her turn is over. Player 2 takes a turn in the same manner. Alternate play continues until one player claims three spaces in a diagonal, horizontal, or vertical row and is declared the winner, or until all the spaces are claimed and the game is declared a draw.

Kathy Hamby
Smiths Station Primary School
Smiths, AL

How Tall?

Nonstandard measurement

Invite students to size up their heights in two different ways! Place at a center a supply of two different-size manipulatives and recording sheets similar to the one shown. For each student, cut a length of adding machine tape that is equal to his height and write his name on it. Instruct each child to use the manipulatives to measure his adding machine tape to the nearest whole unit and have him complete a recording sheet. After each student finishes the activity, prompt a class discussion about the results. Lead students to realize that it takes more small units and fewer large units to measure the same length.

Kate Rader
Governor Bent Elementary
Albuquerque, NM

Name Carson	
Recording Sheet	
How many straws?	How many crayons?
about 6	about 12

Building Math Skills

Divided Equally
Fractions

To prepare this pocket chart activity, cut out a copy of the fraction game cards on page 30 and mount them on colorful tagboard. For each figure, label a blank white card with the corresponding fraction. Place all of the cards in a pocket chart in random order so that the backs of the cards face outward.

To take a turn, a student turns over one colorful card and then one white card. If a Fraction Action card is revealed, he draws a shape on the board, divides it in half, and then sets the card aside. If he turns over two matching fraction cards, he removes them from the chart. If he turns over two fraction cards that do not match, he flips them back over. Students take turns in this manner until the pocket chart is empty. **For an easier version,** make two copies of the game cards and set aside the Fraction Action cards. Have students play as in the traditional game of Concentration and identify the number of equal parts on each card.

adapted from an idea by
    Heather E. Graley
Grace Christian School
Blacklick, OH

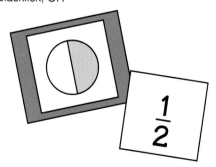

Make Ten!
Number sense

For this number combination game, remove the face cards and jokers from two decks of playing cards. Gather a small group of students and explain that aces are worth one. Deal each player five cards and then stack the remaining cards facedown. Next, ask each player to set aside any tens she has or any two cards that equal ten, such as a six and a four. Then instruct students to continue play as in the traditional game of Go Fish, but have them make combinations that equal ten instead of pairs of matching numbers. **For an easier version,** spread out selected cards faceup and help students create pairs of cards that equal ten.

Danielle Peyton
South Side School
Effingham, IL

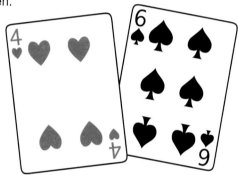

"Cent-sational" Roundup
Money

Cash in on this idea for a variety of coin skills! Twist pipe cleaners together to make two circles several inches in diameter and then place them on a flat surface. Set a different assortment of coins in each circle. Next, have students sit around the circles. Pass a clean flyswatter to one youngster. Then pose a question, such as "Which circle has a quarter?" or "Which circle has the greater value?" and ask the youngster to swat the corresponding circle. After you confirm the correct answer, have him pass the flyswatter to the next student. Continue with different questions as described, periodically changing the assortments of coins.

Maryann Bennett
Goodyear, AZ

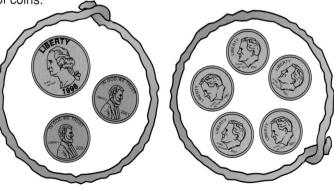

Building Math Skills

Sizing Up Objects
Comparing lengths

To prepare for this measurement activity, gather a ruler, several objects that are longer than the ruler, and several objects that are shorter than the ruler. Lay the ruler on a work surface and have students sit facing it. Place the objects nearby. Next, have a youngster hold a chosen object near the ruler. Ask him to compare the lengths of the object and ruler with his classmates' input. If the object is longer than the ruler, have the youngster place it above the ruler. If the object is shorter than the ruler, instruct him to place it below the ruler. Have students sort the remaining objects in the same manner. **For more advanced students,** after youngsters sort the objects, invite them to arrange the objects from the shortest to the longest.

Maryann Bennett, Goodyear, AZ

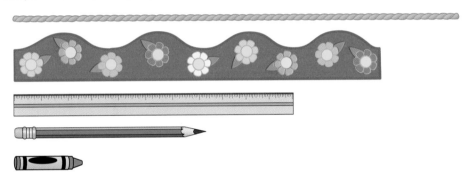

How Many Consonants?
Subtraction

No doubt students will love using their names with this letter-perfect approach to writing number sentences! Give each youngster a copy of a recording sheet similar to the one below. Next, write a student's first name on the board. Have each child write the name in the first column on her paper. Instruct her to circle the vowels. Then have her subtract the number of vowels from the total number of letters. Confirm the correct subtraction sentence. Write another child's name on the board to continue. Repeat the activity as needed to feature each student's name.

Angelika Marquis
Amanda Rochell Elementary
Rockwall, TX

Recording Sheet	
Stefano	7 - 3 = 4
Mark	4 - 1 = 3
Mario	5 - 3 = 2

Follow the Shapes!
Identifying solid figures

Give geometry a festive flair with this party-themed trail game! Color a copy of the gameboard on page 31 and a copy of the game cards on page 32. Cut out the cards and gather two game markers. Arrange for two students to play the game at one time. To begin, players stack the cards facedown and place the game markers on Start. To take a turn, a player takes the top card and names the solid figure pictured. Then he advances his marker to the closest corresponding figure on the path. If there are no corresponding figures ahead on the path, his turn is over. Students take turns as described, reusing the cards if needed, until one player reaches Finish.

Karen Cook
McDonough Primary School
McDonough, GA

Booklet Pages

Use with “Shapes Everywhere” on page 20.

A square is like

____

A circle is like

____

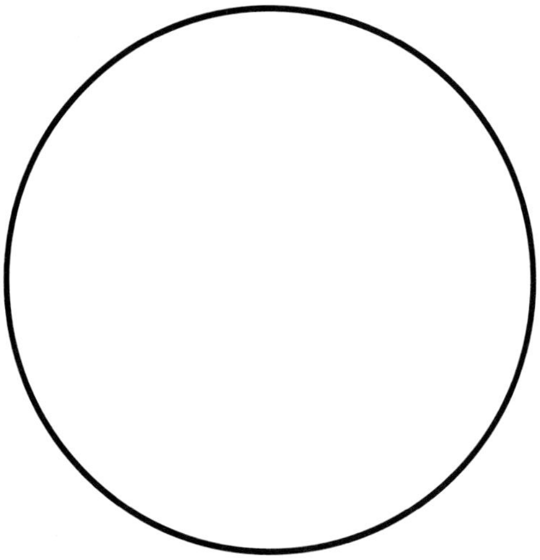

A triangle is like

____

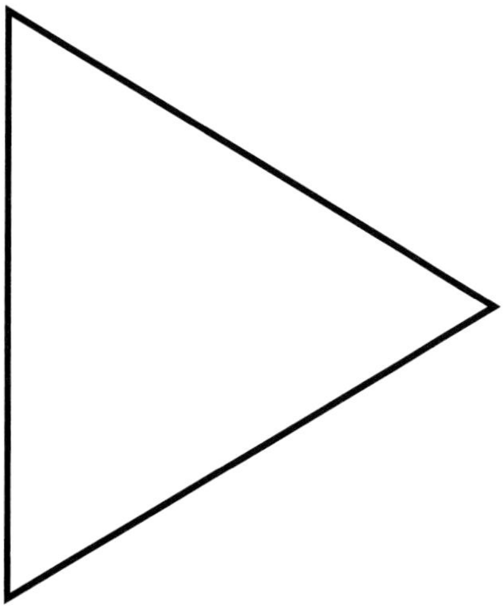

A rectangle is like

____

©The Mailbox® • TEC42026 • Aug./Sept. 2006

Carrot Number Line

Use with "Hopping Ahead" on page 21.

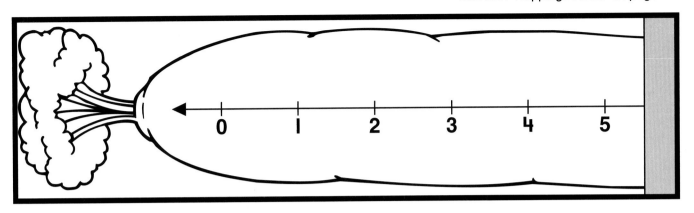

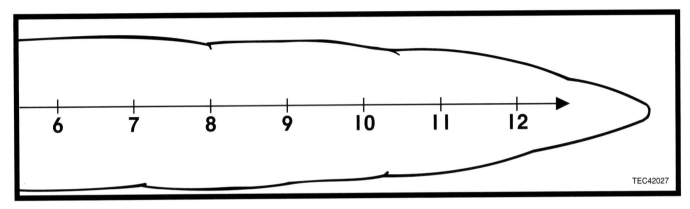

TEC42027

Rabbit Patterns

Use with "Hopping Ahead" on page 21.

Apple Card

Use with "Guess Who!" on page 21.

TEC42027

TEC42027

TEC42027

Chant Card
Use with "At the Bakery" on page 22.

Cookies

[Five] yummy cookies at the bakery shop,

Round and sweet with sprinkles on top.

A child came in with some money in her hand.

She bought [one] cookie(s), and away she ran.

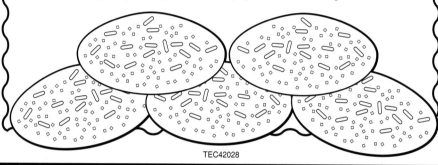

TEC42028

Symbol Cards
Use with "Bear Facts" on page 22.

Bear Cards
Use with "Bear Facts" on page 22.

| **Papa Bear** | **Mama Bear** | **Baby Bear** |

Three in a Row

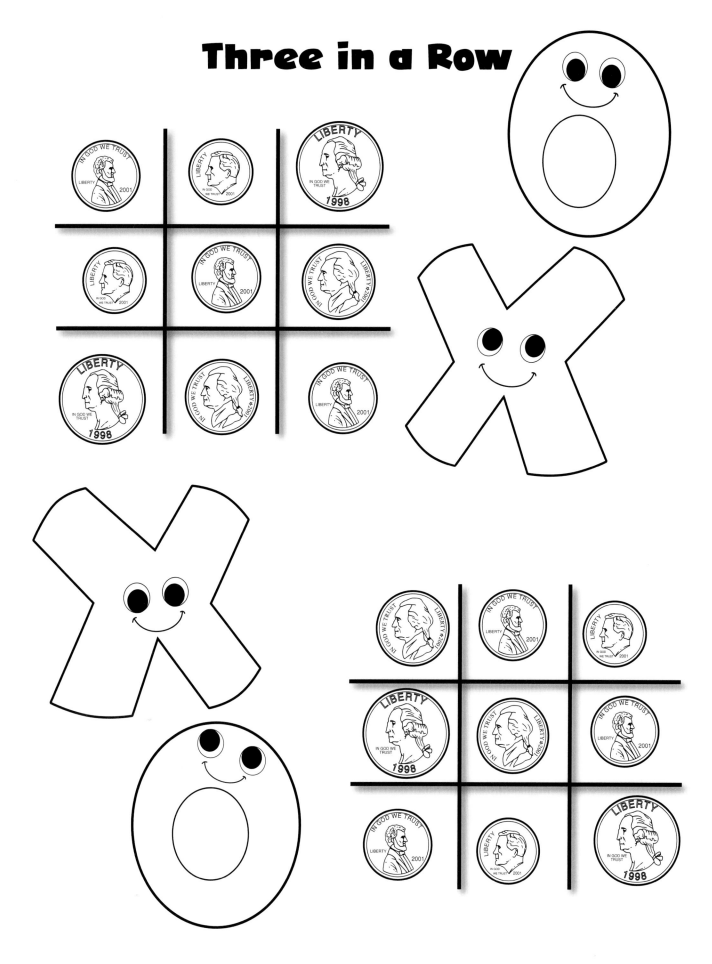

Note to the teacher: Use with "Three in a Row" on page 23.

29

Fraction Game Cards

Use with "Divided Equally" on page 24.

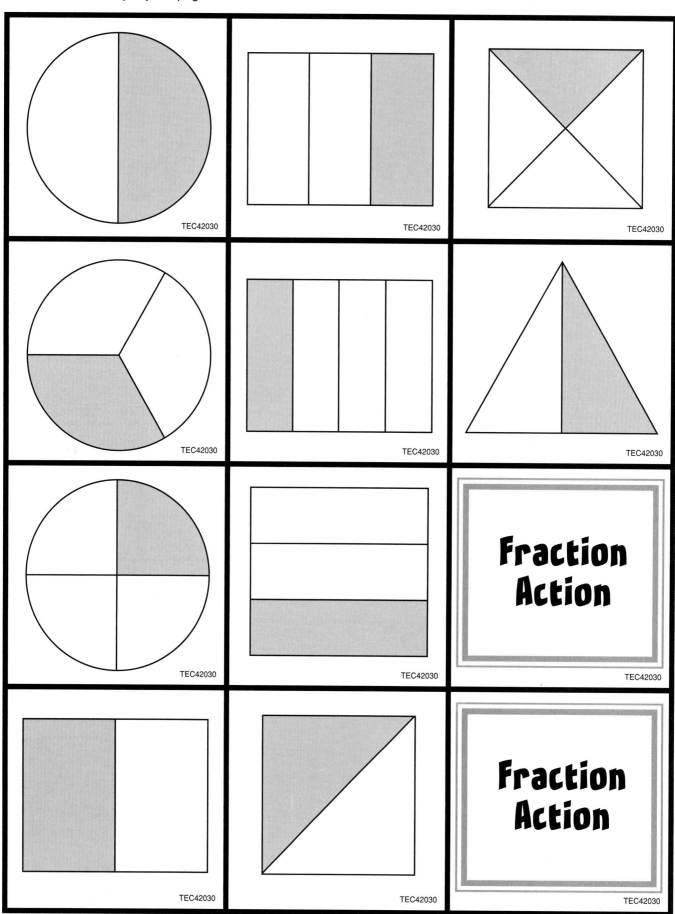

TEC42030

TEC42030

TEC42030

TEC42030

TEC42030

TEC42030

TEC42030

TEC42030

Fraction Action

TEC42030

TEC42030

TEC42030

Fraction Action

TEC42030

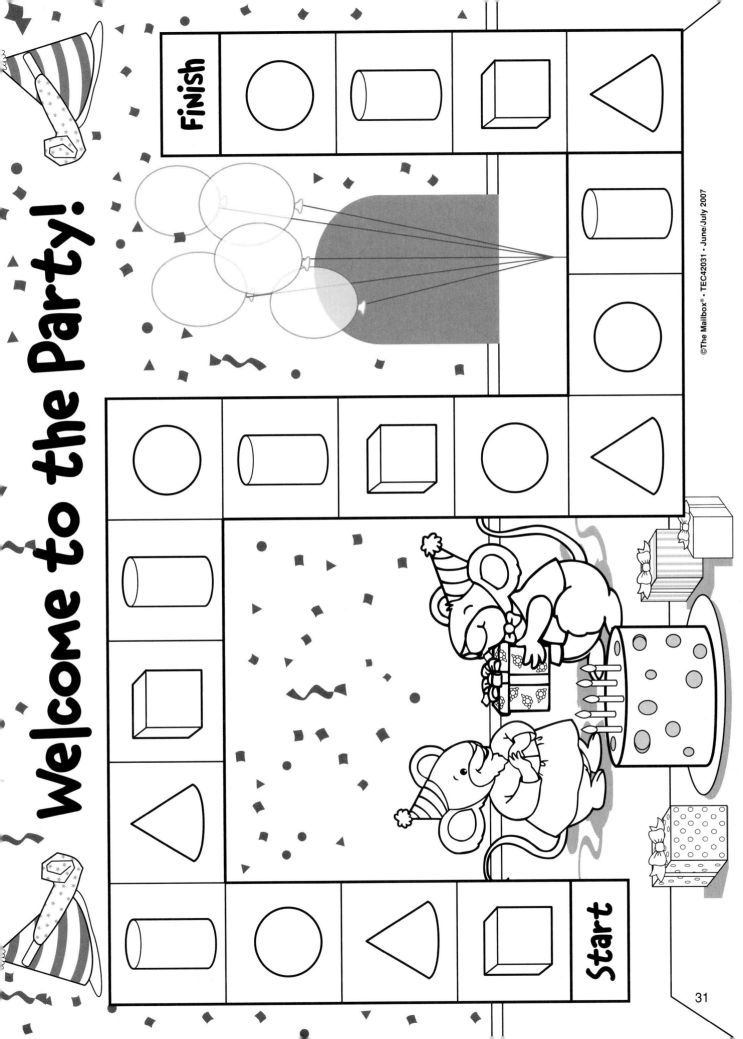

Welcome to the Party!

Finish

Start

©The Mailbox® • TEC42031 • June/July 2007

Solid Figure Game Cards

Use with "Follow the Shapes!" on page 25.

TEC42031

TEC42031

TEC42031

TEC42031

TEC42031

TEC42031

TEC42031

TEC42031

TEC42031

TEC42031

TEC42031

TEC42031

Classroom Displays

CLASSROOM DISPLAYS

Hooray For School!

Jon

Marcel

Cara

Livvy

Look to the left
And then look to the right.
See all of us smiling,
So happy and bright.

"Why are you all smiling?"
You may ask right away.
The answer is easy:
We are at school today!

Veronica

Luis

Nick

Joelle

At the beginning of the school year, have each student draw a self-portrait. Mount each drawing on construction paper and label it with the child's name. Post the poem and title shown on a hallway wall. Then arrange students' artwork as desired to the left and right of the poem.

Margaret Elliott, Madison-Ridgeland Academy, Madison, MS

Our Class Roundup

Get year-round use out of this display by periodically updating it with seasonal decorations. Use a digital camera to take an individual photo of each student (head-and-torso view). Crop the photos and enlarge them as desired. Or have each student illustrate a head-and-torso cutout to resemble himself. Display the photos or illustrations above a fence on a hallway wall. Add hats, a title, and any desired decorations.

Becky Lance, Covington Elementary, Ft. Wayne, IN

Here's a stellar way to welcome students. Cover a board with blue or black paper. Post a rocket and a title similar to the one shown. Write each student's name on a separate star and add it to the board. Then embellish the display with adhesive foil stars.

Mary Delak
Washington Elementary
Ely, MN

It's full speed ahead with this birthday timeline! Post the title shown and a train engine. Label a separate boxcar for each month of the year. Then arrange the boxcars in chronological order and add balloons for decoration. Glue a photo of each student on a separate construction paper gift box. Label each box with the child's name and birthdate. Then load each boxcar with the appropriate gifts!

LeChelle Garnes, Sheehy Elementary, Tampa, FL

For this fun word review, frame a board or wall space with bulletin board trim. Post the title shown and arrange eight word cards around it. Number eight pumpkins from 1 to 8 and add curling ribbon to resemble vines. Then conceal each card with a pumpkin, securing the pumpkin only at the top. Have youngsters spin a spinner like the one shown. After each spin, lift the corresponding pumpkin and ask students to read the word revealed.

Elaina Hall
Mapleton Elementary
Mt. Sterling, KY

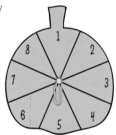

No patterns are needed to create this Halloween display! Instruct each student to tear a sheet of white paper to resemble a ghost. Have him accordion-fold four strips of colorful paper and glue them to his ghost to create arms and legs. Then ask him to add two construction paper hands, two construction paper ovals for shoes, and a personalized trick-or-treat bag. Showcase students' resulting trick-or-treaters on a titled board.

Pam Ingram, Davenport A+ School, Lenoir, NC

To make this Veterans Day display, ask each student to color a copy of a United States flag. Invite her to write holiday-related words or sentences on the white stripes. Curl lengths of red, white, and blue curling ribbon and attach them to each flag as shown. Post students' completed flags on a titled board and then embellish the display with stars.

Linda Teagarden, Dennett Road Elementary, Oakland, MD

A Feast of Good Work

These cute gobblers show off student work samples. Have each youngster illustrate a brown circle and glue it to a scalloped shape to resemble a turkey as shown. Then write each student's name on his turkey's feathers. Post a title and each student's turkey along with a sample of his best work.

Here's a "de-light-ful" way to welcome the holiday season. Ask each youngster to position a construction paper holiday lightbulb with the base at the top. To personalize the lightbulb, have her write her name and draw and/or write a holiday wish. Post a desired title. Then display students' lightbulbs on ribbon around the title.

Hope Nolte
Elizabeth Waters Elementary
Fond du Lac, WI

Spark creative thinking with this imaginative display. Have each student use chosen arts-and-crafts materials to make a snowpal. Then ask him to write on a speech bubble a sentence that his frosty friend might say (or dictate the sentence for you to write). Showcase each youngster's snowpal with his sentence on a titled board.

Stephanie Schmidt, Lester B. Pearson Public School, Waterloo, Ontario, Canada

Use this cool idea to follow up any penguin book. Cover the top portion of a board with blue paper and the lower portion with snowy hills. Add snowflakes, a title, and a sign with a chosen book title. Have each student write about her favorite part of the book on a penguin (pattern on page 46) and draw a relevant illustration on a sign. Instruct her to color the penguin, cut it out, and then glue the sign to it. Arrange students' penguins on the board as desired.

Annalisa C. Parent, Saint Mary's School, Middlebury, VT

Warm Up to Math Facts!

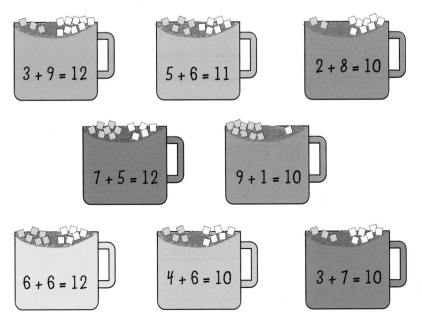

To create this math display, have each student color the top part of a colorful mug to resemble hot chocolate. Ask him to write an addition fact on the mug and glue on pink and white rectangles (marshmallows) to illustrate it. Post students' mugs with the title shown. **For an easier version,** choose a number. Have each child use pink and white marshmallows to make that number on his mug. Then label the mugs with the corresponding combinations.

Melissa Polashock
Hillcrest Elementary
Somerset, NJ

To create this sweet holiday display, ask each student to glue a heart on a diagonally positioned square as shown. Then have him use paint to make a handprint on the heart. Cover a bulletin board with squares of alternating colors and arrange students' work on them as shown. Post a jumbo heart with a title in the center of the display. Then staple crepe paper along the edges of the heart and the board to resemble ruffles.

Maureen Glennon, Faller Elementary, Ridgecrest, CA

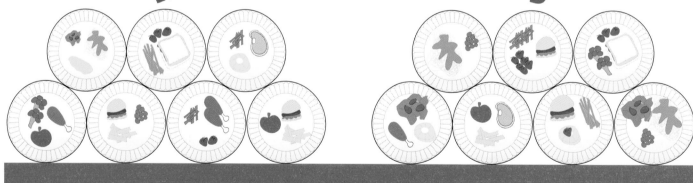

After students are familiar with the different food groups, have each youngster illustrate a nutritious meal on a white paper plate. Post a jumbo balance scale on the wall. Arrange the student-illustrated plates on the scale and then add a title.

Candice Marshall, Kensington Parkwood Elementary, Bethesda, MD

Soar With Math!

$$\begin{array}{r} 8 \\ +2 \\ \hline 10 \end{array}$$

$$\begin{array}{r} 6 \\ +6 \\ \hline 12 \end{array}$$

$$\begin{array}{r} 6 \\ +5 \\ \hline 11 \end{array}$$

$$\begin{array}{r} 3 \\ +8 \\ \hline 11 \end{array}$$

$$\begin{array}{r} 8 \\ +4 \\ \hline 12 \end{array}$$

$$\begin{array}{r} 3 \\ +7 \\ \hline 10 \end{array}$$

$$\begin{array}{r} 9 \\ +2 \\ \hline 11 \end{array}$$

Here's a way to help students solve vertical addition problems with flying colors. Give each youngster a kite programmed with a problem. Have her tape colorful rectangles to a length of yarn to model the problem. Then instruct her to write the answer on the kite and tape the yarn to the back of it. Post students' kites and some clouds on a board with the title shown.

Janet Boyce, Cokato, MN

For this reading motivation idea, post a titled cloud on a bulletin board covered with a light color of paper. Add grass and then draw two leafless stalks that are a little taller than the grass. Post a giant's head and hands above the cloud as shown. After you read a book aloud or a youngster reads a book independently, staple a leaf (pattern on page 47) programmed with the appropriate information to a stalk. As you add more leaves, extend the stalks and watch students' interest in reading grow!

Tammi Ayres
Fairfield Elementary
Leesburg, OH

Watch Our Book Stalks Grow!

Spring Is in Full Bloom!

Decorate your classroom for spring in a jiffy! Have each youngster crisscross four strips of colorful paper and glue them together. Instruct him to add a stem and triangular leaves. Then invite him to glue crumpled tissue paper to the center of the flower. Display students' shapely posies with a desired title.

Anne Cromwell-Gapp, Memorial School, Winchendon, MA

To make this easy-to-adapt display, have each student color a personalized paper plate green and then glue an illustrated frog head, two front legs, and two back legs to it (patterns on page 48). Then instruct her to write an assigned letter on a lily pad and add labeled illustrations of words that begin with that letter. Display students' work as shown. **For a math variation,** have each child label a frog with the numbers of a fact family and write the facts on a lily pad.

Megan Carney, Multiple Intelligences School, Worcester, MA

For this science display, each child completes a riddle like the one below to describe a chosen oviparous animal. He mounts the riddle on colorful paper and glues it to the front of an egg that has been cut from a folded piece of paper. Then he opens the egg and illustrates the animal inside. Display each youngster's egg on a titled board as shown, and post pictures of oviparous animals to jump-start students' guesses.

Tracy Lowe
Des Moines, IA

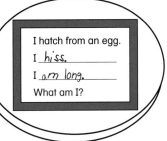

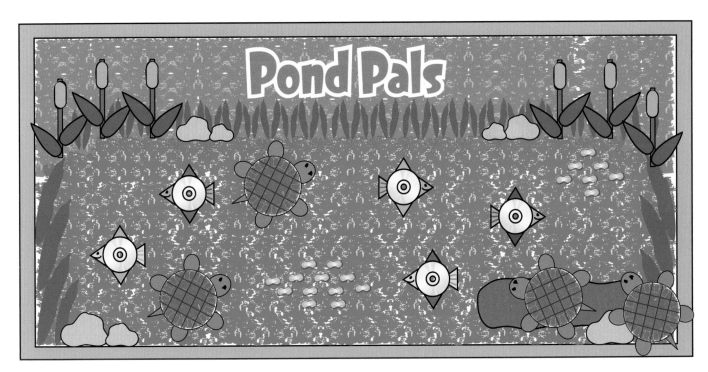

Spark students' creativity with this pond project! Instruct students to sponge-paint a white-backed board green and blue. Then have them paint grassy plants and post paper rocks and logs. Over the next several days, invite youngsters to add desired details to the scene. For example, they might make construction paper cattails and paper plate turtles. They might also glue triangles to old CDs so that the CDs resemble fish and cover packing peanuts with foil to make minnows. The possibilities are endless!

Ruth Rigenhagen, Quality Schools International, Kosice, Slovakia

Fishbowl Mystery

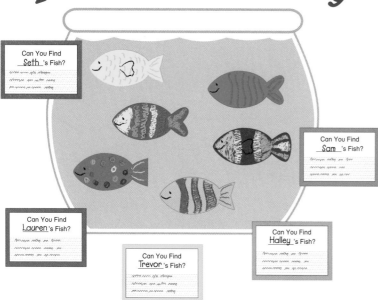

Get students in the swim of descriptive writing! Ask each youngster to decorate a construction paper fish as desired. Have her complete a paper similar to the one below with her name and a description of the fish and then mount it on colorful paper. Display students' fish on a paper fishbowl. Post a title and the descriptions. Everyone who sees the display will be eager to match the clues with the correct fish!

Katie Klipp
Bob Jones Elementary
Greenville, SC

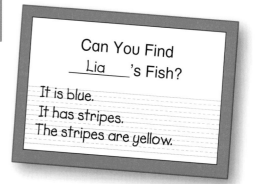

Can You Find _Seth_'s Fish?

Can You Find _Sam_'s Fish?

Can You Find _Lauren_'s Fish?

Can You Find _Halley_'s Fish?

Can You Find _Trevor_'s Fish?

Can You Find
Lia's Fish?

It is blue.
It has stripes.
The stripes are yellow.

Red, Ripe Strawberries?

My disguise is a bean
Raul

Promote creativity with this follow-up to *The Little Mouse, the Red Ripe Strawberry, and the Big Hungry Bear* by Don and Audrey Wood. Instruct each child to glue a leafy top to a strawberry cut from a folded piece of paper. Have him use arts-and-crafts materials to disguise the top berry as desired. Ask him to unfold the paper and then write about the disguise and sign his name inside. Title a jumbo strawberry and arrange students' berries around it.

Cindy Barber, Fredonia, WI

For this seasonal idea, cover a bulletin board with blue and tan paper as shown. Post a sun on the horizon and add twisted crepe paper streamers for the sun's rays. Help each youngster poke the ends of pipe cleaners into two shoe cutouts and secure the pipe cleaners to make flip-flops. Ask him to write his name on one flip-flop and illustrate a favorite summer activity on the other flip-flop. Display each youngster's flip-flops and a title as desired.

Jami Foster, Early Education Center of Perry County, Duncannon, PA

Honor the Stars and Stripes with this festive display. Glue a large white paper cake to a plate that you have cut from bulletin board paper. Have students embellish the cake with construction paper candles and decorations in patriotic colors. Post the cake on the board. Then complete the display with a title and student-made stars.

Cindy Barber
Fredonia, WI

Penguin Pattern

Use with "Penguin Promenade" on page 39.

TEC42028

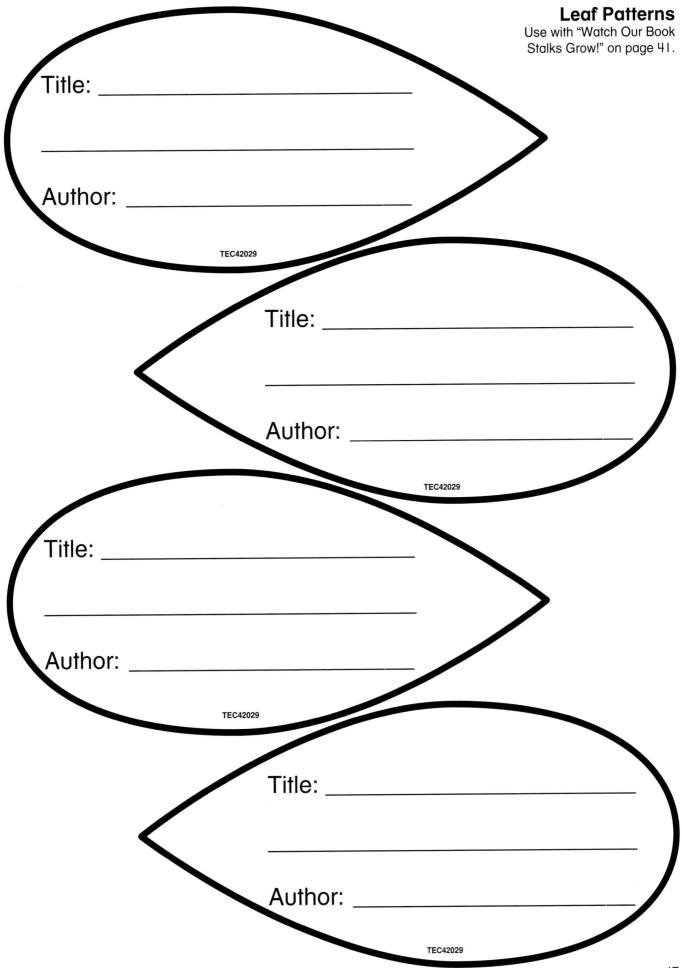

Title: _____

_____

Author: _____

TEC42029

Title: _____

_____

Author: _____

TEC42029

Title: _____

_____

Author: _____

TEC42029

Title: _____

_____

Author: _____

TEC42029

Frog Patterns
Use with "Hop to It!"
on page 42.

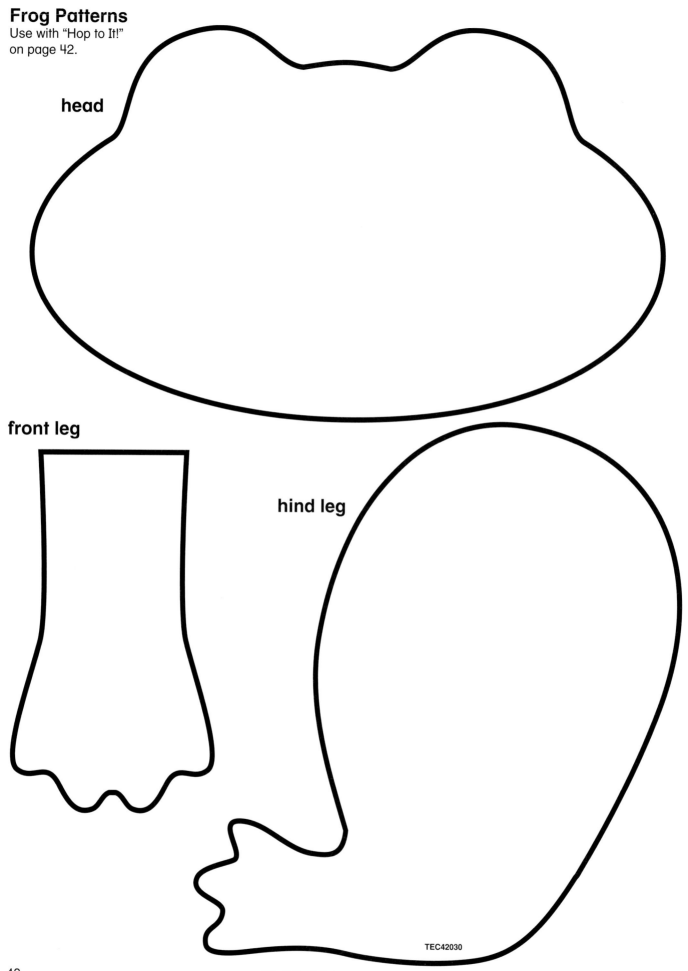

head

front leg

hind leg

TEC42030

GROUP TIME

Group Time

Tune In to a New Day
Number Sense

It's all aboard for the first 100 days of school with this morning melody! Write the song shown on sentence strips, leaving a blank space for a number. Write the numbers 1 to 100 on individual cards that fit in the blank space. Display the sentences in a pocket chart and place the cards nearby. Each morning, have a youngster update the chart with the appropriate number card; then lead the group in singing the song. After students are familiar with the activity, incorporate additional skill reinforcement, such as comparing numbers or adding.

Jana Murphy
Primavera School
Prescott, AZ

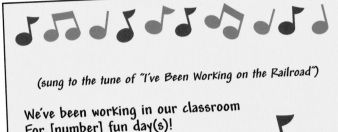

(sung to the tune of "I've Been Working on the Railroad")

We've been working in our classroom
For [number] fun day(s)!
We've been working in our classroom.
Let's all shout, "Hooray! Hooray!"
We are ready for a new day,
Even better than the rest!
Do you think that we can learn more?
We can! We'll do our best!

Musical Introductions
Speaking in a Group

Help your students get acquainted with this version of the traditional hot potato game. Hold a small stuffed animal (class mascot) as you sit with students in a circle. Help the youngsters agree on a name for the mascot. Then explain that the mascot will help with student introductions.

Next, have the children pass the mascot around the circle as you play some music. After a few moments, stop the music and invite the child holding the mascot to announce her name. After the class greets her, resume the music. Continue the activity as described until each child has introduced herself. During later rounds, encourage each youngster to tell the group her favorite color, food, or game.

Andrea Singleton
Waynesville Elementary
Waynesville, OH

LILY.

Math Motion
Shape Identification

Energize a review of geometric figures with this lively chant. To prepare, make a class supply of assorted construction paper shapes. To begin, sit with students in a circle. Give one shape to each student and confirm that he can identify it. Then lead students in the chant below, substituting the name of a different shape if needed. Repeat the chant with each featured shape. **To modify the activity for different skill areas,** feature letters, numbers, or sight words in the chant instead of shapes.

[Square], [square] is the shape I see.
If you have a [square], please show it to me.
Stand up and turn around.
Show your [square] and then sit down.

Lucille Iscaro
P.S. 257
Bronx, NY

Group Time

Hickory Dickory Clock
Literacy

To review number words, write the featured nursery rhyme on a sheet of chart paper, replacing the number word with a Velcro dot. Display the poem. Then post two shapes that resemble the top and bottom of a grandfather clock as shown. Add a clockface with movable hands and a mouse for decoration. Use Velcro dots to post the number words *one* to *twelve* in order beside the clock. Next, complete the rhyme with a chosen card and have students identify the number word. After you model the corresponding time on the clock, lead students in reading the rhyme. **For more advanced students,** display the number words in random order.

Deb Shank
Greencastle-Antrim Primary School
Greencastle, PA

one
two
three
four
five
six

eight
nine
ten
eleven
twelve

Hickory, dickory, dock,

The mouse ran up the clock.

The clock struck seven.

The mouse ran down,

Hickory, dickory, dock.

Pairs, Pronto!
Literacy

Students try to beat the clock during this versatile game. Program a class supply of blank cards to create pairs of rhyming words, colors and color words, or uppercase and lowercase letters. Place the cards in an unlidded box.

To play, invite each student to take a card at random and then quickly return to her seat without revealing the card to her classmates. After each student has a card, set the timer for a chosen amount of time. At this signal, each student tries to quickly find the child with the card that forms a pair with her card. When she finds her, the two students sit together. After all of the students are paired in this manner or when the timer goes off, invite each twosome to name its pair of cards.

Dawn DiPietro
Lafayette-Pershing School
Carney's Point, NJ

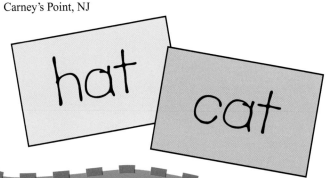

Orderly Changes
Math

For this ordinal number idea, arrange three large disposable cups upside down in a row. As students watch, place a small object under one cup. Then describe the object's location with an ordinal number. Next, slide the cups around to vary their order. Ask a volunteer to use an ordinal number to describe where he thinks the object is. Then lift the named cup to check whether he is correct. If he is correct, invite the youngster to hide the object during the next round of play. If he is not correct, scramble the containers and have youngsters guess again. **For more advanced students,** use five cups.

Janet Boyce
Cokato, MN

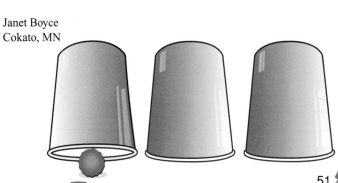

Group Time

Soup's On!
Literature

January is a perfect time to add this monthly idea to your calendar routine. On the first school day of each month, read aloud that month's poem in *Chicken Soup With Rice: A Book of Months* by Maurice Sendak. Over the next few days, reread the poem with students and reinforce chosen calendar concepts and literacy skills. For additional reinforcement, leave the book in your calendar area along with highlighting tape and writing paper. Invite students to revisit the book and complete tasks such as highlighting designated words and writing chosen rhymes.

Laura Titsch
P.S. 171
Long Island City, NY

Plenty of Purchases
Letter-Sound Associations

Letter cards give students clues during this memory game. Have students sit in a circle. Give each student a letter card and have her place it facedown. To begin, one student holds up her card and names the letter. She says, "I went to the store and bought…" Then she names something that begins with her letter. The next student holds up his card and names the letter. He uses the modeled sentence format to identify a purchase that begins with his letter. Then the group repeats the previous student's purchase, looking at her card for a reminder. The activity continues around the circle as described, with each youngster naming a new purchase before the group recalls each previous purchase.

For more advanced students, encourage each youngster to recall the previous purchases on his own rather than have the group name them.

Deanne D'Imperio
Martin Luther King School
Paterson, NJ

Before and After
Number Sense

For this kid-pleasing activity, number a class supply of blank cards, beginning with the number 2. Arrange the cards in random order in a large circle on the floor. To begin, play some lively music and have students walk around the cards. After a few moments, stop the music and instruct each student to stand at the nearest card. Next, call out a student's name and ask her to identify her number. Then have the group name the number that comes just before it and the number that comes just after it. Resume the music to continue. **For an easier version,** post a number line for student reference. Have students name only the number that comes after each identified number.

Patrice Bryson
Hawk Ridge Elementary
Charlotte, NC

I went to the store and bought pizza.

14 comes just before 15.

LEARNING CENTERS

Learning Centers

Paper Plate Puzzler
Literacy Center

This self-checking activity can be used for two different skills. Use one of the options below to program several paper plates. Then puzzle-cut between the programming. Have each center visitor assemble the puzzles and name the letters or read the words.

For letter knowledge, program each plate with the uppercase and lowercase forms of a letter, leaving space between the two letters.

For high-frequency words, use two different colors of markers to write a word two times on each plate as shown.

Erin Roeske
Woodbury, MN

Goody, Goody Gumball!
Math Center

Here's a sweet approach to number words. Copy the gumball machine cards on page 65 to make 11 cards. Leave one gumball machine empty. Draw one colorful gumball on one card, two gumballs on another card, and so on until all of the cards have been programmed. Color the gumball machines. Then cut out the cards and mount them on tagboard rectangles for durability. Also, write the number words *zero* through *ten* on separate sentence strips. Write the corresponding number on the back of each sentence strip and card to make the activity self-checking. Display the gumball machine cards in order in a pocket chart. Set the sentence strips nearby.

Students place each word beside the appropriate gumball machine. Then they flip the sentence strips and cards to check their work. **For an easier version,** write the appropriate numeral beside each number word.

Jackie Wright, Summerhill Children's House, Enid, OK

Stamp, Spell, and Read!
Spelling Center

Reinforce familiar words with this easy-to-prepare center. Draw a grid similar to the one shown. Then write a different word in each row of the first column. Place copies of the grid at a center stocked with lowercase letter stamps and a washable ink pad. To complete the activity, a student reads a word, spells it by stamping the corresponding letters in the provided space, and then reads the stamped word. She continues with the remaining words in the same manner.

For more advanced students, prepare a list of words, replacing one letter in each word with a blank. Have students complete the words by stamping each missing letter.

Vicki Shannon, Benton Elementary
Marshall, MO

Mischievous Mice
Storybook Center

Pair literature and math with this follow-up to *Mouse Count* by Ellen Stoll Walsh. Cut a jar-shaped opening from the front of a file folder as shown. Draw grass around the jar and label the folder with the book title. Next, open the folder and glue a piece of construction paper to the intact half. Laminate the folder and then staple the sides closed. Color and cut out ten mouse cards (patterns on page 65). To prepare a snake, use a permanent marker to draw two eyes near the toe of an old sock and then glue on felt decorations. Set the snake, mice, folder, and book at a center.

A student uses the props to act out the story, counting the mice as he puts them in the jar and as he takes them out. He may also practice skills such as counting backward, adding, or subtracting.

Kim Connell
McKitrick Elementary
Lutz, FL

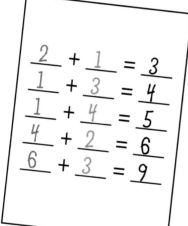

$$\underline{2} + \underline{1} = \underline{3}$$
$$\underline{1} + \underline{3} = \underline{4}$$
$$\underline{1} + \underline{4} = \underline{5}$$
$$\underline{4} + \underline{2} = \underline{6}$$
$$\underline{6} + \underline{3} = \underline{9}$$

Roll a Sum!
Math Center

Colorful dice make this idea a surefire approach to addition. Place at a center two different colors of dice, the corresponding colors of crayons, and copies of a recording sheet similar to the one shown. To complete the activity, a student rolls one die. He uses the matching crayon to write the corresponding number in the first blank on his paper. He rolls the other die and writes that number in the second blank with the matching crayon. He writes the sum with a pencil. Then he counts the pips on the dice to check his answer. He continues writing and solving addition problems in this way to complete his paper.

adapted from an idea by Jennae Snow
Panorama Elementary
St. George, UT

In the Clouds
Literacy Center

It's up, up, and away with beginning sounds! Color a copy of the center mat on page 66 and a copy of the activity cards on page 67. Cut out the cards. Label the back of each card with the letter for the corresponding beginning sound. Place each set of cards in a separate resealable plastic bag and decide which set each student should use.

A student stacks the cards picture side up beside the mat. She names the picture on the top card and then places the card in the box below the corresponding initial consonant. She sorts the remaining cards in the same manner. Then she flips them to check her work.

Learning Centers

Letter Search
Literacy Center

Whether students complete this alphabet activity alone or with a partner, it's sure to please! Place one magnetic letter for each letter of the alphabet in a large, shallow plastic container. Conceal the letters with packing peanuts or shredded paper. When a student visits the center, he closes his eyes and removes a letter from the container. Then he opens his eyes and places the letter on a work surface. He continues removing the letters as described, arranging them in alphabetical order as he sets them down. When the alphabetical lineup is complete, he will know that he has found all of the letters!

To make the activity easier, set out a large sheet of paper on which you have written the alphabet. Have students set each magnetic letter they find on the corresponding letter.

adapted from an idea by Randi Austin, Gasconade C-4 Elementary, Falcon, MO

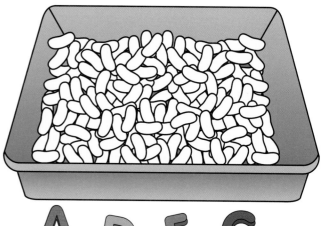

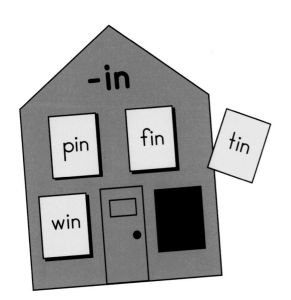

A Full House
Literacy Center

Here's a cozy sorting activity for word families. Make three 9" x 12" construction paper house shapes. Label each roof with a different rime and draw a door on each house. To make windows, cut out 12 identical yellow rectangles and 12 identical black rectangles. Glue four black windows on each house. Write a word on each yellow window so that there are four words per rime.

A student covers the windows on each house with yellow windows whose words have the same rime as the house. Then she reads each group of words. **To make the activity easier,** use only two houses and glue a picture whose name has the featured rime at the top of each house.

Karen Nelson, H.O.M.E. Center for Education, Kissee Mills, MO

Versatile Cutouts
Math Center

Put extra calendar cutouts to use with the skill-building ideas below.

Patterning: Set out two or more types of cutouts. Have a student arrange them in a pattern and then use letters to record the pattern on provided paper.

Skip-counting: Use two different types of cutouts. Number alternating types of cutouts by twos or fives. Instruct a youngster to arrange the cutouts in number order and then write the number sequence on provided paper.

adapted from an idea by Jennifer Gaynor, Hickory Grove/Sharon Elementary
Hickory Grove, SC

L L P L L P

Learning Centers

Lift to Check!
Math Center

Use this bright idea for either addition or subtraction. Cut several index cards in half. Tape the top of each card half to a whole index card as shown and decorate the card half with a sticker. Next, program the left-hand side of each whole card with an addition or a subtraction problem. Then lift each card half and use a yellow highlighter to write the answer as shown. (The number will not show through the card.) Place the cards at a center stocked with paper and a highlighter.

A student writes a chosen problem on his paper and solves it. Then he lifts the card half to check his answer. If his answer is correct, he draws a smiley face with the highlighter. If his answer is not correct, he corrects it with the highlighter.

Donna Pollhammer, Charles Carroll Elementary
Westminster, MD

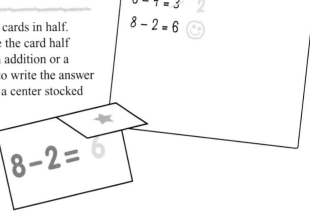

Syllable Scoops
Literacy Center

Phonological awareness is the focus of this cool activity. Use the patterns on page 68 to make three ice-cream treats: a one-scoop cone, a two-scoop cone, and a three-scoop cone. Number the cones from 1 to 3. Color and cut out a copy of the picture cards on page 68. On the back of each card, write how many syllables the corresponding word has.

A student stacks the cards picture side up. She names the picture on the top card. She identifies the number of syllables, turns the card over to check her answer, and then places the card on the cone with the correct number. She sorts the remaining cards in the same manner.

Pamela Ballingall, Gossler Park School, Manchester, NH

Blast Off!
Math Center

Watch students' number word skills skyrocket with this activity! Color a copy of the center mat on page 69 and a copy of the activity cards on page 70. Cut out the cards. Write the corresponding number on the back of each card to make the activity self-checking.

A student spreads out the star and word cards faceup. He takes a star card and places it on the rocket. He sets the matching word card in place and then turns over the two cards. If the numbers on the back of the cards match, he places the cards at the bottom of the mat. If they do not match, he tries again. He continues in the same manner until he correctly pairs all of the cards.

Learning Centers

Snowball Sequence
Spelling Center

This pocket chart activity can be used with any words. Write a different familiar word on each of several copies of the snowpal card on page 73. Add desired crayon details. Then display the cards in separate rows of a pocket chart. Beside each card, place a scrambled set of snowballs labeled with the letters for the corresponding word. To complete the activity, a student reads the word on the first snowpal. She arranges the snowballs to form the word and then spells the word aloud. She continues with the remaining words in the same manner. *Spelling*

Susan Strauss, Tyngsboro Early Childhood Center
Tyngsboro, MA

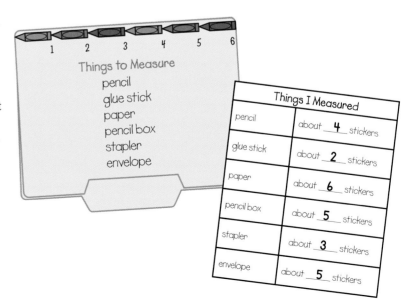

Hundred Chart Match
Math Center

Count on this partner activity to reinforce two-digit numbers. To prepare, place in a shoebox two number cards for each of the numerals 0 to 9. Gather crayons and a class supply of hundred charts.

Partner 1 takes two number cards at random, arranges them to form a two-digit number, and then names the number. Both partners color the corresponding box on individual hundred charts. Next, Partner 2 rearranges the cards to form a different two-digit number and names the number. After the youngsters color the corresponding boxes on their charts, they return the cards. They continue in the same manner as time allows. *Two-digit numbers*

Kristin Webber, Eagle Heights Academy, Youngstown, OH

Sizable Lengths
Math Center

For this measurement activity, adhere equal-size stickers end to end along the fold of a file folder. Number the stickers as shown. Below the stickers, list several items for students to measure. To create an answer key, write inside the folder how many stickers long each item is. Place at a center the folder, the listed items, and a supply of recording sheets similar to the one shown. When a student visits the center, she arranges the items from shortest to longest. She measures each item, in turn, along the labeled edge of the folder and records the measurement. Then she checks her work with the answer key. *Nonstandard linear measurement*

Alessa Keener, Reisterstown, MD

Learning Centers

Begging for Bones
Literacy Center

Use these pooches to reinforce a variety of skills. Make a supply of dog cards and an equal number of bone cards (page 71). Choose an option below and program the cards as described. Then color and cut out the cards. To make the activity self-checking, number the backs of the cards so that each pair has the same numeral and have the child flip the cards to check his work.

Concepts About Print: Write a different uppercase letter on each dog dish. Write each corresponding lowercase letter on a different bone. A child pairs the cards and names the letters.
Reading: Program pairs of dog and bone cards with antonyms or rhyming words. A child pairs the cards and reads the words.

Mary Corcoran, St. Leo the Great School, Pawtucket, RI

Dinnertime!
Math Center

To serve up practice with addition combinations, label the largest section of a divided disposable plate with a chosen sum. Gather that many small plastic vegetables or orange cubes (carrots). Prepare copies of a recording sheet similar to the one shown. To complete the activity, a student divides the vegetables or cubes between the two small sections of the plate as desired. Then she writes the corresponding numbers in the first two blanks on her recording sheet. She models and records three more combinations in the same manner. **For more advanced students,** provide blank paper and have students find all of the combinations. *Addition*

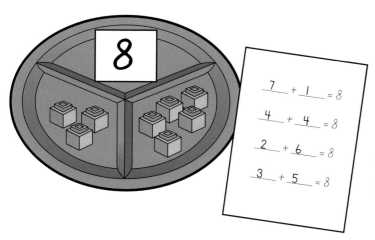

$$7 + 1 = 8$$
$$4 + 4 = 8$$
$$2 + 6 = 8$$
$$3 + 5 = 8$$

Deborah Patrick, Park Forest Elementary, State College, PA

Tall Treat
Literacy Center

To prepare this tempting word sort, color a copy of the center mat on page 72 and a copy of the activity cards on page 73. Cut out the cards. Place the *–at* and *–an* cards in one resealable plastic bag and the *–og* and *–ock* word cards in a different plastic bag. To complete the activity, a student takes a set of cards. He places a picture-word card at the top of each column on the mat and stacks the word cards faceup nearby. He sorts the words by rime and then reads each column of words. *Word families*

Learning Centers

First-Class Words
Literacy Center

Students at this center deliver mail to families—word families, that is! Collect three empty cereal boxes. Push the top box flaps inside each box. Cut from construction paper three mailbox shapes that are slightly taller than the cereal boxes. Label each mailbox with a different rime. Secure each mailbox to the front of a cereal box and then cut an opening in the box for delivering mail. Program a supply of blank cards with words that have the rimes, writing one word per card. To complete the activity, a student sorts the mail into the appropriate mailboxes. Then she empties each mailbox, in turn, and reads that batch of mail. *Word families*

Mandy Yan, Anchorage, AK

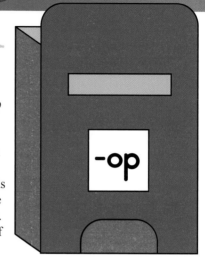

Golden Coins
Math Center

To give students valuable skip-counting practice, glue together two identical black construction paper pots along the sides and bottom. Label the pot "twos," "fives," or "tens." Use a glitter glue pen to program several construction paper or craft foam coins with a corresponding skip-counting sequence, writing one number per coin. Then embellish the coins as desired. After the glitter glue dries, place the coins in the pot and set the pot at a center stocked with paper. When a student visits the center, he arranges the coins in the correct sequence and then writes the numbers in order. *Skip-counting*

Sue Fleischmann, Sussex, WI

Best in the West
Writing Center

What's corralled at this center? An arts-and-crafts project sure to spark enthusiasm for writing! To prepare, make a class supply of white construction paper copies of the horse pattern on page 74. Place the patterns at a center along with a class supply of the writing forms on page 74, crayons, yarn, scissors, glue, and two wooden clothespins per student. (If desired, clip the clothespins to the sides of a box to resemble a fence.)

A student colors a horse pattern, cuts it out, and then colors the back of the pattern if desired. She glues yarn to the pattern to resemble a mane and tail. Then she clips two clothespins to the horse to make it self-standing. Finally, she writes about her horse on a writing form. *Writing with sentence starters*

Katie Klipp, Bob Jones Elementary, Greenville, SC

Learning Centers

Handy Gardening
Literacy Center

Count on students' syllable-segmenting skills to grow at this sorting center! Color and cut out a copy of the picture cards on page 75. Place the cards in a plastic flowerpot. Divide a sheet of paper into three columns and number them as shown. Set the paper, the flowerpot, and a pair of gardening gloves at a center.

A student takes a card from the pot and places it on the work surface. As she names the picture, she claps once for each syllable. Then she places the card in the column that corresponds with the number of syllables. She sorts the remaining cards in the same manner. To check her work, she puts on the gloves and claps the syllables again. **For more advanced students,** have students segment words into individual sounds, using different picture cards and an appropriately numbered sheet of paper. *Phonological awareness*

Cindy Foreman, Three Points Elementary, Orlando, FL

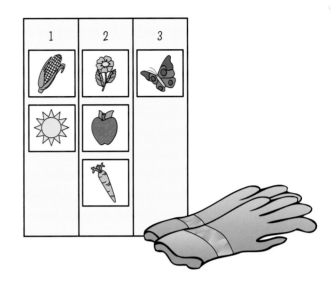

Lots of Spots
Math Center

To prepare this partner addition activity, make a ladybug similar to the one shown. Place the ladybug, a supply of black pom-poms (spots), and a die at a center stocked with paper.

Each partner, in turn, rolls the die and puts that many spots on a different half of the ladybug. The students write the corresponding addition sentence on their papers and then count the spots to check their work. They model, write, and check different addition sentences in the same manner. **For a subtraction version,** the students put spots on the ladybug as described. Then they remove one set of spots and write the corresponding subtraction sentence. *Addition or subtraction*

Heidi Gross, Avoca Central School, Avoca, NY

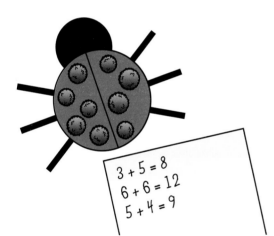

Words, Words, Words!
Literacy Center

Program a set of spiral-bound index cards, and you'll be ready to reinforce your students' word skills in a variety of ways! Simply write a different familiar word on a desired number of index cards, keeping the cards bound together. Then choose from the options below. *Word recognition, spelling*

Reading: Two students read the words to one another.
Manipulatives: Set out letter manipulatives or alphabet stamps and paper. A student reads each word, forms it, and then spells it aloud.
Computer: A student types the words and reads the resulting list.

Karen Almond
Royston Elementary
Royston, GA

Daily Routine
Math Center

A digital camera makes it a snap to prepare this time-telling activity. Take several photos of your students during routine activities at different times of the day. Mount each photo on tagboard. Then label it with the activity and the digital time to the nearest hour (or half hour). For each photo, stamp a clock-face on a blank card and draw clock hands to show the time. Place matching stickers on the backs of each pair of photo and clock cards for self-checking. To complete the activity, a student spreads out the cards faceup. He pairs each clock card with the corresponding digital time. Then he flips the cards to check his work. *Telling time*

Angie Kutzer, Garrett Elementary, Mebane, NC

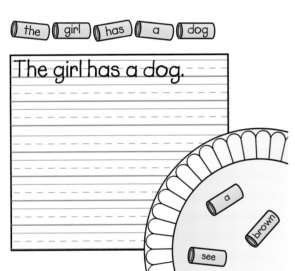

Nifty Noodles
Literacy Center

This tempting center not only reinforces sight words, but also serves up practice forming sentences. Use a permanent marker to program a supply of uncooked tube-shaped pasta with words, writing one word per noodle. Put the pasta and a large spoon in a pot. Place the pot, a paper plate, and writing paper at a center.

To complete the activity, a student spoons a serving of pasta onto the plate and reads the words. She writes a sentence including three or more of the words, using correct capitalization and punctuation. Then she returns the pasta to the pot and serves herself another helping of sentence-forming fun. **For an easier version,** a student lists on her paper the words she spoons onto the plate instead of forming and writing sentences. *Sight words*

Becky Morlan
J. A. Maxwell Elementary
Thomson, GA

Bug's Bargain
Math Center

For "cent-sational" skills practice, color a copy of the center mat on page 76 and a copy of the activity cards on page 77. Cut out the cards. On the back of each coin card, write the corresponding value.

A student spreads out the cards faceup. He takes a coin card and places it in the large box on the cash register. He counts the coins and places the corresponding value card in the small box. Then he flips the coin card. If the cards match, he places them on the flowerpot. If the cards do not match, he tries again. He continues as described with the remaining cards. **To make the activity easier,** set aside selected cards. *Counting coins*

Learning Centers

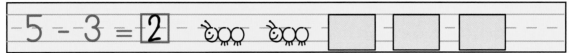

$$5 - 3 = 2$$

Disappearing Act
Math Center

For this beginning subtraction activity, write a different problem on each of several sentence strips. Illustrate each strip with a number of shapes or simple seasonal illustrations that is equal to the first number in the problem. Laminate the strips for reuse. Place the strips, a wipe-off marker, and a supply of sticky notes at a center. To complete the activity, a student reads a problem. She uses sticky notes to cover the number of items being subtracted. Then she writes the answer. She models and solves different problems in the same manner. *Subtraction*

adapted from an idea by Amy Lindley
Greensboro, NC

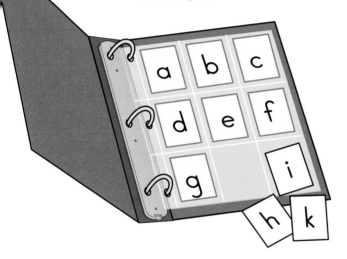

From A to Z
Literacy Center

Improved letter knowledge is in the cards! Place in a three-ring binder a few plastic page protectors with pockets like the ones used for holding sports cards. (You need 26 pockets in all.) Gather a set of alphabet cards sized to fit the pockets. To complete the activity, a student puts the cards in the pockets in alphabetical order. **To modify the activity,** place several letter cards in the correct pockets and have students fill in the missing cards. Or have students alphabetize several word cards instead of letter cards. *Alphabetical order*

Mardina Blake, Charity Dye Elementary #27, Indianapolis, IN

Clear Comparisons
Math Center

To prepare for this partner activity, gather ten blank cards of one color and ten blank cards of another color. Number each set of cards from 6 to 15. Cut out a copy of the fish patterns and bucket card on page 78. Place the fish, the bucket card, the number cards, and 30 plastic worms at a center stocked with paper.

The students sit beside one another. Each student stacks a set of cards facedown in front of him. Next, each youngster turns over his top card and places that many worms near the card. Then the students place a fish or the bucket card between the numbers to compare them using the appropriate symbol (greater than, less than, or equal to). Each student writes the number comparison on his paper. Then he returns the bait and turns over his next card to continue. *Comparing numbers*

Kristin Bynum, Vivian Fowler Elementary
Mt. Pleasant, TX

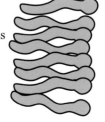

Learning Centers

Read and Graph!
Literacy Center

This high-frequency word idea doubles as a math activity. Draw a 12-space grid on the back of a box lid. Write a different high-frequency word in each grid space. To prepare a recording sheet, make a 12-row graph with several columns and label the rows with the high-frequency words. Place copies of the graph, the lid, a supply of crayons, and a pom-pom at a center. Arrange for two or more students to visit the center at a time.

To take a turn, a youngster drops the pom-pom on the grid. He reads the word in the grid space where the pom-pom landed. Then he colors the corresponding box on the graph. (The students share one graph.) The youngsters take turns as time allows or until they color one entire row of the graph. **For more advanced students,** have youngsters complete a tally chart instead of a graph. *High-frequency words, graphing*

adapted from an idea by Rebecca Needham
Luce Road Early Childhood Learning Center, Alma, MI

saw	could	them	very
where	now	some	been
with	over	said	which

Sizable Stems
Math Center

To give students practice with using either nonstandard or customary units, draw four flowers of different heights on a large piece of paper. Letter the flowers for easy identification. Place at a center the paper, chosen measurement tools, and recording sheets similar to the one shown. To complete the activity, a student measures each stem to the nearest whole unit and writes each length on a recording sheet. *Measuring lengths*

Name   *Darius*

Recording Sheet

A. about _5_ inches

B. about _9_ inches

C. about _4_ inches

D. about _8_ inches

Take a Look!
Literacy Center

Pair sequencing and writing with this picture-perfect idea. Color a copy of the center mat on page 79 and a copy of the activity cards on page 80. Cut out the cards. Number the backs of the cards in each set to make the activity self-checking. Put each set in a separate resealable plastic bag. Place the mat and cards at a center stocked with writing paper.

A student spreads out one set of cards faceup. She arranges the cards in order on the mat. Then she turns them over to check her work. After she corrects any errors, she writes about the pictures, using words such as *first, next, then,* and *lastly.* **For an easier version,** have students use paper programmed with the transition words. *Sequencing, writing*

Gumball Machine Cards
Use with "Goody, Goody Gumball!" on page 54.

Mouse Cards
Use with "Mischievous Mice" on page 55.

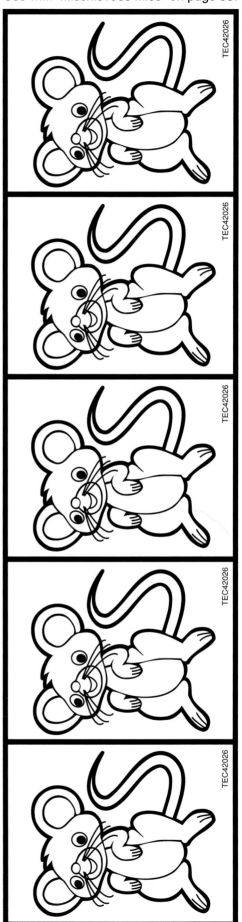

In the Clouds

Sort by beginning sounds.
Check.

d

c

r

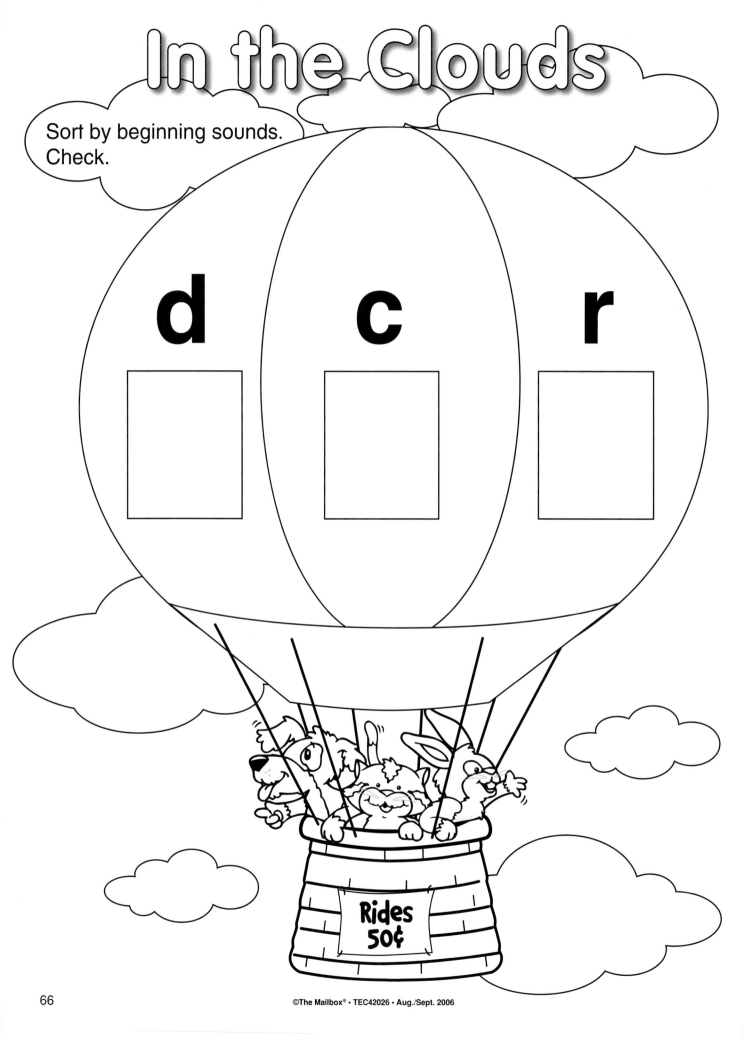

Rides
50¢

___uck	___oor	___esk	___ice
___ake	___ar	___an	___orn
___ing	___ain	___ope	___ake

Ice-Cream Cone Patterns and Picture Cards

Use with "Syllable Scoops" on page 57.

TEC42027

Blast Off!

Put a star card.
Put the matching word card.
Check.

69

Activity Cards

Use with "Blast Off!" on page 57.

one	two	three	four
five	six	seven	eight
nine	ten	eleven	twelve

TEC42028

TEC42028

TEC42028

TEC42028

TEC42028

TEC42028

TEC42028

TEC42028

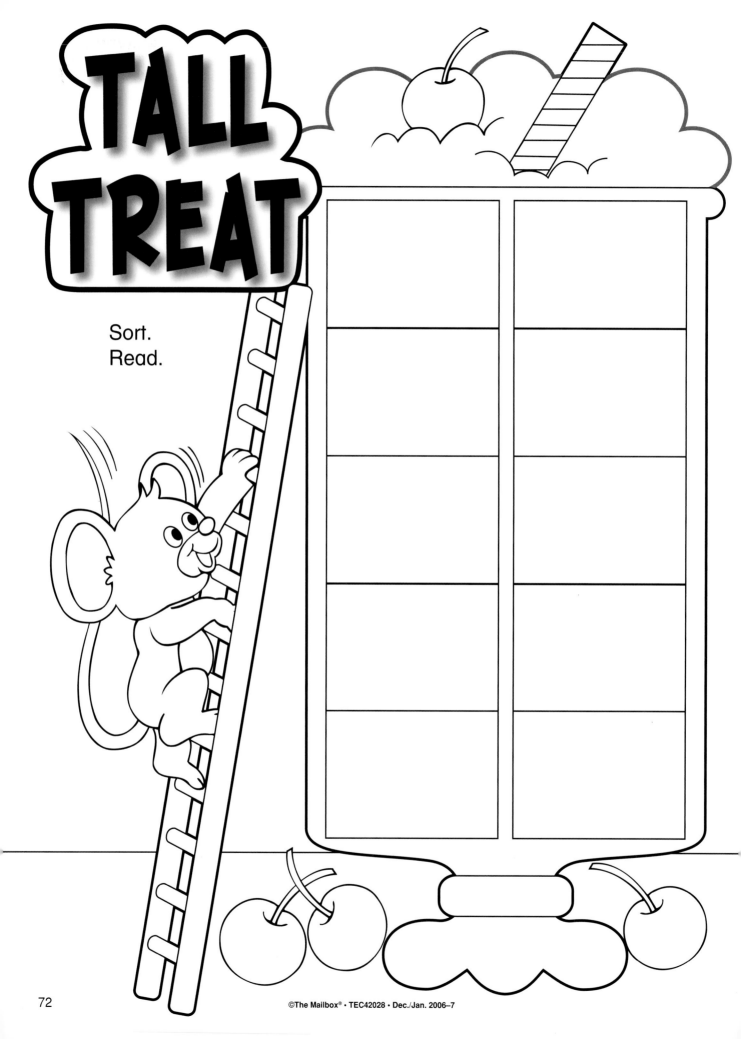

TALL TREAT

Sort.
Read.

mat	hat	bat	sat
man	pan	ran	fan
log	fog	jog	frog
rock	lock	dock	clock

cat

can

dog

sock

TEC42028

Horse Pattern and Writing Form

Use with "Best in the West" on page 60.

TEC42029

Name_____ Writing

The Best in the West

_____

_____

My horse's name is _____

_____

_____

I like my horse because _____

_____

_____

_____

_____

_____

TEC42030

TEC42030

TEC42030

TEC42030

TEC42030

TEC42030

TEC42030

TEC42030

TEC42030

TEC42030

TEC42030

TEC42030

Bug's Bargain

Put a coin card in the big box.
Put a matching card in the small box.
Check. If correct, put the cards on the flowerpot.

		3¢	4¢
		6¢	5¢
		10¢	14¢
		24¢	30¢
		46¢	50¢

Fish Patterns and Bucket Card

Use with "Clear Comparisons" on page 63.

TEC42031

TEC42031

TEC42031

Take a Look!

Put the cards in order.
Check.
Write.

MUSEUM GIFT SHOP

MANAGEMENT TIPS & TIMESAVERS

Color-Coded Centers

This display idea makes it a snap to manage learning centers. Create a two-column poster, similar to the one shown, with a different-colored section for each center. Label and illustrate each section. Then clip color-coded clothespins to the edges of the poster to indicate how many students can visit each center. At center time, have each child take a clothespin, clip it to his shirt, and then visit the corresponding center. *Shannon H. Bass, Moore Haven Elementary, Moore Haven, FL*

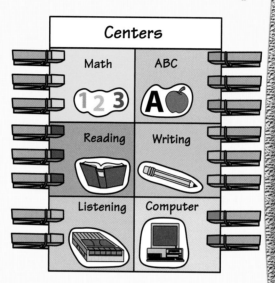

Centers

Math	ABC
Reading	Writing
Listening	Computer

Forms and Such

Here's a handy way to keep track of the paperwork you collect from students at the beginning of the school year. Write each child's name on a divider tab and then place the dividers in a three-ring binder. Hole-punch each student's forms (or copies of them) and file them behind the corresponding tab. Not only does this filing system make quick work of finding student information, but it also makes it easy to take the forms on field trips. *Ashley Cagle, Hill City Elementary, Jasper, GA*

A Full Fishbowl?

Count on this school of fish to help you take attendance. Write each student's name on a separate fish cutout and attach a piece of magnetic tape to the back of it. Draw the outline of a large fishbowl on a magnetic board and then display all of the fish nearby. When each youngster arrives at school, she moves her fish into the bowl. You can tell at a glance whether a student is absent! *Nicole Snyder, Parkway Elementary, Paramus, NJ*

Ready to Go!

Streamline fire drill preparations with this simple tip. Glue a copy of your emergency procedures to a large, clasp closure envelope. Place in the envelope a pen, a copy of your class list, and any other items needed during a drill. Hang the envelope from its flap on a hook near your classroom door. During a drill or an emergency, take the envelope as you leave the room and you'll have what you need at your fingertips. *Rita Skavinsky, Minersville Elementary Center, Minersville, PA*

Emergency Procedures

Clean Classroom

Let students know it's time to clean up by singing this variation of an old favorite. Once cleanup is complete, reward your youngsters' hard work with star stickers or stamps. *Cathy Welwood, Learning Experience, Calgary, Alberta, Canada*

(sung to the tune of "Twinkle, Twinkle, Little Star")

Twinkle, twinkle, little stars,
Time to clean up where you are.
Put each thing back in its place.
Keep a smile upon your face.
Twinkle, twinkle, little stars,
Time to clean up where you are!

Management Tips & Timesavers

What's for Lunch?

This idea allows youngsters to indicate their lunch choices without teacher assistance. Write each letter *A–C* on a separate sentence strip and on a separate container. Laminate the strips; then post the strips within student reach. Place the containers and a class supply of personalized craft sticks nearby.

Each morning, use a wipe-off marker to program the sentence strips with the lunch choices and use reusable adhesive to add corresponding pictures. (Old magazines and image Web sites are good sources of pictures.) As you tend to various morning tasks, have each student indicate her lunch choice by placing her stick in the appropriate container. Count each group of sticks to determine the lunch choice totals. *Lana Hart, Lettie Brown Elementary, Morton, IL*

Efficient Assessment

Instead of setting aside a special time to assess your students' calendar skills, record their progress during your regular routine. First, prepare a checklist with your students' names and chosen objectives. Then, during your regular calendar time, ask students questions based on the objectives and mark the checklist to indicate each youngster's accuracy. Repeat the process on each of several days to complete the assessments. It's a simple way to make the most of your instructional time! *Stacey Helders-Pevan, Somerset Elementary, Somerset, WI*

Centers to Go

If you have limited space for learning centers, try this! Label a sturdy container for each center and stock it with the appropriate supplies. Store the containers within student reach. At center time, set each container at a different work area and assign students to the activities as desired. When center time is over, have the youngsters return the materials to the appropriate containers and then set them in their original locations. *Sue Frederick, W. W. Evans Elementary, Bloomsburg, PA*

Stretch Break

As you lead students in this transition chant, have them perform the appropriate actions. It's sure to get the wiggles out!

Reach for the sky,
Then touch your nose.
Wiggle your fingers,
Then touch your toes.
Put your hands on your head,
Then turn around.
Now that we have all stretched,
Let's sit down!

Susan Taffar, Claysville School, Guntersville, AL

Perfectly Organized Posters

Keep your posters in good condition with this storage idea. For every two posters, cut a paper towel tube in half as shown. Roll up the posters separately, slide each poster into a separate tube, and then label the tubes. When it's time to update your displays, you'll be able to find the posters you want in a jiffy! *Kristy Mestrich, St. Thomas More School, Munster, IN*

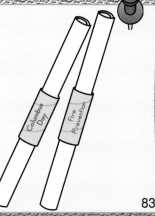

Management Tips & Timesavers

Picture-Perfect Behavior

Here's a positive way to motivate students to follow classroom rules. Divide a coloring page or a simple black-and-white illustration into a desired number of sections. Then post the paper in a prominent classroom location. Each time your students exhibit exceptional behavior, color one section of the paper. After all of the sections are colored, give the class a reward such as an extra recess or an inexpensive treat. *Bobi Miller, Tuloso-Midway Primary School, Corpus Christi, TX*

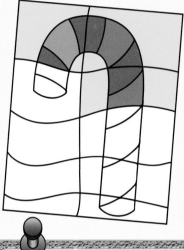

Welcome Back Folders

Use this handy folder system to ensure that absent students get important notices and assignments. When a student is not at school, set a designated folder at his workspace. Place a copy of each paper that is passed out during his absence in the folder. When the youngster returns to school, have him take the folder home, complete any enclosed assignments, and then return his work in the folder. *Stephanie Summers, McBride Elementary, Springfield, MO*

Busy Buckets

Looking for an easy way to help early finishers use their time wisely? Try this! Label several buckets for easy reference. Place in each container a variety of skill-based materials, such as letter manipulatives, flash cards, and file-folder games. Set the buckets around the room and specify the number of students allowed at each location. When a youngster finishes her work with time to spare, she uses the materials in a designated bucket for skill practice. At the end of the allotted time, she returns the materials and rejoins the group. *Nikki Buwalda, Randolph Elementary, Randolph, WI*

Busy Bucket #3

Easy-to-Maintain Display

This strategy for showcasing student work makes it a snap to update a display. Personalize a separate sheet of construction paper for each student. Add any desired decorations and then laminate the papers for durability. After you hot-glue two clothespins to each paper as shown, post the papers on a wall. Then clip a corresponding work sample to each paper. To update the display, simply replace the work samples. *Heather Teasley, Haskins Elementary, Pratt, KS*

Elise

Whose Paper?

Lead your students in this catchy song as a reminder for them to write their names on their papers. Every few assignments, modify the lyrics to reinforce listening skills and different positional words. Later in the year, simply hum the melody to prompt students to write their names! *Jana Miller, Katy Elementary, Katy, TX*

(sung to the tune of "London Bridge")

Write your name [at the top],
[At the top], [at the top].
Write your name [at the top]
Of your paper.

Management Tips & Timesavers

Grade A Behavior

Promote positive behavior with this "egg-ceptional" idea! Write a different class reward on each of several small strips of paper. Then fold each strip and place it in a separate plastic egg. Set the eggs in a basket lined with cellophane grass and display the basket in a prominent classroom location. When your class exhibits especially good behavior, invite a child to open an egg and announce the reward to the class. *Patrice Bryson, Hawk Ridge Elementary, Charlotte, NC*

extra recess time

Dismissal Reminders

Keeping track of changes in students' dismissal routines is easy with this idea. When you find out about a change such as a student riding a different bus, jot a brief reminder on a sticky note. Adhere each note to the classroom door frame at your eye level. The notes will catch your attention at dismissal time and remind you of the changes! *Marla Cobb, Barhitte Elementary, Burton, MI*

Reusable Titles

Use this tip to save precious time putting up displays that you use each year. Arrange the letters for a display title on a piece of laminating film as you would like them to appear on a board. Laminate the arrangement and then trim the laminating film, keeping the title intact. Simply attach the laminating film to the board to post the title in one easy step. After you change the display, save the title to be used again. It's a timesaving alternative to creating a new title and posting it one letter at a time! *Millie Lentz, Forest Hill Elementary, West Palm Beach, FL*

Organized Letters

Here's a quick way to pass out letter manipulatives for activities such as making words. Sort the manipulatives by letter and store each set of letters in a different container. When it's time for students to use the manipulatives, list on the board the letters each child needs. (If each youngster needs more than one of a certain letter, note the quantity.) Place the corresponding letter containers within student reach and instruct each youngster to take the designated letters. At the end of the activity, have each child return his letters to the appropriate containers. *Greta Merrick, Kyrene De Las Manitas School, Tempe, AZ*

Ready to Color

Looking for a way to keep crayons at students' fingertips? Use flowerpots! Gather a supply of small, clean, plastic flowerpots (about three inches in diameter). Stock the flowerpots with crayons and then set them at centers and other work areas where students need easy access to crayons. Whenever students need to color, they can get right to work! *Lucille Iscaro, P.S. 257, Bronx, NY*

April Showers Bring May Flowers!

Management Tips & Timesavers

Ready and Waiting

When your students are ready for dismissal or another transition with time to spare, use this supersimple idea. Announce a topic—such as summer words, action words, or things that are green—or have a youngster suggest a topic. Then toss a foam ball to a student. Have him name a word that fits the topic and then toss the ball back to you. Toss the ball to another student and have him name a different word to continue. It's a great way to make the most of the time and keep students from becoming restless! *Katy Hoh, W. C. K. Walls Elementary, Pitman, NJ*

Let's see how many summer words we can name!

Tuneful Trip

Looking for a way to manage student excitement on a field trip ride? Try this! During the bus ride, lead students in familiar songs or play recordings of songs and invite students to sing along. The music is sure to engage youngsters and help them pass the time. *Sue Denny, Pleasant Hope Elementary, Pleasant Hope, MO*

Writer's Signal

This idea makes it a snap to keep your writing time running smoothly. Write each student's name on a separate index card. Adhere magnetic tape to one side of each of several clothespins. Place the clothespins and cards near a magnetic board. When a youngster is ready for you to edit her work, she clips a clothespin to her name card and secures the clothespin to the board. Then she starts a new piece of writing. You'll know at a glance who is ready to meet with you! *adapted from an idea by Lisa Maucione, Acushnet Elementary, Acushnet, MA*

Take a Bow!

Here's an approach to positive reinforcement that makes students feel like stars. At the end of the day, announce the name of a student who exhibited exceptionally good behavior or achieved a goal. After you explain why the youngster deserves to be recognized, have his classmates give him a standing ovation and invite the honored youngster to take a bow. Each day, recognize one or two students in this manner to give each youngster a turn in the spotlight. *Faith Sukoff, Sunrise Drive Elementary, Sayville, NY*

Party Pleasers

Prepackaged snack foods make it a breeze to serve refreshments during classroom parties. Invite parents to donate drink boxes and single-serving packages of crackers or other snack foods. You'll cut down on the time it takes to serve party treats to students. Plus, you won't need to refill any cups! *Casey Cooksey, Bruce Elementary, Bruce, MS*

OUR READERS WRITE

The ABCs for a Great Year

Each fall a new group of students means a new group of parents with questions. So, on the first day of school, I send home an ABC booklet similar to the one shown with information about my classroom. (I give Spanish-speaking families a Spanish version.) I save an electronic copy so that I can easily make changes each year. Sharing information in this way reduces the number of phone calls and notes from parents. Plus, it gets rave reviews from parents and administrators!

Kay Chabot, Long Beach Elementary, Long Beach, WA

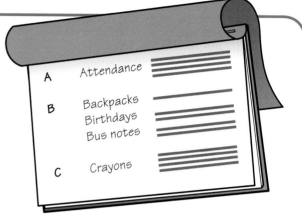

A	Attendance
B	Backpacks
	Birthdays
	Bus notes
C	Crayons

Grandparents Day Tea

I invite my students' grandparents to our classroom to give them an idea of what a typical school day is like. During the visit, the family members observe a daily activity and look at class projects on display. Also, my students and I take our guests on a school tour. Near the end of the visit, students practice good manners as they serve their grandparents tea. The event is always a hit with the adults as well as the students!

Nancy Malik, Eagle's Nest Christian Academy, Naples, FL

loop cereal crayons
glitter pie tins
cotton balls paper plates

Wish Fish

My wishes for classroom donations come true with these unique fish. I put several fish cutouts labeled with different supplies in a nonbreakable fishbowl. During the school's open house and parent-teacher conferences, I invite each parent to take a fish anytime throughout the year as a reminder of a classroom need. As the bowl empties and classroom needs change, I restock the fishbowl.

Katie Zuehlke, Bendix Elementary, Annandale, MN

Constitution Day Fun

Creating a class constitution links the past with the present! To prepare a scroll, I dab a large piece of white paper with a damp tea bag. I let the paper dry and then I roll it up. To introduce the activity, I read aloud a book on the topic, such as *We the Kids: The Preamble to the Constitution of the United States* by David Catrow. After a class discussion, I write student-generated classroom rules on the scroll. Then I have each child sign his name. My students take great pride in the official-looking document!

Jamie Goehring, Hermes Elementary, La Grange, TX

We the People of Room 12

Birthday Box

Use this simple idea to celebrate students' birthdays in a big way. Decorate a large box with a removable lid to resemble a gift. Place in the box a supply of inexpensive treats, such as erasers, party favors, and novelty pencils. On a child's special day, lead the class in singing a birthday song. Then invite the honored youngster to open the box and take a treat.

Diane Bonica, Deer Creek Elementary, Tigard, OR

Less Mess Mats

Foam trays make great workmats when students work with messy materials. I give each student a large tray for painting projects. When we work with play dough, I give each youngster a tray programmed with a letter, number, or shape. I invite him to roll play dough on the tray to make a snake shape and then I have him lay it along the programming. Cleanup is a breeze!

Patty Henderson, Early Childhood Learning Center, Titusville, PA

Colorful Hugs

My students enjoy this sweet follow-up to *Little Blue and Little Yellow* by Leo Lionni. First, I give each child two vanilla wafers: one with a drop of blue decorating icing and one with a drop of yellow decorating icing. (I use the icing—not gel—that is sold in tubes.) Then I have the children use the props to imitate the part of the story when the characters hug. When they press the wafers together, the icing turns green just as the characters do!

Jennifer Curtin, Early Childhood Center, Islip Terrace, NY

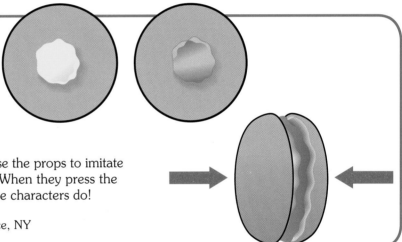

Graphing in a Jiffy

To make reusable blank graphs, cut a solid-colored shower curtain in half lengthwise. Tape one end of each curtain half to a separate dowel. Then use a permanent marker to create a blank graph on each curtain. Have students complete the graphs with sticky notes or other removable items. For easy storage, roll up the graphs.

Kristen Gregory, Binger-Oney Public School, Binger, OK

Sky-High Words

I have limited space for a word wall, so I use this supersimple alternative. I threaded a length of yarn through a roll of adding machine tape. I secured the yarn to a hook high on a classroom wall. Next, I gently pulled the paper across the wall and tacked the free end. Then I wrote chosen words on it. Whenever I introduce more words, I untack the paper and extend the display as needed.

Sharon Vandike, Visitation Inter-Parish School, Vienna, MO

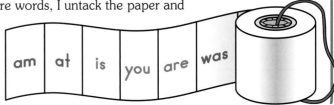

Our Readers Write

Sunny Conference Notes

Here's a bright way to conclude parent-teacher conferences. Set out markers, sun-themed notepaper, and a basket for collecting messages. At the end of each conference, invite the parents to write an encouraging message to their child and then have them deposit it in the basket. On the next school day, privately present each message to the intended recipient. Students' faces are sure to brighten at the positive words!

Marla Cobb, Barhitte Elementary, Burton, MI

Dear Emma,

Thank you for working so hard at school. We liked reading your journal.

Love,
Mom and Dad

Start Here!

To help children with their handwriting, I use red sticker dots. I place a dot on each letter of my classroom alphabet display to show its correct starting point. When students are unsure how to form a letter, they refer to the display.

Janette Crowley, St. Agatha School, Columbus, OH

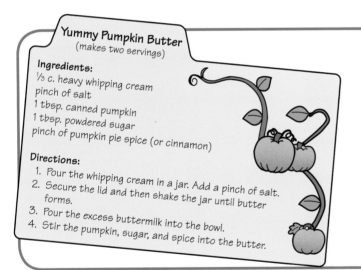

Yummy Pumpkin Butter
(makes two servings)

Ingredients:
⅓ c. heavy whipping cream
pinch of salt
1 tbsp. canned pumpkin
1 tbsp. powdered sugar
pinch of pumpkin pie spice (or cinnamon)

Directions:
1. Pour the whipping cream in a jar. Add a pinch of salt.
2. Secure the lid and then shake the jar until butter forms.
3. Pour the excess buttermilk into the bowl.
4. Stir the pumpkin, sugar, and spice into the butter.

A Seasonal Treat

As students prepare this simple snack, they'll observe a tasty transformation! Give every two students one lidded plastic jar and a spoon. Set out one bowl (for excess buttermilk). Help each student pair follow the recipe shown. Then invite the youngsters to spread their resulting butter on rolls or graham crackers. Refrigerate any leftover butter.

Terri Myers, Ringgold, GA

Literature Attractions

This display idea is perfect for building enthusiasm for books during Children's Book Week or any time of year. Decorate a titled board with paper strips and white lights or yellow circles to resemble a marquee. Throughout the week, place each completed read-aloud near the board. At the end of the week, poll students to determine which book they like the most. Feature the top pick on the board along with relevant student comments and drawings. For a variation, collaborate with other teachers and create a hallway display with a section for each participating class.

Tara King, Highland Park Elementary, Sheridan, WY

This Week's Main Attraction

The "Write" Supplies

This portable center makes students feel like professional writers! Collect an assortment of writing supplies, such as decorative paper, envelopes, and novelty pens and pencils. Place the supplies in an old briefcase (or a box with a handle). When you assign students to the writing center, have them take the briefcase to a chosen work area. It's sure to spark loads of writing motivation!

Denise Wright, Truman Elementary, Norman, OK

Recycling Caps

Before you throw away dried-out markers, save the caps. Students can use the caps as game pieces when they play teacher-made or store-bought games. They are easy for youngsters to handle, and students love the variety.

Diane Pillari, Carteret School, Bloomfield, NJ

Purposeful Painting

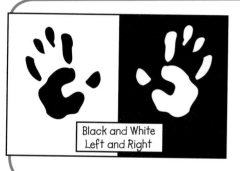

Black and White
Left and Right

Try this handy approach to three topics: left and right, color words, and opposites. To begin, have each student glue a half sheet of black paper to a half sheet of white paper as shown. Instruct him to use his left hand to make a black paint print on the white paper. Then ask him to use his right hand to make a white print on the black paper. After the youngster cleans his hands, give him a paper strip with the phrases shown and have him glue it to his paper.

Kris Murphy, Athens Elementary, Athens, AL

Chair Decorations

Painted pillowcases make honored students easy to find in my classroom. I have two special pillowcases—one for student birthdays and one for the student of the week. I used fabric paint to label and decorate each pillowcase. To recognize an honored student, I slide the appropriate pillowcase over the back of her chair. Classroom visitors always notice the pillowcases and congratulate the honored students!

Sherri Hoar, West Washington Elementary, Campbellsburg, IN

Teacher's Scrapbook

At the beginning of each year, I label a scrapbook with my name, my grade level, and the school year. Whenever a student gives me a special note or card, I mount it in the scrapbook and label it as appropriate. The scrapbook shows students that their mementos are special to me. Plus, it's a tidy alternative to displaying the notes on a bulletin board!

Carol Grant Barrett, John Adam Memorial School
Delson, Quebec, Canada

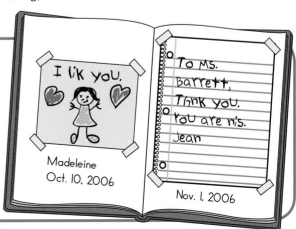

I lik you.

Madeleine
Oct. 10, 2006

To MS.
Barrett,
Thnk you.
You are nis.
Jean

Nov. 1, 2006

Festival of Lights

Celebrate Hanukkah with this poetic approach. To make simple props, form play dough or clay into a large ring. Cut drinking straws to make eight candles. Then glue a construction paper flame to one end of each candle. On eight consecutive school days, invite a student to place a candle in the wreath. Then lead the class in reciting the poem below.

Hanukkah is a special time
That lasts eight days and nights.
It's celebrated by Jewish friends
And called the Festival of Lights.

Deborah Garmon, Groton, CT

Box Bonus

Here are two great ways to reuse holiday gift boxes. For class book projects, cut away the sides of the box lids. Then use the remaining pieces as book covers. To make puzzles, cut out illustrations from chosen box lids. Puzzle-cut each illustration and then place each set of puzzle pieces in a separate resealable plastic bag. Students love to assemble the puzzles during indoor recesses!

Annette Hamill, Collins Elementary, Collins, MS

We have fun reading together
And we learn a lot too!
Enjoy this book
From me to you.

When you're ready to start reading,
This pointer you may need
To help you follow
The words you read!

Love, Ms. Henderson
December 2006

Christmas Pointers

At this time of year, I like to give my students small gifts. For each youngster, I sign a copy of the poem shown and label it with the date. I tie the poem to a plastic candy cane ornament. Then I attach each ornament to an inexpensive book. It's a sweet way to promote reading and help my students track print!

Patty Henderson, Early Childhood Learning Center, Titusville, PA

Wintry Snack

Making this fruit snowpal is a treat! Ask each student to arrange three banana slices on a disposable plate to form a snowpal. Then have him add a few M&M's Minis candies (eyes, mouth, and buttons) and short pieces of string licorice (arms). Finally, invite him to spread a spoonful of whipped topping below the snowpal to resemble snow.

Allison Pratt, Onalaska Kindergarten Center, Onalaska, WI

Looking at Locations

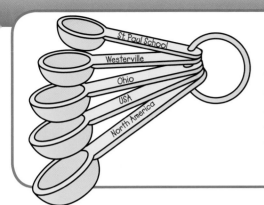

A set of measuring spoons is a wonderful visual aid for developing geographical awareness. Label the smallest spoon with the name of your school. Label the next largest spoon with the name of your school's city, the next largest spoon with the name of your school's state, and so on. Since the spoons fit inside one another, they clearly show the relationship among the locations.

Melanie Ridgway, St. Paul School, Westerville, OH

Word Wall Placemats

To make the most of snacktime, I incorporate reading practice. For each student, I glue a list of familiar words on a large sheet of construction paper. On the back of the paper, I glue a list of words that are suitable for later in the year. Then I laminate the papers. The resulting placemats are fun for students to read, and they keep youngsters' desktops clean!

Charise Carthy, Maddock Elementary, Burbank, IL

Recycled Calendars

December is a perfect month to ask families to save old calendars. I encourage parents to help their children use the calendars for activities such as the ones shown. Parents like having new ideas for reinforcing skills. Plus, they appreciate having the needed materials at their fingertips!

Laura Hamons, Pawnee Elementary, Overland Park, KS

Calendar Activities
Color the box with the number 15 red.
Circle the number that is one less than 20.
Cut apart the numbered boxes and then put them in order.
Color every other box; count by twos.

Serving Simply

I keep a supply of coffee filters in my classroom for snacktime and parties. I use the coffee filters as inexpensive bowls for foods such as pretzels, crackers, and dry cereals. They hold plenty of goodies and they don't tip easily!

Marci Bryan, Lake Placid, FL

Two students are reading books.
Two more students start reading.
How many students are reading now?

$2 + 2 = 4$

"Sum" Book!

Photos make story problems special for my students. I have students work in small groups to create story problems. To illustrate the problems, I photograph each group. Then I help the group members make a page for a class book with their photo, their story problem, and the corresponding number sentence. I bind all of the pages into a book. It's a class favorite in both our math center and our reading area!

Lynn Lupo-Hudgins, Austin Road Elementary, Stockbridge, GA

Coin Connections

My approach to coin identification is perfect for Presidents' Day or any time of year. I enlarge patterns of both sides of the coins that my students need to know. When I introduce a coin, I display the appropriate patterns and tell students a fact or two about the corresponding president. It helps youngsters distinguish the coins as well as identify them!

Katy Hoh, W. C. K. Walls Elementary, Pitman, NJ

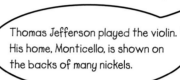

Thomas Jefferson played the violin. His home, Monticello, is shown on the backs of many nickels.

Books From the Heart

In early February, I ask each student to bring in two gently used books for a book swap and giveaway. (I have books available for youngsters who do not bring any.) Just before Valentine's Day, each child chooses one book to take home and one book to donate to a local children's hospital. We send the donations to the hospital along with student-created Valentine's Day cards. It's always a heartwarming project!

Katy Hoh

Party Preparation

Channel student excitement before a class celebration with this decorating idea. Cover a tabletop with bulletin board paper. As youngsters wait for the festivities to begin, invite them to draw party-related illustrations all over the paper. The resulting tablecloth is both appealing and useful!

April Wensko, Jeffrey Clark Elementary, Mickleton, NJ

Funny Face

Fruit and pretzels are the ingredients for this unique portrait. To make one, a youngster arranges several pieces of fruit on a disposable plate to resemble a face similar to the one shown. Then he arranges several pretzel sticks at the top of the plate for hair. Students love the silly snack!

Karen Chilton, Arlington, TX

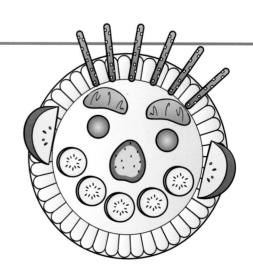

The Sky's the Limit!

Motivate students to reach class goals with this kite display. Establish a behavioral or an academic goal. Then mark several increments in a column on your board or a small bulletin board. Embellish the endpoint as desired and post a kite at the lowest point. Each time students make progress toward the goal, move the kite up one increment. After the kite reaches the top, celebrate students' success with a class reward, such as an extra recess.

Ada Goren, Winston-Salem, NC

Tagboard Tools

Don't throw away old file folders; they're perfect for making tracers! The tracers are easy for students to handle. Plus, they're so durable that they can be reused year after year.

Amber Baker, Martinsville, IN

Pleasing Paper

Looking for a supersimple way to promote independent writing? I set out cute thematic notepads and stationery. Sometimes I assign a relevant writing prompt, and other times I invite students to choose their own topics. Either way, the novelty of the paper sparks students' imaginations, and they're eager to write!

Sonia Day, Weatherford Elementary, Plano, TX

Count and Collect

When it's time to gather manipulatives after a math activity, I use this idea to keep students engaged. I ask the first child to count aloud as she drops into a container each manipulative that she used. Then I have each remaining student, in turn, count on as she adds her manipulatives to the container. For example, the first student might say, "One, two." Then the second student might say, "Three, four." This strategy not only helps me know whether all of the manipulatives are returned, but it also gives students practice counting to higher numbers.

Ann Ebert, Oostburg Elementary, Oostburg, WI

Choo-Choo or Shhhh?

Here's how I help my students distinguish between the sounds associated with *ch* and *sh*. I divide a large sheet of paper in half and title each half as shown. I illustrate each half with a relevant picture. Then I display the resulting poster in a prominent classroom location. Whenever students need help spelling or sounding out words with the digraphs, they refer to the poster.

Amy Hernandez, Wagoner School, Sauk Village, IL

Our Readers Write

"Hand-some" Follow-Up

I use this activity for National Poetry Month (April), but students love it anytime of year! Read aloud "Thumb Face" from *A Light in the Attic* by Shel Silverstein. Next, instruct each student to trace his hand on a small sheet of story paper. Have him use washable ink to make a thumbprint on his tracing as shown. Ask him to draw a face on the thumbprint and add desired details to complete his illustration. Then invite him to write about his unique artwork.

Dawn Hurley, Bethel Memorial Elementary, Bethel Park, PA

I have a lion face on my thumb. It has orange fur.

Ready to Take Home

My students have trouble taking large projects home without damaging them, so I use tubes to protect their work. I cut paper towel tubes in half to make a supply. When a child has a large poster or paper project to take home, I roll it up, slide it into a tube, and then label the tube with the child's name. Students are always pleased to know that their special projects will arrive home safely!

Penny Miller, Jefferson School, Princeton, IL

Thank you, Ms. O'Dell!

From Ms. Wilkinson's Class

Growing Appreciation

Looking for a creative way to thank a classroom volunteer or school staff member? Try this! I use this idea to create thank-you notes for Administrative Professionals Day. To make one thank-you note, I glue a small, circular photo of each of my students on a large circle. (The photos may overlap slightly.) I glue student-made petals to the circle and add a stem and two leaves. After I write a message on the leaves, the classy blossom is ready to be delivered!

Lisa Wilkinson, Benjamin Banneker Elementary, Loveville, MD

Just Hatched!

This bird nest is easy for students to make and a treat for them to eat! To make one, spread green frosting on a sugar cookie. Arrange chow mein noodles on the frosting to resemble a nest. Then spread a small amount of frosting on the bottom of a marshmallow chick and place it in the nest.

Bonnie Elizabeth Vontz, Cheshire Country Day School, Milldale, CT

Flower for Mom

To make this adorable Mother's Day bookmark, write a chosen message at the bottom of a tagboard strip. Have a child draw a flower center and stem, as shown, and then make fingerprint petals and leaves with paint. After the paint dries, ask her to glue a photo of herself to the flower center. Then help her punch a hole in the bookmark and thread a length of yarn through it as shown.

Patricia Murphy, Broadway Elementary, Elmira, NY

Happy Mother's Day 2007!

Rainy-Day Recess

When the weather doesn't allow your students to have recess outdoors, invite them to help you create unique bulletin board borders. Use rubber stamps and ink to decorate a supply of white borders. Then have children color the stamped images. Not only will students have a quiet recess, but they'll also enjoy being teacher's helpers!

Victoria Cavanagh, Troy Hills School, Parsippany, NJ

Activities

Monday (Fun Day): Tell about your weekend.
Tuesday (News Day): Talk about a teacher-chosen picture from a newspaper or magazine.
Wednesday (Friends Day): Enjoy a book with a reading buddy.
Thursday (Verse Day): Recite a favorite poem or sing a song.
Friday (My Day): Tell about your favorite part of the week.

Day by Day

To keep my students excited about school, I designate a different theme for each day of the school week. (See the examples.) My students always look forward to the special activities!

Mary Jane Rochford, East School, Long Beach, NY

Teachers for Tests

Here's a supersimple way to motivate students to study spelling words: invite them to take turns giving the tests! A day or two before a test, I choose a youngster to take my role during the test. To prepare for his special responsibility, I encourage him to practice using each spelling word in a sentence. Students study harder when it's their turn to give a test, and they look forward to when their friends play teacher!

Katy Hoh, W. C. K. Walls Elementary, Pitman, NJ

Picture-Perfect Directions

Gameboards make it fun for my students to use cardinal directions. I arrange digital photos of students in rows and columns around a compass rose. (For a variation, write students' names instead.) I give each child a copy of the resulting gameboard and have him place a game marker on the compass rose. Then I give students directions to follow, such as, "Move two spaces south." It's easy to check their work since each student's marker should be on the same familiar face!

Gena Pittman Heffner, Singing River Elementary, Gautier, MS

Picture-Perfect Memento

My students and I give one of these cute gifts to each of our classroom volunteers. To make one, we back a class photo with heavy paper. We glue four craft foam strips in one or more of our school colors to the front of the photo to frame it. Then we glue a craft foam star to each corner of the frame. On the back of the gift, we glue a thank-you note and attach magnets for easy display. Students are as pleased to present the gifts as the volunteers are to receive them!

Jennifer Varano, Centennial Elementary, Olympia, WA

Thank you for helping us. You brightened our year!
Ms. Varano's Class
June 2007

Keeping in Touch

To promote writing, I give my students my email address before summer vacation. I receive a lot of wonderful letters from students throughout the summer. Email makes our correspondence easy to manage since there is no need for stamps, envelopes, or trips to the post office!

Kathy Levy, Jacksonwald Elementary, Reading, PA

Song of Appreciation

I plan a special celebration at the end of the year to thank classroom volunteers. My students offer the helpers muffins and cookies and give them thank-you cards. Then, as the youngsters sing a song like the one shown, students hold up corresponding letter and word cards at the appropriate times. The volunteers love it!

Beth Vondran, East Elementary, St. Marys, OH

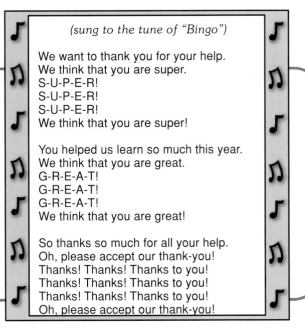

(sung to the tune of "Bingo")

We want to thank you for your help.
We think that you are super.
S-U-P-E-R!
S-U-P-E-R!
S-U-P-E-R!
We think that you are super!

You helped us learn so much this year.
We think that you are great.
G-R-E-A-T!
G-R-E-A-T!
G-R-E-A-T!
We think that you are great!

So thanks so much for all your help.
Oh, please accept our thank-you!
Thanks! Thanks! Thanks to you!
Thanks! Thanks! Thanks to you!
Thanks! Thanks! Thanks to you!
Oh, please accept our thank-you!

Find Your Groups!

Get students excited about group work with this strategy for randomly dividing a class. Collect manipulatives of two colors to make a class supply. Then put each manipulative in a separate film canister. Ask each student to take a canister, look inside it, and then gather with the other students who have manipulatives of the same color. To create smaller groups, use manipulatives of more colors.

Sue Page, Thompsontown-Delaware Elementary, Thompsontown, PA

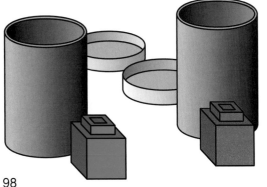

Rhyme, Sing, and Chant!

Rhyme, Sing, and Chant!

Traveling Butterflies

Add this delightful song to a study of migrating monarchs.

(sung to the tune of "My Bonnie Lies Over the Ocean")

Verse
A monarch laid eggs on some milkweed,
Then silently fluttered away.
Soon out came a caterpillar
That ate and ate milkweed all day.

Chorus
Monarchs, monarchs,
They are orange and white and black.
Monarchs, monarchs,
We love to see them come back.

Verse
The caterpillar ate lots of milkweed,
Then hung upside down like a *J*.
There soon was a chrysalis hanging
With a pupa hidden away.

Repeat chorus.

Verse
The chrysalis hung there so pretty
For many bright sunny days.
Then out came a pretty butterfly
That silently fluttered away.

Repeat chorus.

Michelle Beckley
Calvin Coolidge Elementary, Binghamton, NY

Hooray for Constitution Day!

Celebrate an important date in United States history with this kid-pleasing tune. It's a perfect way to launch a discussion about concepts such as freedom and rights!

(sung to the tune of "London Bridge")

The Constitution is the law,
Is the law, is the law.
The Constitution is the law for Americans.

It was written long ago,
Long ago, long ago.
It was written long ago for America.

It gives people freedoms and rights,
Freedoms and rights, freedoms
    and rights.
It gives people freedoms and
    rights all across the land.

Now it's time to celebrate,
Celebrate, celebrate.
Now it's time to celebrate
    Constitution Day!

adapted from an idea by Melissa Eck
Curtisville Primary Center
Tarentum, PA

Apple Picking

Post this fall song in your group area for bushels of learning fun. After you teach students the lyrics, have them find the word *apples* each time it appears. If desired, invite them to find selected high-frequency words as well.

(sung to the tune of "Twinkle, Twinkle, Little Star")

Pick some apples from the trees,
Some for you and some for me.
Red and green and yellow too,
Apples are so good for you.
Eat them plain or in a cake.
There is a lot that you can make.

Apple cider, apple pie,
Apple muffins, my oh my!
Apples are so nice and sweet.
Apples are a tasty treat.
Pick some apples from the trees,
Some for you and some for me.

Andrea Hildenbrand, Willow Road Elementary, Franklin Square, NY

Rhyme, Sing, and Chant!

Harvesttime

Once students are familiar with this fall song, they'll be eager to suggest additional verses!

(sung to the tune of "The Wheels on the Bus")

The apples on the tree are round and red,
Round and red, round and red.
The apples on the tree are round and red.
It's harvesttime!

The pumpkins in the field are big and orange,
Big and orange, big and orange.
The pumpkins in the field are big and orange.
It's harvesttime!

Julie Granchelli
Lockport, NY

A Look at Books

Before you begin a read-aloud, lead students in this toe-tapping tune. Then have them identify the title, author, and illustrator of the book.

(sung to the tune of "The Farmer in the Dell")

Books are fun to read.
Books are fun to read.
Hey, ho, we all know
Books are fun to read.

The title is the name.
The title is the name.
Hey, ho, we all know
The title is the name.

The author writes the words.
The author writes the words.
Hey, ho, we all know
The author writes the words.

The illustrator adds pictures.
The illustrator adds pictures.
Hey, ho, we all know
The illustrator adds pictures.

adapted from an idea by Joyce Bishopp
Ocean Palms Elementary
Ponte Vedra Beach, FL

In the Field

Encourage students to use plenty of expression when they sing this cute song!

(sung to the tune of "I'm a Little Teapot")

I'm a silly scarecrow on a post.
Guarding corn is what I like the most.
When the crows come flying, hear me cry,
"Shoo! Go away! Don't even try!"

Elizabeth Schechter
Herbert Hoover Elementary
Kenmore, NY

Rhyme, Sing, and Chant!

Seasonal Fun

After students are familiar with this delightful poem, help them write their own wintry verses.

Winter means shorter days
When chilly north winds blow.

Winter means building snowmen
In the sparkling white snow.

Winter means skating on ice
And sliding down hills too.

Winter means a lot of fun;
There is so much to do!

Deborah Garmon
Groton, CT

Holiday Excitement

Invite students to name various Christmas sights and sounds before leading them in this cheerful tune.

(sung to the tune of "Jingle Bells")

Christmastime has come.
What a happy time of year!
We cannot wait to see
Santa and his deer.
Lights are shining bright,
Making houses glow.
The tree has been put up just right,
And presents are below. Oh!

Christmas trees, greeting cards,
Gifts of every kind.
Candy treats, lots to eat,
And new toys on my mind.
Christmas lights in the night,
Tinsel, elves, and more.
Pretty stockings, songs, and bells,
And a wreath hung on the door!

Charlotte Sellers
Lebanon, MO

Point the Way!

Use this simple song to familiarize youngsters with the cardinal directions.

(sung to the tune of "Are You Sleeping?")

North, east, south, west.
North, east, south, west.
Tell which way.
Tell which way.
Directions on globes and maps
Point the way in a snap.
Point the way.
Point the way.

adapted from an idea by Sharon Vandike
Visitation Inter Parish School, Vienna, MO

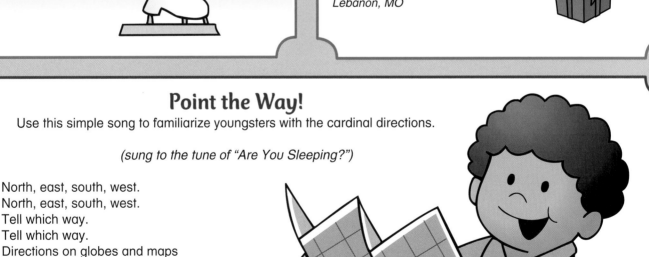

Rhyme, Sing, and Chant!

Watching for Shadows

Familiarize students with both verses before Groundhog Day. Then, after Punxsutawney Phil appears on February 2, have students sing the verse that corresponds with his appearance, modifying the verb tense and words as appropriate.

(sung to the tune of "If You're Happy and You Know It")

Will the groundhog see its shadow, yes or no? Yes, yes!
Will the groundhog see its shadow, yes or no? Yes, yes!
If the groundhog sees its shadow, count on six more
    weeks of winter.
Will the groundhog see its shadow, yes or no? Yes, yes!

Will the groundhog see its shadow, yes or no? No, no!
Will the groundhog see its shadow, yes or no? No, no!
If it doesn't see its shadow, then spring will soon be here.
Will the groundhog see its shadow, yes or no? No, no!

Rebecca Needham
Luce Road Early Childhood
*   Learning Center*
Alma, MI

Read, Read, Read!

Celebrate the anniversary of Dr. Seuss's birthday (March 2) with this catchy song.

(sung to the tune of "Row, Row, Row Your Boat")

Read, read, read a book.
We read all the time.
We all love books by Dr. Seuss.
We love the way they rhyme.

Read, read, read a book.
Read about the cat.
The naughty cat makes such a mess!
What do you think of that?

Read, read, read a book.
We know just the one:
Green Eggs and Ham
    with Sam-I-Am.
Reading is such fun!

Doreen Scheetz
C.A. Dwyer School
Wharton, NJ

Valuable Verses

Count on this "cent-sational" tune to sharpen students' math skills!

(sung to the tune of "Are You Sleeping?")

Penny, penny. Penny, penny.
Worth one cent. Worth one cent.
Nickels are worth five.
Nickels are worth five.
Dimes are ten. Dimes are ten.

Quarter, quarter. Quarter, quarter.
Twenty-five. Twenty-five.
That's what they are worth.
That's what they are worth.
Let's count coins! Let's count coins!

Kristin Webber
Eagle Heights Academy
Youngstown, OH

Rhyme, Sing, and Chant!

Fascinating Fireflies

Brighten an insect unit with this science song. Then encourage students to look for fireflies on summer evenings.

(sung to the tune of "Twinkle, Twinkle, Little Star")

Watch the fireflies out at night.
See them glowing—what a sight!
Two antennae and six legs,
They are insects and lay eggs.
Watch the fireflies out at night.
See them glowing—what a sight!

adapted from an idea by Renee Ferner
St. Ignatius Elementary
Cleveland, OH

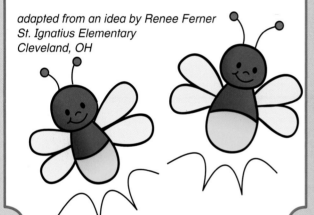

Proud and Free!

After students sing this patriotic tune, help them write about ways to celebrate Independence Day.

(sung to the tune of "He's Got the Whole World in His Hands")

The Statue of Liberty stands so tall.
The Statue of Liberty stands so tall.
The Statue of Liberty stands so tall.
For freedom it stands oh, so tall.

The U.S. flag waves high in the sky.
The U.S. flag waves high in the sky.
The U.S. flag waves high in the sky.
The Stars and Stripes wave in the sky.

Oh, celebrate independence in July!
Oh, celebrate independence in July!
Oh, celebrate independence in July!
Independence Day is in July!

Dayle Timmons
Jacksonville Beach, FL

Name That Shape!

Count on these geometry songs to help students identify cones and cylinders.

(sung to the tune of "Mary Had a Little Lamb")

A cone is my favorite shape,
Favorite shape, favorite shape.
A cone is my favorite shape
Because it holds ice cream!

(sung to the tune of "This Old Man")

Here's a shape, flat and round.
It can roll along the ground.
But it can stand when placed upon
   an end.
It's a cylinder, my friend!

adapted from an idea by Judy Knapp
Wilcox Primary School
Twinsburg, OH

SIMPLE SCIENCE

Bright Observations

"Whoooo" is wise about the sun and light? Your students will be after these investigations!

ideas contributed by Angie Kutzer, Garrett Elementary, Mebane, NC

The Super Sun

Identifying the sun as a source of light and heat

On a sunny day, draw a large sun on the board. Write the word *light* on it and tell students that the word names something that the sun provides. Use clues such as rhyming words to help youngsters identify the word.

Next, tell students that they will do an experiment to learn about another thing that the sun provides. Instruct each student to label a piece of black paper with his initials. Pair students and then take them outdoors. Have one student in each pair leave his paper in a sunny location and have his partner leave his paper in a shady location. About 15 minutes later, ask the partners to return to the locations and feel their papers. Guide youngsters to notice that the papers in the sunshine are warmer than the ones in the shade. When you return to the classroom, add the words *heat* and *shade* to the sun illustration and review with students how the three listed words relate to the sun.

Shadowy Shapes

Understanding how shadows are created

Once students understand that shade is created by blocking sunlight, explain that a shadow can also be created by blocking artificial light. Tell students that they will investigate shadows with owl puppets. To make a puppet, have each youngster adhere two yellow adhesive circles to a 3" x 5" brown construction paper oval as shown. Ask her to color two black pupils and draw two wings. After she glues a beak and two ears to her owl, instruct her to tape a craft stick to the back of it to create a handle.

To establish a shadow station, post a large moon on a wall. Place a flashlight nearby and dim the lights. Then arrange for a few students at a time to visit the station. Invite them to determine how to cast shadows on the moon with their puppets. Also challenge them to answer questions such as "How can you make a shadow bigger?" and "What happens to the shadows when you turn the puppets?"

•FUN FACT•
Owls can see much better in the dark than people can.

SIMPLE SCIENCE

Daily Forecast

Observing and recording changes in weather

Create a blizzard of learning opportunities with this weather station. To set up the station, display a pocket chart. Prepare sentences such as the ones shown for students to complete, and set out corresponding word and picture cards. Post a blank graph for recording each day's weather and a laminated sign with the sentence starter "Today's meteorologist is…." Also, gather several weather-related props such as a winter scarf, an umbrella, and a pair of sunglasses.

Each day, place the current local newspaper weather forecast at the weather station. To designate a student as the meteorologist, use a wipe-off marker to write his name on the sign. Help him complete the remaining sentences and record the appropriate information on the graph. Then have him use the provided materials to present a weather report to the class.

Carol Gabriel, Rocky Mount Elementary, Marietta, GA

Fascinating Frost

Recording observations, exploring the properties of water

You don't need cold weather to do this frosty experiment! Gather a small group of students. Give each youngster a recording sheet similar to the one below and give every two students a nine-ounce colorful disposable cup. Instruct each twosome to place a tablespoon of salt in its cup and then partially fill the cup with ice cubes. Next, have the partners pour in another tablespoon of salt, fill the rest of the cup with ice cubes, and then sprinkle a tablespoon of salt on top.

Encourage each youngster to observe how her cup looks and feels. Have her record her observations on the first half of her paper. Then guide students to describe how their cups and the contents change. (After a few minutes, the ice melts and frost appears on the cup.) Once students complete the second half of their papers, explain that on clear, freezing cold nights when the air has moisture, frost may form on objects outdoors. No doubt students who have seen frost will be eager to tell about it!

Erika Mora
Sullivan Elementary
Chicago, IL

Ice Experiment

First	Later
The cup has ice in it. It is cold.	The ice trnd to wtr. The cup has white stuf. It is very cold.

SIMPLE SCIENCE

Watch the Wind!
Understanding that wind can move things

This predict-and-check activity makes it a breeze to spark students' interest in science. Gather a small electric fan and several objects that vary in size, weight, or shape, such as a sheet of paper, a craft feather, some blocks, a pencil, and a ruler. Make a recording sheet similar to the one shown and give each child a copy.

To begin, explain to students that wind is moving air. Briefly turn the fan on to demonstrate. Next, place the first numbered object in front of the fan. Ask each student to write "yes" or "no" in the first box on his recording sheet to indicate whether he thinks the wind will move the object. Next, turn the fan on for a few moments. After students record the results, put the object aside. Repeat the predicting and checking process with the remaining objects. Then recap the results and guide students to draw conclusions about the objects that the wind moves.

Sharon Glos
Rosemont Elementary
Virginia Beach, VA

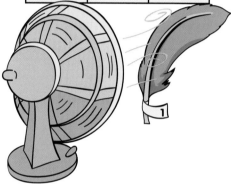

Will the Wind Move It?		
Items	Guess	Check
1	no	yes
2		
3		
4		
5		
6		

High or Low?
Distinguishing sounds

Tune students in to high- and low-pitched sounds with this simple idea. Gather two identical drinking glasses. Nearly fill one glass with water. Pour only a small amount of water in the other glass. Tap the side of each glass with an unsharpened pencil and guide students to notice that the sounds vary in pitch. (The glass with more water has a lower pitch because it vibrates more slowly.)

Next, stand a large book in front of the glasses or place a box in front of them to block them from students' view. Then ask each student to stand and hold her arms out to her sides. Tap one glass. If the sound is low, each student rotates her arms slowly to represent slow vibrations. If the sound is high, she rotates her arms more quickly. Tap the glasses several more times and have students distinguish between the sounds as described.

Cindy Barber
Fredonia, WI

SIMPLE SCIENCE

Jumbo Blossom
Identifying parts of a flower

Plant the seeds for a class discussion with this fun project! In advance, cut colorful crepe paper streamers into two-inch lengths. Also, make a class supply of labels for the following plant parts: flower, stem, leaf, and roots.

To begin, a student glues streamers to the center of a nine-inch white paper plate, overlapping them slightly. Then he glues streamers along the edge of the plate to resemble petals. To add a stem, he punches a hole at the bottom of the plate. Then he threads one end of a green pipe cleaner through the hole and twists the pipe cleaner to secure it. Next, he cuts two leaves from construction paper and punches a hole in each leaf. He attaches each leaf to the stem with a small piece of a pipe cleaner. Then he ties yarn to the stem to make roots. Finally, he uses glue or clear tape to attach a label to each featured plant part. **For more advanced students,** also have each youngster write about the functions of the plant parts.

Dee Wilkerson
Cord-Charlotte Elementary
Charlotte, AR

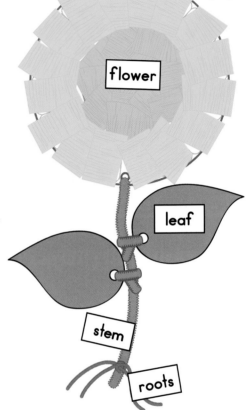

Looks Like Rain!
Making and recording observations

Here's a simple way to help students understand the connection between clouds and precipitation. Collect a facial tissue, an eyedropper, and a disposable cup containing water. To begin, loosely gather the corners of the tissue to make a ball. Encourage students to imagine that the tissue is a cloud, and explain that clouds are made of tiny water droplets.

Next, use the eyedropper to squeeze a drop of water on the cloud. Ask students to predict what will happen if more water is added to the cloud. After students share their thoughts, invite them to watch closely as you add water to the cloud one drop at a time. Continue adding water until the cloud becomes so saturated that drops of water fall from it. Explain that the water droplets in a cloud may join, growing larger. When they get too heavy, they fall as precipitation. Then arrange for students to repeat your demonstration in small groups. Have each youngster write and illustrate her observations and explain what she learned.

Sharon Vandike
Visitation Inter-Parish School
Vienna, MO

SIMPLE SCIENCE

Marbles in Motion
Observing properties of liquids

To prepare for this demonstration, obtain two or more liquids of various consistencies, such as water, cooking oil, shampoo, and corn syrup. Partially fill separate plastic water bottles with the liquids. Then label each bottle with the name of the liquid it holds. To begin, tilt each bottle back and forth as students observe the liquid inside. Then ask students to predict what will happen if you drop a marble into each bottle. To guide their thinking, ask questions about the marble in each bottle, such as "Will the marble drop to the bottom of the bottle?" and "Will the marble drop quickly or slowly?"

After students share their ideas and reasoning, drop a marble into each bottle and secure each bottle's cap. Then move each bottle, in turn, to swirl and tilt the liquid inside. Invite youngsters to take turns moving the bottles in a similar way. After students observe each marble, stand the bottles upside down and encourage youngsters to compare how the marbles move. Guide students to realize that the thicker the liquid, the more slowly a marble moves in it.

Amy Morris, Oakville Elementary, Mechanicsville, MD

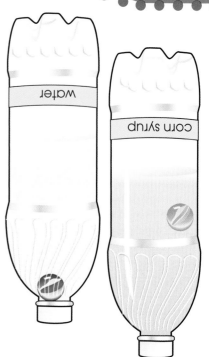

Whose Home?
Knowing that animals live in different habitats

This simple song helps students learn a new vocabulary word! Familiarize students with the song and explain that animals live where they can find food, water, and shelter. Then ask youngsters to look through old magazines to find pictures of various animal habitats. After each student finds a picture and cuts it out, invite each youngster, in turn, to show his picture to the group. Have him point out any animals in the picture and name different animals he thinks would be well suited for that habitat. Then help students create a collage with the pictures.

Christopher Lee
Thelma Crenshaw Elementary
Midlothian, VA

(sung to the tune of "Camptown Races")

H-A-B-I-T-A-T,
Habitat, habitat.
H-A-B-I-T-A-T,
A place where animals live.

In a lake or in a tree,
On land or in the sea.
H-A-B-I-T-A-T,
A place where animals live.

SKILLS FOR YOUNG READERS

Skills for Young Readers

Shoe, glue!

Secret Pair
Rhyming

What could it be? That's what students ask themselves with this mystery bag activity. Give each student an empty paper lunch bag. Have him take the bag home along with a note asking that he place in the bag two items (or pictures) whose names rhyme.

After each student returns his bag to school, invite a youngster to remove one of his items from his bag. Have him name the item and show it to the class. Then remind his classmates that the name of the second item rhymes with the name of the first item. Prompt students to guess what it is. After students correctly guess the item or when they have no more guesses, ask the volunteer to reveal what is in the bag. Repeat the guessing process over the next few days until each student has shared his rhyming pair in this manner.

Susan Weaver
West Side Kindergarten
Magnolia, AR

Name Some Words!
Letter-Sound Associations

Whether you use this song as part of a letter introduction or a review, it's sure to be a hit! In advance, gather four pictures whose names begin with a chosen letter. (Old phonics workbooks are a good source of pictures.) Mount each picture on a blank card. To begin, have four volunteers stand in front of the group and give each of them a different card to hold. Then, as you lead students in the song shown, substitute the chosen letter and the names of the pictures, and have each cardholder raise his card at the appropriate time. At the end of the song, invite youngsters to name additional words that begin with the featured letter.

Carolyn Bryant
First Baptist Church of Powder Springs
Powder Springs, GA

(sung to the tune of
"Did You Ever See a Lassie?")

Do you know some words that start with [b],
Start with [b], start with [b]?
Do you know some words that start with [b]?
Let's say them right now.

There's [balloon] and [baseball]
And [baby] and [bird].
Oh, those are words that start with [b];
Who can name some more?

112

A "Purr-fect" Booklet
-at *Words*

This curious cat is an adorable reading buddy. For each student, prepare a 5½" x 8½" booklet that has several pages programmed as shown. To decorate her booklet, each student draws a cat face on a four-inch construction paper circle. She cuts two ears and two paws from construction paper. After she glues the ears in place, she glues the face and paws to her booklet as shown. To complete the booklet, she writes a title and her name on the front cover. She completes each sentence with one or more *-at* words. Then she illustrates each page.

adapted from an idea by Lynda Hoefer
Sedalia Park Elementary
Marietta, GA

Yellow Brick Roads
Sight Words

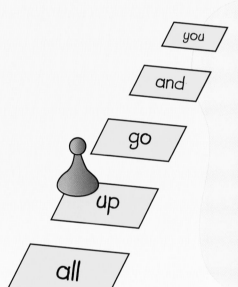

Here's a fun alternative to traditional flash cards. Prepare a supply of yellow construction paper rectangles (bricks). When a student acquires a sight word, have him write it on a brick and then store it in a personalized resealable plastic bag. After he accumulates several bricks, ask him to arrange them to resemble a road. Then have him read each word from the beginning of the road to the end.

For a small-group review, have each student create a separate brick road and give each youngster a game marker. Instruct each student, in turn, to advance his game marker one brick and read the corresponding word. Continue in the same manner as time allows or until each youngster "travels" to the end of his road and back.

Kim Lavery
Sacandaga Elementary
Scotia, NY

Where, Oh Where?
High-Frequency Words: **is, on, the**

Keep reading interest high with busy bees! Make several copies of a clip art bee and program an equal number of blank cards as shown. Have a volunteer tape a bee to a chosen classroom item. Then, with students' help, complete a programmed card to describe the bee's location. After students read the sentence, ask the volunteer to place the card near the bee. Display and label the remaining bees in a similar manner. During center time, have students visit each bee's location and use a pointer as they read the cards.

Coramarie Marinan
Howe School
Green Bay, WI

Skills for Young Readers

/b/ - /at/

Hand Jive
Phonological Awareness

This quick and easy blending idea is sure to be a favorite, hands down! Tell students that they will repeat some sounds in a special way and put them together to form a word. To demonstrate, say a one-syllable word, dividing it into the onset and rime. As you repeat the onset, hold out your left hand with the palm up. As you say the rime, hold out your right hand in the same manner. Then clap your hands together as you blend the onset and rime. For example, say, "/b/" as you extend your left hand and "/at/" as you extend your right hand. Then clap your hands and say, "Bat." Present several words for students to blend in the same manner.

To reinforce letter-sound associations, write each onset and rime on the board and point to them as you lead students in saying and blending the sounds.

Janet Boyce
Cokato, MN

On a Roll
Letter Knowledge or Word Recognition

For this small-group activity, choose an option below. Program six blank cards as described and tape each card to a different side of a small tissue box. (Loosely taping the cards will allow you to substitute different cards as students' skills progress.) **To manage the activity for different skill levels,** program a box for each level with a different color of marker.

Letter Knowledge: Program each card with a different uppercase letter. Give each student an individual whiteboard and writing supplies. To take a turn, a student rolls the prepared box and names the letter. Then each group member writes the corresponding lowercase letter.

Word Recognition: Write a different familiar word on each card and list the words on the board. After a student rolls the prepared box and reads the word, have another youngster make a check mark near the word on the board. Continue the activity for a desired number of words and then have students determine which word was rolled most often.

Heather Graley
Grace Christian School
Blacklick, OH

Mix-and-Match Sandwiches
Consonant-Vowel-Consonant Words

Here's an idea that is made-to-order for decoding practice. Make several construction paper bread slices and cut out five orange rectangles (cheese slices). Label each cheese slice with a different vowel and each bread slice with a chosen consonant. Have students use the bread and cheese slices to form designated words in a pocket chart. For additional vowel reinforcement, have students change selected words by substituting different slices of cheese. **To make the activity easier,** use various initial consonants but only one vowel and final consonant.

Nancy Delia Cushing
Our Lady of Hope School
Philadelphia, PA

Carousel Ride
High-Frequency Words: up, down

Word cards are the only things needed to operate this unique ride! Gather ten identical blank cards. Write the word *up* on five of the cards and the word *down* on the remaining cards. Shuffle the cards. Ask students to stand facing you and to imagine that they are on a carousel ride. Explain that to make the ride go, they need to act out the words on the cards. Then show each card, in turn, pausing for students to read the word and either crouch down or stretch up as indicated.

Marjorie Conrad
Kaysville, UT

Top the Pizza!
Onsets and Rimes

Who can resist this appetizing approach to forming words? To prepare this small-group activity, cut white paper plates into triangular pieces (pizza slices) so that there is one piece per student. Write a rime on each pizza slice, allowing space for an onset. Label each of several red circles (pepperoni slices) with a consonant that forms a word with one or more of the rimes. (Be sure that there is at least one consonant per rime.) Place the pepperoni facedown on an intact paper plate.

To begin, have each youngster color his pizza slice. Then ask him to position a slice of pepperoni on it to form a word. Instruct each youngster, in turn, to read aloud his word and tell whether it is a real word. Write each real word on the board. To announce another round, say, "Pass the pepperoni!" Then have the youngsters pass the plate of pepperoni and ask each student to exchange his pepperoni for a different slice. Continue the activity as described for a desired number of rounds.

Susan Johnson
Zion Lutheran School
Belleville, IL

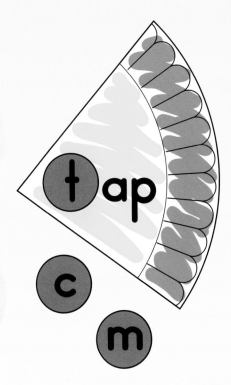

Skills for Young Readers

Load the Train!
Phonological Awareness

All aboard for segmenting fun! Glue a construction paper train engine to a cardboard tube, as shown, to make it self-standing. Number three construction paper train cars from 1 to 3. Tape each train car to the side of a small unlidded box or a plastic container. Arrange the train engine and cars to resemble a train as shown. Collect several small items (or pictures of items) whose names have up to three syllables.

Gather a small group of students. Have a volunteer take an item and name it. Then ask his classmates to repeat the word as they clap one time for each part (syllable). After the students determine how many parts the word has, instruct the volunteer to place the item in the corresponding container. Continue as described until all of the freight is loaded!

Helen Fuller
Wilmington, NC

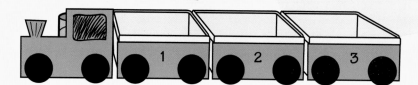

On the Move
Letter-Sound Associations

Review chosen alphabet letters with this fast-paced activity. In advance, gather several large blank cards and write a different letter on each card. Post each letter card in a different part of the classroom. Gather a supply of pictures whose names begin with the chosen letters (or write words that begin with each letter on separate cards). Stack the picture cards facedown.

To begin, point out the letter cards to students and ask them to stand. Next, have each youngster move quickly to a letter card of her choice as you count to five. Then take the top picture card and name the picture. If a student is at the corresponding initial letter, she gives a thumbs-up. If she is not at the corresponding letter, she gives a thumbs-down. Scan students' responses and then confirm the correct letter. To resume play, have each student move to a different letter as you count again. **For more advanced students,** modify the activity to reinforce initial consonant blends.

Kristin Ganoung
Sandhills Elementary
Halsey, NE

House!

Changing Caterpillar
Forming Words

To prepare this hands-on activity, write on the board several letters that can be used to form different words. Then give each student one circle per letter plus one more. Have each student write the designated letters on separate circles. To create a caterpillar head, ask him to illustrate a face on a blank circle and glue on two narrow paper strips (antennae).

Next, instruct each student to place his caterpillar head on a work surface. Have him create the caterpillar's body as shown by using his lettered circles to form a word you name. Confirm the correct spelling. Then announce another word for students to form in a similar manner. **For more advanced students,** have youngsters form words on their own and write them on provided paper.

adapted from an idea by Stephanie Affinito
Glens Falls, NY

Family Reunion
Word Families

This quick and easy idea can be used to reinforce any rimes. Gather a class supply of blank cards. Write on each card a familiar word with a chosen rime so that there are three or more words per rime. Randomly distribute the cards to students. Next, call out, "Family time!" At this signal, each youngster walks around the room to find students whose words have the same rime as her word. Students with matching rimes stand together. After all of the students are grouped in this manner, ask each group to introduce its word family to the class. To do this, have the group members name their rime and read their words aloud.

Liana Mahoney
Beaver River Central School
Beaver Falls, NY

Remote Control Reading
Comprehension

Here's a reading strategy that students can relate to. Before beginning a read-aloud, ask students to imagine that they have invisible remote controls that can help them understand books. Pantomime pressing the fast-forward button on an imaginary remote control and then "fast-forward," or preview, the book with students. Then, to model using a remote control as you read the book, press an imaginary pause button when you come to an unfamiliar word or when you want to question something. If it's helpful to look back in the story for information, press an imaginary rewind button. Encourage students to use their remote controls in a similar manner whenever they read. It's a surefire way for them to self-monitor their reading!

Donna Pollhammer
Hampstead Elementary
Hampstead, MD

Let's press "pause."

Skills for Young Readers

Read and Bowl!
Letter Knowledge or High-Frequency Words

This partner review game is in a league of its own! To program a copy of the bowling pin cards on page 124, write a different letter or word on each card except for the "Wow!" cards. Have each pair of students cut apart two copies of the prepared cards and then place the cards in a small paper bag. Give each student a copy of the gameboard on page 125 and ten counters.

To play, Student 1 takes a card at random. If it is a letter or word card, he reads it aloud and then "knocks down" a bowling pin on his gameboard by placing a counter on it. If it is a "Wow!" card, he "knocks down" two bowling pins. After he sets the card aside, Student 2 takes a turn in the same manner. Alternate play continues as described until one player "knocks down" all of his pins. Then the students work together to finish clearing the pins on the second gameboard in the same manner.

Emily Ryherd
Helen Baker Elementary, Glencoe, MN

Stepping Ahead
Consonant Digraph: **Ch**

Get students up and moving with this simple class activity. For your reference, list on a sheet of paper several words that begin with the /ch/ sound and several words that do not. To begin, have students stand. Tell students that when they hear a *ch* word, they will say, "Cha-cha-cha!" as they do a dance called the cha-cha. Explain that when they hear a word that does not begin with the featured sound, they will put their hands on their hips and shake their heads. Model the two responses and have the students imitate you. Then announce the words you wrote, pausing after each word for youngsters to respond as appropriate. **For more advanced students,** use only *ch* and *sh* words.

Andrea Lovejoy
Goodrich Elementary, Milwaukee, WI

Cha-cha-cha!

Word Safari
Phonics Review

This one-of-a-kind search is easy to adapt for long and short vowels, word families, and other phonics elements. On each of several blank cards, write a different word that has a chosen phonics element. Program several other blank cards with words that do not have the featured element. Scramble the cards and display the words around your classroom.

To begin, announce that students will go on a chosen type of safari, such as a Short *i* Safari. Then pair students and give each twosome a sheet of paper and a clipboard or another portable writing surface. Have the partners look for words that have the designated phonics element. Whenever they find one, they write it on their paper. To conclude the safari, gather students near a sheet of chart paper and compile a list of their findings.

Sheila Criqui-Kelley
Lebo Elementary, Lebo, KS

Words We Found
on Our Short i Safari

it

bib

pig

is

dish

will

Long a Words

Short a Words

Booklets Beyond Compare
Short and Long Vowels

Whether you make these booklets as a class or have each student make his own, they're sure to help youngsters zero in on vowel sounds! To make a short-vowel booklet, staple quarter sheets of white paper between two construction paper covers. To make a long-vowel booklet, cut white paper in half lengthwise. Then sandwich the papers between two construction paper covers and staple them as shown. Title the front cover of each booklet and invite students to add corresponding illustrations.

Guide students to refer to resources, such as a word wall or word family lists, to find words for each booklet. Then have youngsters write the words in the appropriate booklets. As students become familiar with more words, encourage them to make additional entries.

Rachel Dabbert
Transfiguration School, Wauconda, IL

"De-light-ful" Phonics
Blending Sounds

Put decodable words in the spotlight! Write a chosen word on the board and then dim the lights. As you slowly shine a flashlight on each letter in turn, lead students in saying the corresponding sounds. Review the letter-sound relationships one or two more times in the same manner. Then have students blend the sounds to say the word as you sweep the light across the letters.

Erin Clendenny
Woodside School, River Vale, NJ

Skills for Young Readers

ABC Caterpillar
Letter-Sound Associations

This review activity results in an alphabetical display. Write each letter of the alphabet on a separate nine-inch paper plate. Assign each plate to a student and have him color it. (A child may have more than one plate.) Next, explain that each child will decorate his plate with pictures whose names begin with his assigned letter. Then have each youngster cut out appropriate pictures from magazines or create his own illustrations. Instruct him to glue the pictures to his plate, keeping the letter visible.

To showcase students' completed work, illustrate a blank paper plate to resemble a caterpillar's head. Display the head on a wall or bulletin board. Then arrange students' plates in alphabetical order to create the caterpillar's body. **For more advanced students,** help students create a similar caterpillar for consonant blends.

Amy Flori
Grace Lutheran Child Development Center
Paris, IL

Gumballs Galore
Phonics Review

You can use this sweet word-sort center for a variety of skills. Choose two or more categories of words, such as -ack and -uck words. Make a gumball machine for each category. To make one, cut two construction paper copies of the gumball machine pattern on page 126 along the bold outlines and the dashed inner lines. Next, laminate the machines. (Leave the laminating film intact on the globes of the machines.) Cut across the top of one machine. Then staple the cut machine to the intact machine as shown, leaving the top open to create a pocket.

To allow for later reprogramming, use a wipe-off marker to label each machine with a chosen category. Program several construction paper gumballs with words in each category, writing one word per gumball. Place the gumballs and gumball machines at a center. To complete the activity, a student reads each gumball and puts it into the appropriate machine.

Laura Wanke
Pecatonica Elementary
Pecatonica, IL

Poetic Word Search
High-Frequency Words

This word-recognition idea is perfect for National Poetry Month (April). Write a chosen poem on chart paper. Write several high-frequency words that are in the poem on separate blank cards. Then place the cards in a bag. To begin, lead students in reading the poem a few times. Next, invite a youngster to remove a card from the bag. Then ask him to read the word aloud and circle it in the poem. (If the word appears more than once, ask different students to circle each occurrence of the word.) Later, have students use a pointer or clean fly swatter to point out designated words in the poem. Then invite each child to illustrate an individual copy of the poem and circle the featured words.

Lisa Smith
Neshoba Central Elementary
Philadelphia, MS

(sung to the tune of "If You're Happy and You Know It")

Change a letter in the word now, switch and swap!
Change a letter in the word now, switch and swap!
Change a letter in the word, and a new word will be heard.
Change a letter in the word now, switch and swap!

Switch and Swap
Forming Words

Add a kid-pleasing twist to phonics with the help of a puppet! Select a puppet for this purpose and tell students that it likes to change words. Next, use magnetic letters to form a chosen word on a magnetic board. Then, as you lead students in the song shown, use the puppet to change the beginning or end of the word and form a different word. At the end of the song, ask students to read the newly formed word. Repeat the song to begin another round. **For more advanced students,** invite youngsters to take turns as the puppet master.

adapted from an idea by Debbie Reinhardt
Glenn L. Sisco School
Kinnelon, NJ

Pass the Basket!
Word Recognition

To review vocabulary or word wall words, write a different word on each of several blank cards. Place the cards in a basket and ask students to sit in a circle. Have them pass the basket around the circle while you play some music. After a few moments, stop the music. Instruct the student with the basket to take a card and read the word aloud. Then invite youngsters to use the word in a sentence. After you confirm the correct use of the word, ask the cardholder to set the card aside. Resume the music to continue.

Suzanna White
Sycamore Elementary
Cookeville, TN

Skills for Young Readers

C comes before R!

Alphabet Challenge
Letter Knowledge

This partner game is not only a quick review of letters, but also a fun way to reinforce alphabetical order. Each twosome needs two sets of alphabet cards. One student in each twosome shuffles the cards together and then deals them out. Each partner stacks his cards facedown.

To play, each partner turns over his top card at the same time and then names the letter on his card. The player whose letter is closer to the beginning of the alphabet takes both cards and sets them aside. If the players turn over the same letter, a challenge begins. On the count of three, each player turns over his next card. The player whose second letter is closer to the beginning of the alphabet takes all four cards in play and sets them aside. The partners play their cards one time through as described. **For an easier version,** give each twosome an alphabet strip to use as a reference.

Lisa Jensen
Tomball Elementary
Tomball, TX

"Sound-sational" Dachshund
Phonemic Awareness

Students segment words with this dandy dog! Instruct each student to color a copy of the dachshund workmat on page 127. Give each youngster three counters. Next, say a word that has three sounds. As you repeat the word, speak slowly and emphasize each sound. Have each student put one counter on his dog's head when you say the beginning sound, one counter on the middle of the dog's body when you say the middle sound, and one counter on the end of the dog's body when you say the ending sound. Segment different words with students in the same manner.

For more advanced students, ask each youngster to color a copy of the dog bowl workmat on page 127 and cut out the bone cards. Say a word with four sounds and have each student place a bone on the first, second, third, and fourth sections of the dog bowl to correspond with the sounds in the word.

Nancy Randall
Fairmont Elementary
Johnson City, TN

R–u–n!

Name Trevor

Phonemic Awareness

Spot, the Sound Dog

Diving for Treasure
Letter Knowledge or High-Frequency Words

Make a splash with this easy-to-adapt review! Cover a table with blue bulletin board paper or a blue tablecloth and then decorate the covering with fish cutouts. Place a pair of swimming goggles nearby. Decorate a box to make a treasure chest and then stock it with letter or word cards. Put the treasure chest under the table.

To begin, gather a small group of students near the table. Invite one youngster to put on the goggles. As you lead the other group members in the chant below, have the youngster "dive" into the ocean and take a card from the treasure chest. After she correctly identifies the letter or word on the card, have the group respond to a relevant question such as "What is a word that begins with that letter?" or "Who can use the word in a sentence?" Continue with different divers as described.

Nichole Buwalda
Randolph Elementary
Randolph, WI

Ocean diver, ocean diver, dive down deep!
Find a treasure that you can keep!

---

*(sung to the tune of
"Twinkle, Twinkle, Little Star")*

Silent, silent, silent e,
You change words so easily.
You change vowels from short to long.
That is why we sing this song.
Silent, silent, silent e,
You change words so easily!

Presto Chango!
Silent e

A common long-vowel pattern is the topic of this catchy tune. Once students are familiar with the song, list several short-vowel words on the board and have students read them. Then invite students to add an *e* to the end of each word and read the resulting long-vowel words.

Kathy Hannon, Stony Brook Elementary, Brewster, MA

Story Worm
Comprehension

This graphic organizer helps students improve their retelling skills. To complete a copy of page 128, a student writes the title of a recent read-aloud or a book that he has read on his own. He also writes the setting. He uses pictures or words to tell about the beginning, middle, and end of the story on the corresponding sections of the story worm's body. Then he adds desired crayon details. Retelling the story is sure to be a breeze with the resulting reference!

CareyAnne Yager
Lacoochee Elementary
Dade City, FL

123

Bowling Pin Cards

Use with "Read and Bowl!" on page 118.

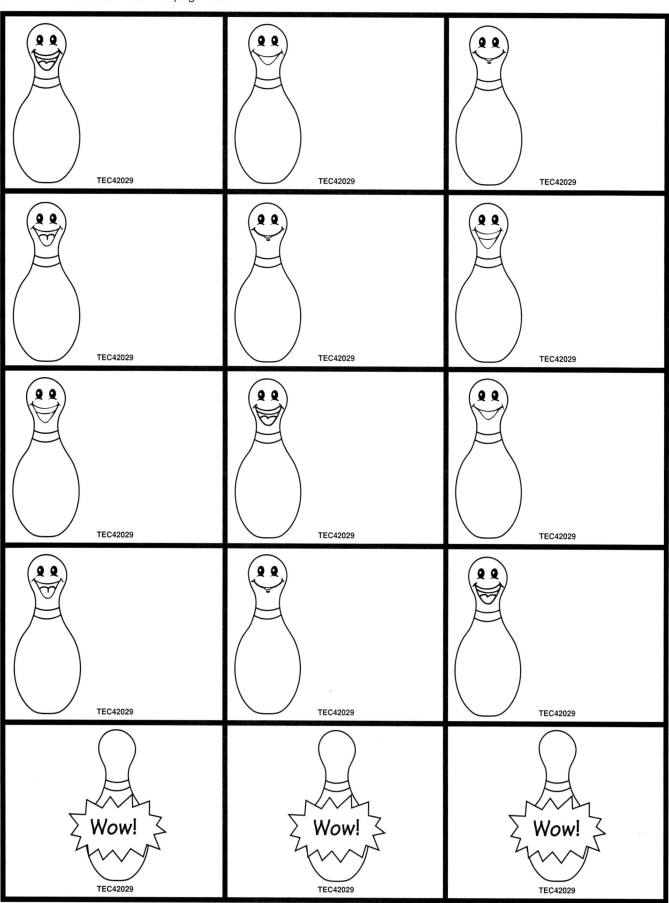

Read and Bowl!

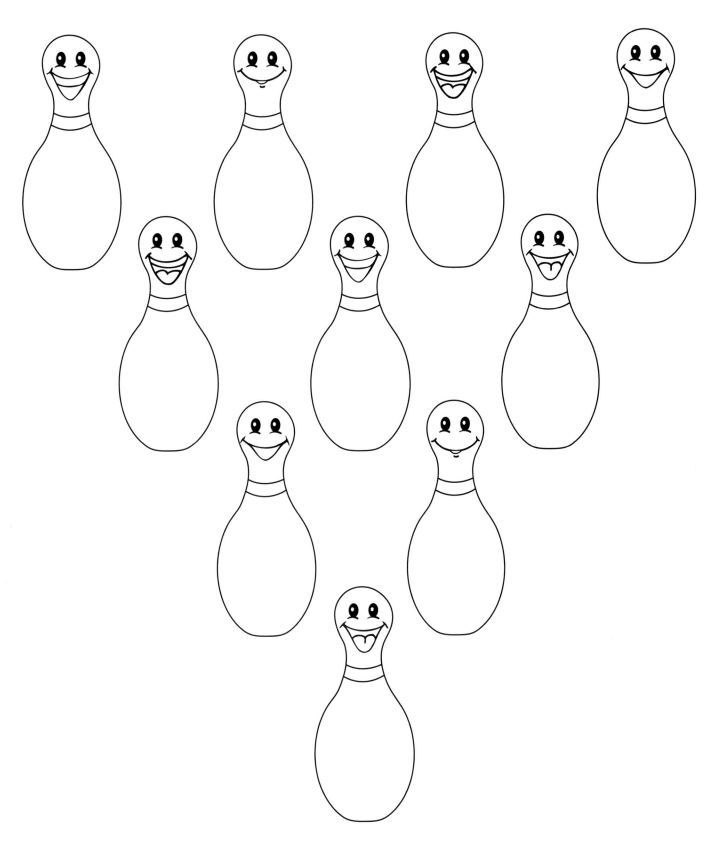

Note to the teacher: Use with "Read and Bowl!" on page 118.

125

Gumball Machine Pattern
Use with "Gumballs Galore" on page 120.

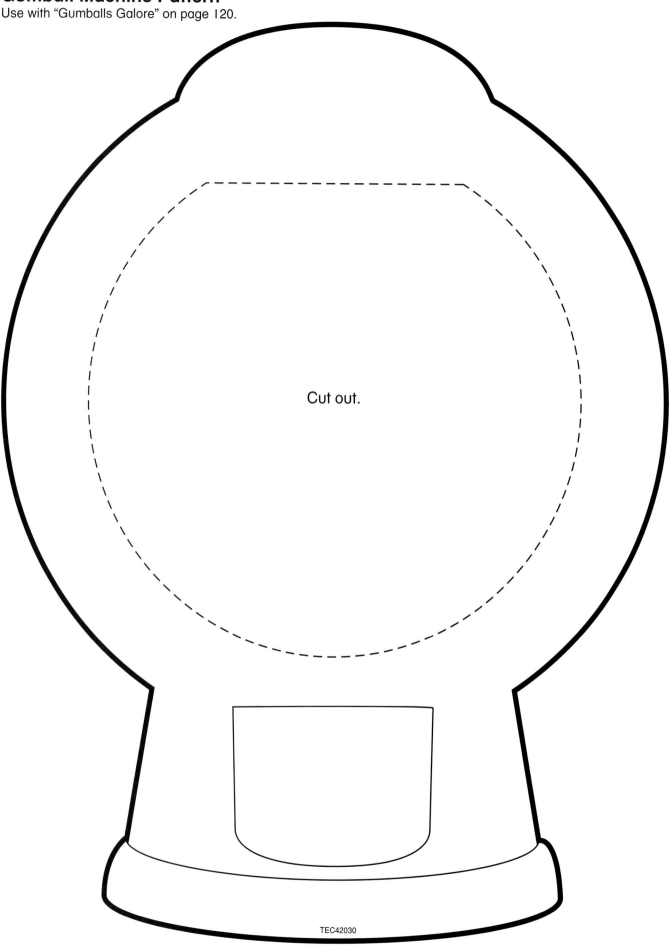

Cut out.

TEC42030

Spot, the Sound Dog

Dinnertime!

Note to the teacher: Use with "'Sound-sational' Dachshund" on page 122.

Comprehension
Graphic organizer

Story Worm

Title: _____

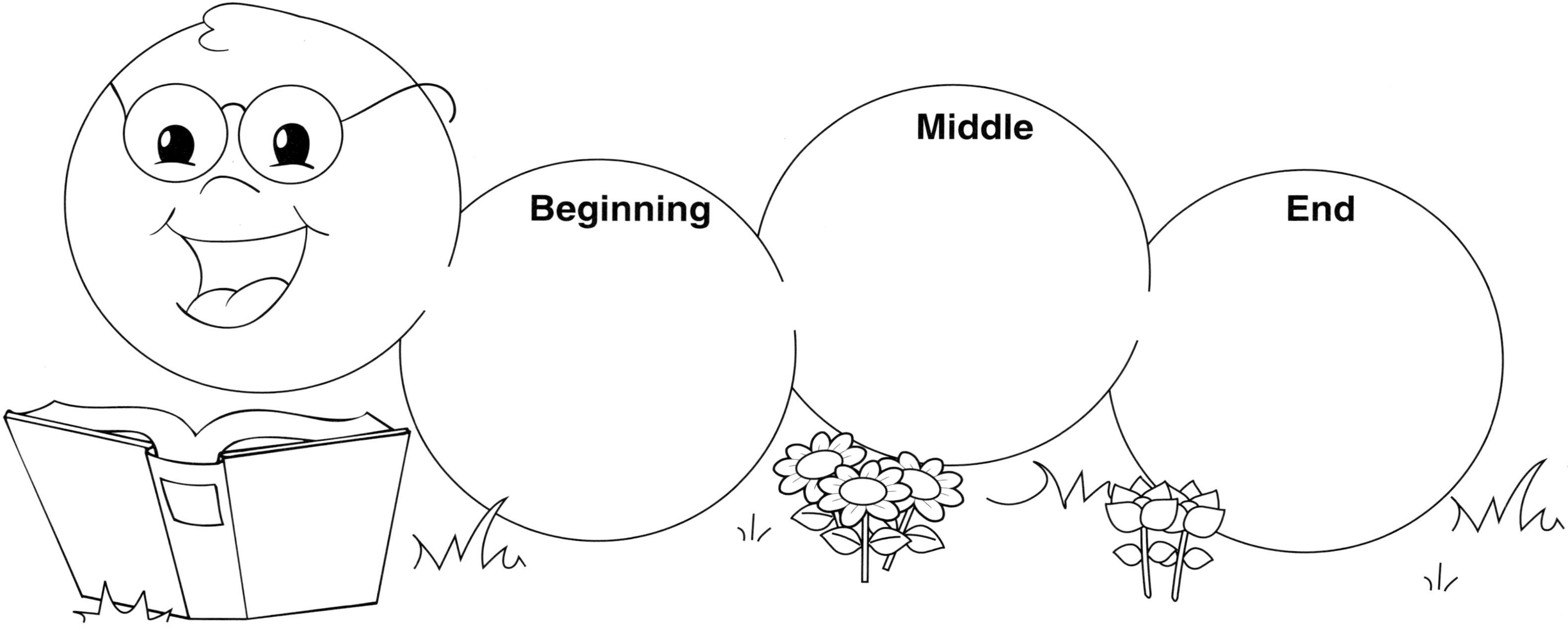

Beginning

Middle

End

Setting: _____

©The Mailbox® • TEC42031 • June/July 2007

Note to the teacher: Use with "Story Worm" on page 123.

'TIS THE SEASON

'Tis the Season

If You Take a Cat to Beale Elementary...

All Around the School

First-day jitters are sure to disappear with this literature-based activity! Read aloud *If You Take a Mouse to School* by Laura Numeroff. Then show students a small stuffed animal. Ask them to imagine what it could do in different parts of the school. Next, take the animal and a camera on a school tour with students. Photograph the animal in various locations and with different staff members. Later, mount each photograph on a separate sheet of paper and add a student-generated caption. Then bind the papers between two covers to make a class book.

Brenda Saunders, Beale Elementary
Gallipolis Ferry, OH

Cool and Colorful

This graphing idea is a great icebreaker for the first day of school. In advance, purchase a class supply of frozen ice pops. Cut a supply of paper strips in colors that correspond with the flavors. Draw and label a grid similar to the one shown, with one row per flavor. To begin, invite students to tell how they stayed cool during the summer. Comment that eating frozen ice pops is a great way to beat the heat. Then post the grid. Help each student show which flavor he likes the most by gluing a corresponding paper strip in the appropriate row. Guide students to read and interpret the resulting graph. Then surprise them with real frozen ice pops!

Deborah Hanes
Lincoln Elementary
Maywood, IL

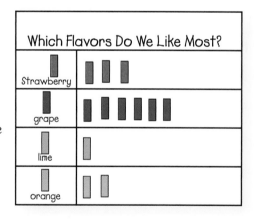

Which Flavors Do We Like Most?					
Strawberry					
grape					
lime					
orange					

I picked an apple from the tree.
Tell me, tell me, whose apple this could be.

Jacob

(Jacob, Jacob), that is me.
Thanks for picking an apple for me!

Bushels of Friends

Here's a fresh way for students to get acquainted. Display a large tree cutout within student reach. Write the name of each student on a separate die-cut apple and then use reusable adhesive to attach it to the tree. To begin, one student takes an apple and shows the name to her classmates. Then she says the first part of the rhyme shown. The student whose name is displayed says the second part of the rhyme and takes his apple. Then he picks another apple from the tree. The activity continues as described until each student has his apple.

Heather E. Graley
Grace Christian School
Blacklick, OH

'Tis the Season

Pumpkin Shell Estimates

To begin, display a pumpkin. Have each student estimate the number of lines (indentations) on the pumpkin shell and write the number on a large sticky note. Then help students arrange their sticky notes on the board in numerical order. Next, trace each line on the pumpkin with a marker and mark a starting point for easy counting. Count the lines with students. Then guide them to compare their estimates with the actual number of lines.

Diane Bonica, Deer Creek Elementary, Tigard, OR

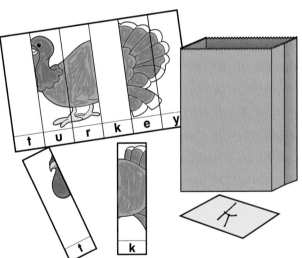

Turkey Puzzler

A Thanksgiving word is the focus of this small-group game. For each group, make a letter card for each letter in the word *turkey* and then place the cards in a paper lunch bag. Have each group member color the turkey puzzle pieces on a copy of page 137. Then instruct him to cut out the puzzle pieces and gameboard, keeping the gameboard intact.

To take a turn, a player takes a card at random. Then he places his corresponding puzzle piece on the matching section of his gameboard and returns the card. (If the piece is already in place, he returns the card and his turn is over.) The players alternate turns as described until one player completes his turkey.

Teresa Gillan, Gouverneur, NY

Fall Fun

It's a breeze to tailor this activity to suit the needs of your students! Color a copy of the gameboard on page 138, using a different color for each variety of leaf. To make game cards, gather a supply of blank cards that are the same colors as the leaves and program them to reinforce chosen skills. For example, you might write letters or words for students to identify or addition problems for them to solve. Arrange for two to four students to play at a time.

To play, the youngsters stack each group of cards facedown. Each player sets a game marker on a different corner of the gameboard. Player 1 rolls a die and moves her game marker clockwise that many spaces. If she lands on a leaf, she takes the top card of the corresponding color. She responds as appropriate and then sets the card aside. If she lands on a corner, she does nothing. The players take turns as described, reusing the cards if necessary, until one player reaches the corner where she started.

Karen Cook, McDonough Primary School, McDonough, GA

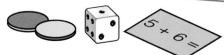

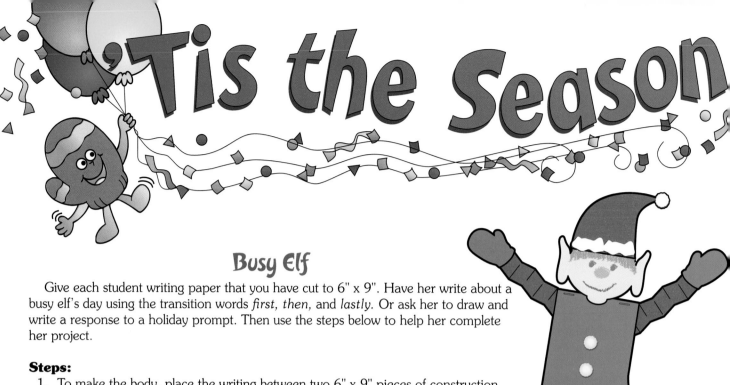

'Tis the Season

Busy Elf

Give each student writing paper that you have cut to 6" x 9". Have her write about a busy elf's day using the transition words *first, then,* and *lastly.* Or ask her to draw and write a response to a holiday prompt. Then use the steps below to help her complete her project.

Steps:
1. To make the body, place the writing between two 6" x 9" pieces of construction paper. Staple the stack at the top.
2. Use the elf patterns on page 140 to make one head, two shoes, and two mittens.
3. Draw a face and hair on the head and then glue it to the body. Cut out a hat from construction paper. Glue it to the head and decorate it as desired.
4. To make the arms, accordion-fold two 1½" x 9" paper strips. Glue them to the back of the body. Glue the mittens in place.
5. To make the legs, color two 2" x 12" white paper strips as desired. Accordion-fold the strips and then glue them to the back of the body. Glue the shoes in place.
6. Glue pom-poms to the body to resemble buttons.

Cindy Barber
Fredonia, WI

Frosty Addition

To make this snowpal project, a student draws a face on a five-inch white circle. He glues the head, a six-inch white circle, and a seven-inch white circle on a large sheet of paper as shown. He cuts a hat and two arms from construction paper and then glues them in place. Next, the youngster rolls a die. He arranges that many identical adhesive dots on the middle snowball to resemble buttons. He rolls the die again. Then he places that many adhesive dots of a different color on the bottom snowball. Finally, the youngster writes a corresponding vertical addition problem on a paper shovel and glues it to his paper.

For an easier version, instead of having the child write on the shovel, ask him to complete a paper strip with this addition sentence: "____ buttons + ____ buttons = ____ buttons."

Joanne Goerler
John M. Marshall Elementary
East Hampton, NY

'Tis the Season

Broken Hearts

Help students learn words by heart! Make a supply of identical die-cut hearts. Draw a zigzag on two or three hearts as shown. Program pairs of hearts with chosen words so that each word appears on two different hearts. To begin, a small group of students arranges the hearts facedown. Player 1 turns over two hearts and reads any words revealed. If the words are the same, she takes the two hearts. If the words are not the same, she turns the hearts back over. If a heart has a zigzag, she exclaims, "I have a broken heart!" Then she puts that heart aside and turns the other heart facedown in its original position. The other players each take a turn in the same manner. Alternate play continues until all of the words have been paired.

Emily Ryherd, Helen Baker Elementary, Glencoe, MN

Wild Weather?

On the first day of March, have students predict whether the month will have more weather that is wild like a lion or more weather that is gentle like a lamb. Next, post a blank two-column graph with about 25 rows. Label the columns with lion and lamb stickers or illustrations. On each school day in March, discuss the day's weather with students and have a volunteer color the appropriate space on the graph. At the month's end, compare the graph with students' predictions.

Ferol M. Empen, Byron, IL

Game Piece Code

0—none
1—one arm
2—one leg
3—head
4—body
5—your choice

Lucky Math

To prepare this small-group subtraction game, have each child color and cut out a copy of the leprechaun game pieces on page 142. Give each group two dice and a code similar to the one shown. To take a turn, a youngster rolls the dice. He announces the numbers rolled and determines the difference, with assistance as needed. If the difference is zero, his turn is over. If it is not zero, he takes a corresponding game piece and begins assembling his leprechaun. (If he does not need the game piece, his turn is over.) Players take turns as described until one player finishes assembling his leprechaun.

For an addition version, have students add the numbers rolled and use a code that corresponds with the possible sums. For example, a sum of either three or four may correspond with the head.

Sue Fleischmann, Sussex, WI

'Tis the Season

Busy Bunnies

For this hands-on approach to story problems, place a large empty tissue box upside down so that the bottom becomes the top. Paint the sides and top brown. Allow the paint to dry and then cut three long slits in the top of the box. Color and cut out eleven construction paper carrots (pattern on page 144). Stand them in the slits. Also, cut out a copy of the story problem cards on page 144.

If desired, read aloud *Muncha! Muncha! Muncha!* by Candace Fleming to introduce the activity. To begin, read aloud a chosen story problem or have a student read it to the group. Then ask volunteers to use the carrots to solve the problem. After you confirm the correct answer, "replant" the carrots for more math practice. **For more advanced students,** after volunteers model a problem, have students write the corresponding number sentence.

Erica Cerwin, Bob Beard Elementary, Helotes, TX

Pitter-Patter!

Turn a rainy day into a bright opportunity for writing! Take photos of small groups of students holding an umbrella outdoors. Afterward, give each youngster a colorful copy of the umbrella pattern on page 145. Ask her to write about a memorable rainy day or favorite rainy-day activities. After she finishes her writing, have her cut out the umbrella and tape a paper handle to the back of it. Showcase students' completed work with the photos and some raindrop cutouts on a bulletin board titled "Rainy-Day Writing."

Michelle Morrow, Red Bank Elementary, Lexington, SC

Beeline to Words

Here's a honey of a way to reinforce reading skills! Draw stripes and eyes on a small yellow pom-pom to make a bee. Trace a hexagon, such as a yellow pattern block, repeatedly on a sheet of paper to make a honeycomb similar to the one shown. Then choose an option below.

High-frequency words: Write a different word on each hexagon. Students take turns dropping the bee on the honeycomb, reading the word on which it lands, and then using it in a sentence.
Antonyms: Write a word from a different antonym word pair on each hexagon. In turn, each student drops the bee on the honeycomb, reads the word on which it lands, and then names an antonym.

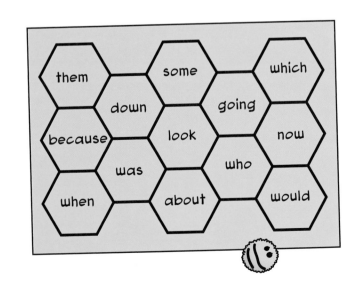

'Tis the Season

Tell a Tale!

Telling stories around a pretend campfire is a great way to promote oral language skills. Make a construction paper campfire in an open area of your classroom. Set up a small tent or decorate a bulletin board with a forest scene to create a backdrop. To begin, dim the lights. Hold a flashlight and sit with students around the campfire. Start telling a summer story. Then say, "Pass!" and hand the flashlight to a student beside you. Have that student continue the story and then pass the flashlight to the next student. Continue around the circle in this manner until the flashlight returns to you. Then conclude the campfire tale.

Andrea Selking
Lantern Farms School
Fishers, IN

Happy Hoppers

Use this frog game to make a splash with addition! Write on each of several lily pad cutouts a number suitable for your students' addition skills. Glue the cutouts on a large paper pond. Set out two plastic jumping frogs or green beanbags to represent frogs. Then arrange for two or three students to play at a time. To take a turn, a youngster makes the frogs jump onto the lily pads or tosses the beanbags onto the lily pads. Then he names the corresponding numbers. (The number for the water is one and the number for outside of the pond is zero.) The youngster determines the sum of the numbers and then passes the frogs or the beanbags to the next player. Students take turns in this manner as time allows.

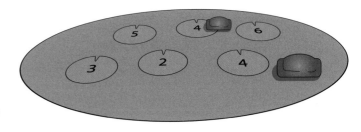

adapted from an idea by Colleen Demarco, Plover-Whiting Elementary, Plover, WI

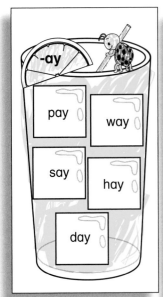

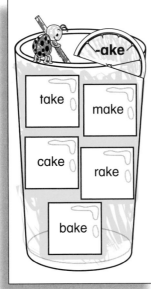

Ice-Cold Lemonade

Here's a refreshing approach to sorting words. Give each child a copy of the lemonade mats and ice cube patterns on page 147. Have her color the mats. Then instruct her to cut out the mats and ice cubes. After she sorts the ice cubes onto the appropriate mats, ask her to read each group of words and write the words on a sheet of paper. For a cool variation on traditional homework, have her take her mats and ice cubes home in a business-size envelope. Encourage her to sort and read the ice cubes with her family.

The reproducible on page 148 was written by Beth Marquardt of Campbellsport, WI.

Name_____

Just Picked!

Cut.

Glue to match the beginning sounds.

TEC42027

| t | u | r | k | e | y |

TEC42027

| t | u | r | k | e | y |

Fall Fun

Pumpkin Patch

✂ Cut. ⬜ Glue to the matching pumpkins.

✏ Write. Read.

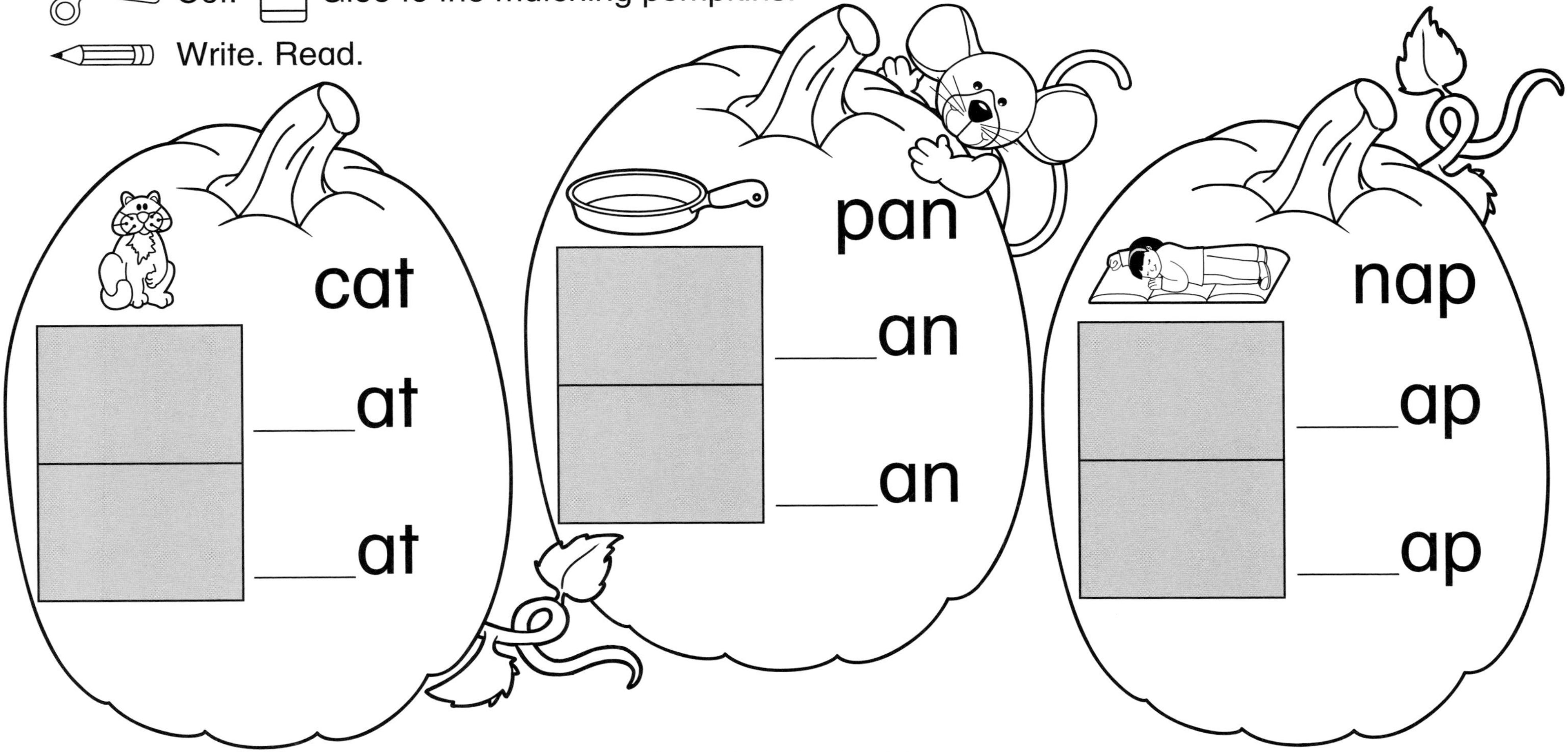

nap

ap ___

ap ___

pan

an ___

an ___

cat

at ___

at ___

TEC42028

Name _____

Fancy Footwork

 Cut.

Glue to match the vowel sounds.

ā as in	ī as in	ō as in

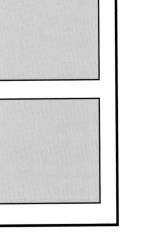

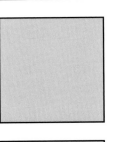

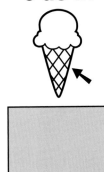

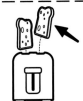

Leprechaun Game Pieces
Use with "Lucky Math" on page 133.

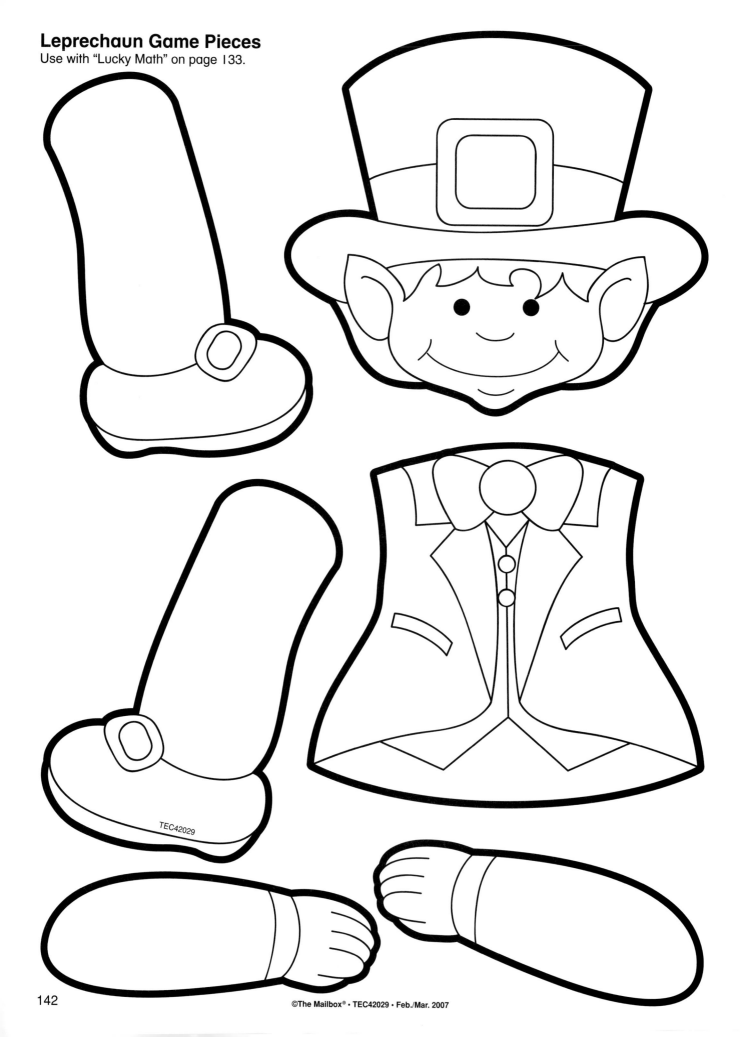

TEC42029

142

Name _____

Holiday Delivery

Read.

Write each word on the correct list.

Word Bank

purple	one	yellow
six	blue	five
nine	green	

red

♡ _____

♡ _____

♡ _____

♡ _____

ten

♡ _____

♡ _____

♡ _____

♡ _____

Bonus Box: Color the heart beside each color word with its matching color. Label the heart beside each number word with the matching number.

Carrot Pattern and Story Problem Cards

Use with "Busy Bunnies" on page 134.

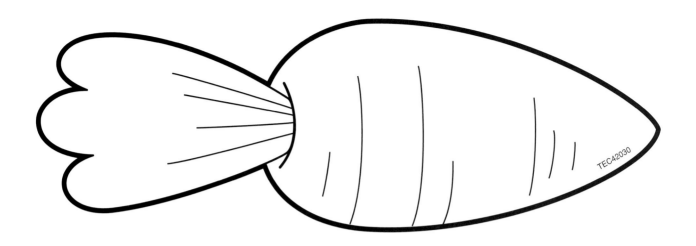

TEC42030

A. Bo Bunny takes 3 carrots.
Bess Bunny takes 2 carrots.
How many carrots do they
take in all?

TEC42030

B. Bo Bunny eats 5 carrots.
Then he eats 3 more.
How many carrots does he
eat in all?

TEC42030

C. Farmer Green plants 10
carrots.
Bo Bunny eats 7 of them.
How many carrots are left?

TEC42030

D. Bo Bunny takes 8 carrots.
He gives 2 of them away.
How many carrots does he
have left?

TEC42030

E. Bo Bunny and Bess Bunny
each take 4 carrots.
How many carrots do they
take in all?

TEC42030

F. Bo Bunny takes 7 carrots.
Bess Bunny takes 4 carrots.
How many more carrots does
Bo have than Bess?

TEC42030

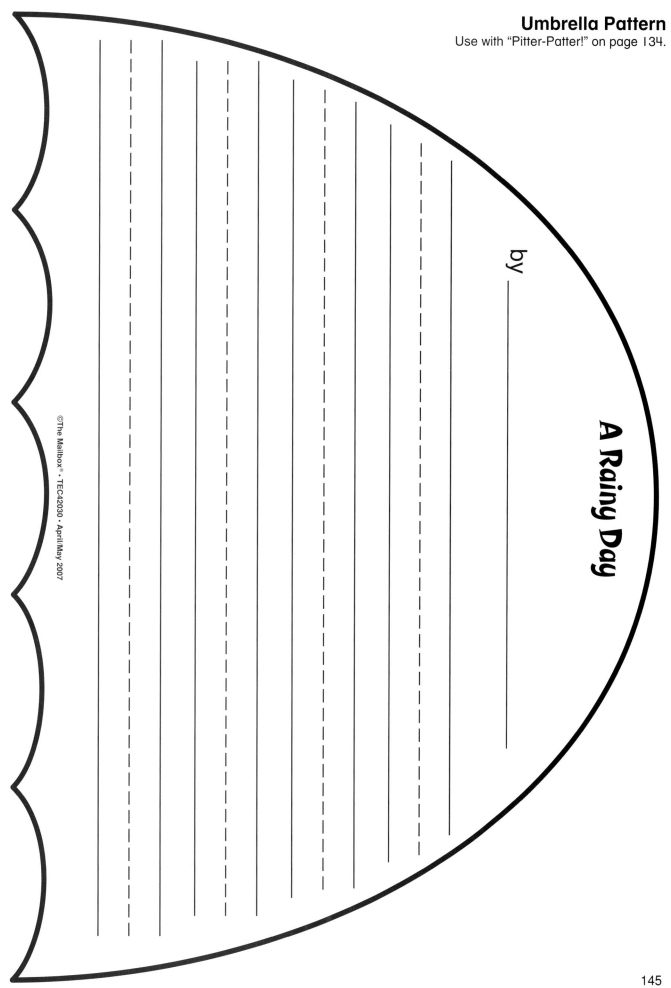

by

A Rainy Day

Flo's Flowers

Count. ✏️ Color the graph.

	Kinds of Flowers			
7				
6				
5				
4				
3				
2				
1				
0	🌼	🌷	🌺	🌾

Circle the correct answers.

1. Are there **more** 🌷 than 🌼 ?   yes   no

2. Are there **more** 🌺 than 🌾 ?   yes   no

3. Are there **more** 🌼 than 🌾 ?   yes   no

-ay

-ake

TEC42031

TEC42031

day	hay	pay	say	way
TEC42031	TEC42031	TEC42031	TEC42031	TEC42031
bake	cake	make	rake	take
TEC42031	TEC42031	TEC42031	TEC42031	TEC42031

Yummy Sums

Cut. Glue to match the sums.

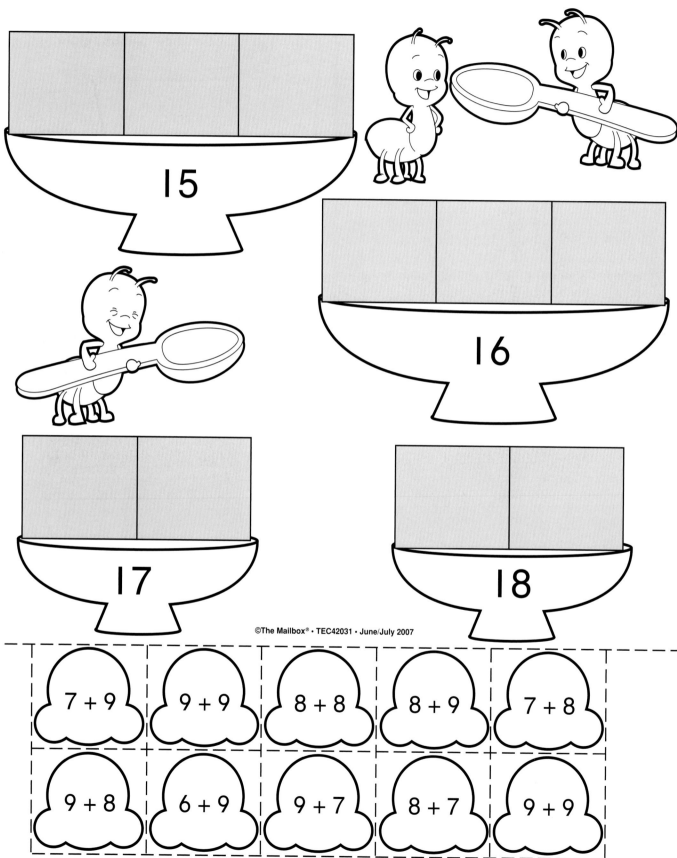

15

16

17

18

©The Mailbox® • TEC42031 • June/July 2007

7 + 9   9 + 9   8 + 8   8 + 9   7 + 8

9 + 8   6 + 9   9 + 7   8 + 7   9 + 9

WRITE ON!

Write On!

September 18, 2006
News Reported
by Carlos

Today is sunny. We will
have P.E.

Now Reporting...

Here's a newsworthy shared-writing activity! Display a sheet of chart paper and write the date near the top. Write "News Reported by" and draw a blank as shown. To begin, designate a student as the news reporter. Have him write his name in the blank and tell the group something about the day. Then write the information, inviting students' input on details such as capital letters and chosen letter-sound relationships. After the report is complete, read it with students and ask the reporter to illustrate it. Prepare reports on several different days as described and then compile them into a class book titled "Our News."

Shirl Bent, Maryvale Primary, Cheektowaga, NY

This is Nicole.

Everyone Is a Star!

Every student has a turn in the spotlight with this sentence-writing idea. Designate a youngster as the star student of the day. Then model how to write the following sentence: "This is [star student's name]." Reinforce chosen skills as you write, such as using capital letters correctly and leaving space between words.

Next, have each student write the sentence on a copy of the booklet page on page 156. (Help the star student write, "This is me.") Ask each youngster to illustrate her page with a drawing of the honored student and color the border. After she cuts out her completed page, instruct her to place it in a personalized folder for safekeeping. Repeat the activity on later days until each student has completed a page about each member of the class. Then stack each student's pages with the page about herself at the bottom and bind them between two covers.

Kim Lavery, Sacandaga Elementary, Scotia, NY

I lik the car. It is nis.

car

Idea Box

Build anticipation for writing with this approach to choosing topics. Collect a class supply of small objects plus a few extra. For example, you might collect shells, toy cars, and plastic animals. Place each object in a separate resealable plastic bag that you have labeled with the corresponding word. Place all of the bags in a decorated box. One day each week, have each student choose a bag from the box before writing time. When it's time to write, he'll have a topic close at hand!

Victoria Cavanagh, Troy Hills School, Parsippany, NJ

Write On!

Pumpkin

orange   heavy

big   round

green   smooth

Tell About It!

Spark interest in describing words with this unique word bank. Create a simple illustration of a seasonal or thematic item on a large sheet of paper. Title the paper with the name of the item and then display it. Guide students to name appropriate describing words; write the words around the illustration. Later, invite students to help you use the words in sentences. **For more advanced students,** ask each youngster to create her own illustration and write describing words around it. Have her write sentences with the words. Then display her artwork with her writing.

Pam Susman, Jenard Gross Elementary, Houston, TX

Stretch It Out!

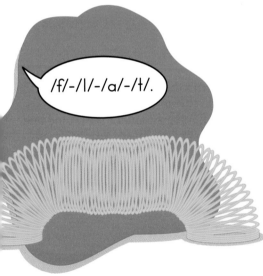

/f/-/l/-/a/-/t/.

Here's an approach to sounding out words that not only works, but is also fun! Bring in a small plastic Slinky toy. When you model sentence writing one day, pause at a chosen word and tell students that the toy will help you spell it. Then slowly stretch the toy as you slowly say the word. Repeat the stretching process and count the number of sounds with students. Then write the word as you repeat the sounds. When students need help sounding out words in their own writing, encourage them to stretch the words and the toy!

Traci Benke, Waynesburg Central Elementary, Waynesburg, PA

"Tree-mendous" Sights

What Grows on Trees?

Red apples grow on trees.

by Tommy

This booklet's patterned text is sure to help students' sentence-writing skills grow. Cut out one copy of the treetop pattern on page 157. Use it as a tracer and make two green treetops for each student. Have each youngster cut out three white copies of the treetop pattern and stack them between his green treetops. Staple the stack at the top. Then instruct the student to glue a construction paper trunk to the back of his resulting booklet. Have him title his booklet "What Grows on Trees?" and sign his name on the trunk.

Next, prompt students to answer the title question by naming items such as red apples, green apples, oranges, and different colors of leaves. Have each student use the sentence pattern shown to write a response on each booklet page. Then instruct him to illustrate his work. **For an easier activity,** create a class book version, enlisting students' help to write as appropriate for their abilities.

Coramarie Marinan, Howe School, Green Bay, WI

Write On!

What's Inside?

No doubt your students are always eager to tell about gifts they receive. So what better writing topic than favorite gifts? To begin this festive project, have each youngster draw a chosen gift on a sheet of story paper. Then instruct him to write about the gift, encouraging him to include details such as who gave it to him and what the occasion was. After his writing is complete, cut a piece of gift wrap that is the same size as the paper. Use clear tape to secure the gift wrap to the top of the writing paper. Then invite the youngster to decorate and label his resulting package as desired. **For an easier version,** give each student paper programmed with appropriate sentence starters.

Bobbie Redd-Hallman, Don Stowell School, Merced, CA

(sung to the tune of "Sailing, Sailing")

End marks, end marks
Finish sentences well.
We always use a period
With sentences that tell.

End marks, end marks
Always are very last.
We always use a question mark
With sentences that ask.

A Good Finish

Here's a fun approach to reviewing punctuation. Post the song shown. After you familiarize students with the song, guide youngsters to dictate a telling sentence and an asking sentence. Write the sentences on separate sentence strips. Then ask volunteers to mark the period and question mark with a highlighter. Display the sentences near the song. Revisit the resulting punctuation reference periodically to keep students' skills sharp.

Beth Marquardt, St. Paul's School of Early Learning, Muskego, WI

"Bear-y" Cute Booklet

Looking for a way to promote simple story writing? Read aloud *Polar Bear, Polar Bear, What Do You Hear?* by Bill Martin Jr. After you point out the patterned text to students, have them brainstorm a list of animal sounds at a place other than a zoo, such as a pet store or a farm. Then give each student an eight-inch round booklet with white covers and several white pages. Instruct him to illustrate a polar bear face on the front cover and glue two ears to the back cover. Then ask him to refer to the brainstormed list as he writes and illustrates a story with a pattern loosely modeled on Bill Martin Jr.'s book. **For an easier version,** create a larger booklet and write one story with students.

Monica Shiba, Indian Trail School, Highland Park, IL

Write On!

Stop and Go

Keep students moving on the road to writing success with this approach to capitalization and end marks. With students' input, write two or more sentences on a sheet of chart paper. Next, suggest that sentences have signals just as traffic lights do: an uppercase letter to signal the beginning and a punctuation mark to signal the end. Then have students check that each sentence has two signals. To do this, ask volunteers to trace the first letter of each sentence with a green crayon and each end mark with a red crayon. **For more advanced students,** encourage youngsters to check their own writing as described.

Katy Hoh and Candy Ware, W. C. K. Wall School, Pitman, NJ

Mail Call!

When it comes to writing motivation, this ongoing idea really delivers! Place a mailbox (or a box decorated to resemble one) in an easily accessible classroom location. Display on a bulletin board a personalized mail pocket, similar to the one shown, for each student, yourself, and any other adults who work in your classroom.

Encourage youngsters to write letters to be delivered to the appropriate pockets. After a youngster proofreads her writing, ask her to place the letter in an envelope. Then have her address the envelope, draw a stamp on it, and deposit it in the mailbox. Each day, have a designated student "cancel" the stamps on the mail with a decorative ink stamp and then deliver the mail. To keep interest high, periodically send each student a letter with questions that encourage a response.

Sheila Criqui-Kelley, Lebo Elementary, Lebo, KS

Wild About Animals

For this caption-writing activity, title a large manila envelope "Mystery Animals" and decorate it as desired. Cut a supply of animal pictures from magazines or calendars and place them in the envelope. Gather students near a sheet of chart paper. Have a volunteer take one picture from the envelope at random and then glue it on the paper. Briefly discuss the picture with students. Then ask a youngster to write a caption with help from you and her classmates as appropriate. After the sentence is complete, invite a different student to remove a picture from the envelope for more caption-writing fun.

Katie Zuehlke, Bendix Elementary, Annandale, MN

Write On!

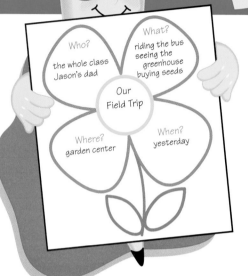

Flowery Plan

Watch stories blossom with this easy-to-adapt prewriting activity. Draw a flower with four or five petals. For a four-petal flower, title the petals with the question words shown. For a five-petal flower, title each petal with a different sense. To complete the resulting graphic organizer, write a topic in the center and one or more corresponding details on each petal. Use the graphic organizer to plan a group story, or have each youngster plan her own story on an individual copy.

Ava Gonick, Cucamonga Elementary, Rancho Cucamonga, CA

Topic Tools

Give writer's block new meaning with this idea for helping students choose writing topics. Gather a supply of blocks and an equal number of blank cards sized to fit the blocks. Program each card with clip art or a writing topic. Attach each card to a different block and then put the blocks in a labeled container. Whenever a child has trouble thinking of something to write about, invite him to take a writer's block. It's sure to jump-start the writing process!

Sarah Scotti, Jefferson Elementary, Schenectady, NY

"Pet-acular" Bugs

Imagine having a pet bug! That's what students do with this descriptive writing activity. Give each child a plastic bug and a resealable plastic bag. Have her trim a 3" x 6" green rectangle to make a leaf, write her name on it, and place it in the bag. Then ask her to put her bug in the bag so that it is in front of the blank side of the leaf.

Next, instruct each student to write about her bug. Encourage her to include a name for it and descriptive details, such as the bug's color, size, and shape. After each youngster edits her writing, post each student's work beside her bag and title the display "Meet Our Pet Bugs!" **For an easier version,** give each child a paper with sentence starters to complete.

Annette Hamill, Collins Elementary, Collins, MS

Write On!

Jump, Roll, and Paddle!

The grin-inducing book *Mrs. Wishy-Washy* by Joy Cowley is a perfect model for using action words and quotation marks. Before you read the book to students, mix equal parts of brown paint and mud in a large shallow container. After you share the book, revisit the pages where the animals see and explore the mud. Have students identify the quotation marks and action words. Then guide youngsters to brainstorm different action words.

Next, arrange for each student to use the prepared mixture to make footprints on the top half of a sheet of paper. After the prints dry, have him write a caption, like the one shown, with his own name and a chosen action verb. Bind students' work into a class book titled "Mud!" **For an easier version,** give each student a sentence frame to complete and glue on his paper.

Coramarie Marinan, Howe School, Green Bay, WI

"Oh, lovely mud," said Spencer, and he crawled in it.

Pet Tales

What's the key to this writing motivation idea? It's allergy-free class pets! Put a stuffed animal in a pet carrier and present it to students as the week's classroom pet. Name the pet with students' input. Then give each youngster a journal with construction paper covers and several blank pages. Throughout the week, encourage each youngster to write about the pet in his journal. You might have him respond to prompts, write a description, or write an imaginative story. At the week's end, invite a student to bring in a stuffed animal to be the next "pet-acular" writing topic!

Katy Hoh, W. C. K. Walls School, Pitman, NJ

This is Stripes. She is our class pet. She likes to play with string.

Count and Confirm!

Here's a hands-on approach to writing complete sentences. Ask a youngster to say a sentence that she would like to write. Have her count the words as you repeat the sentence. Then give her an equal number of sticky notes. Instruct her to write the words on separate sticky notes and then arrange them to form the sentence. After you help her check her work, ask her to write and illustrate the sentence on provided paper.

Yvonne Sturdivant, Vilonia Primary School, Conway, AR

I got a new ~~nu~~ bike last night ~~nite~~

I got a new bike last night.

Booklet Page

Use with "Everyone Is a Star!" on page 150.

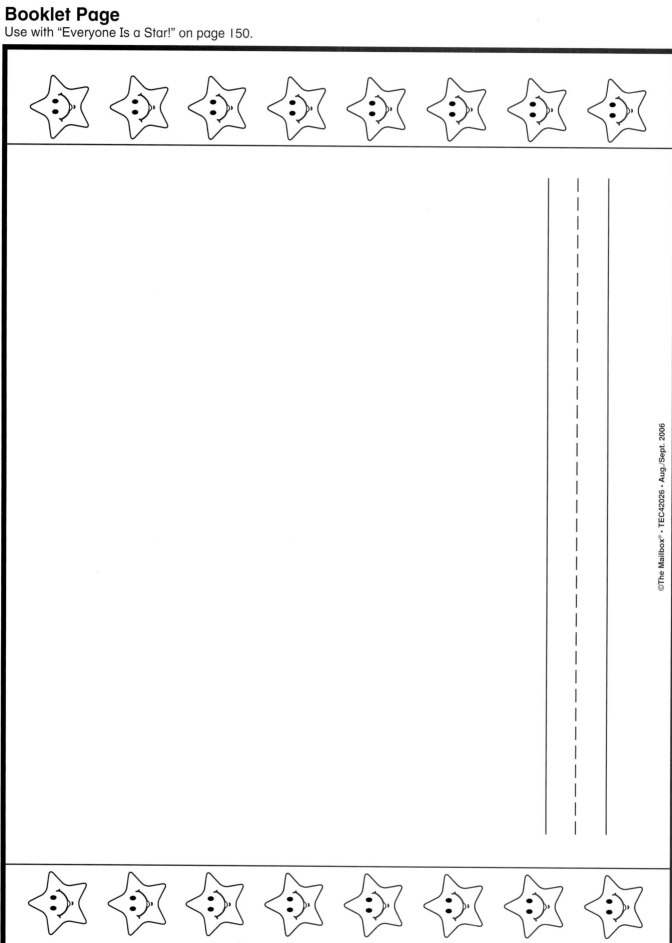

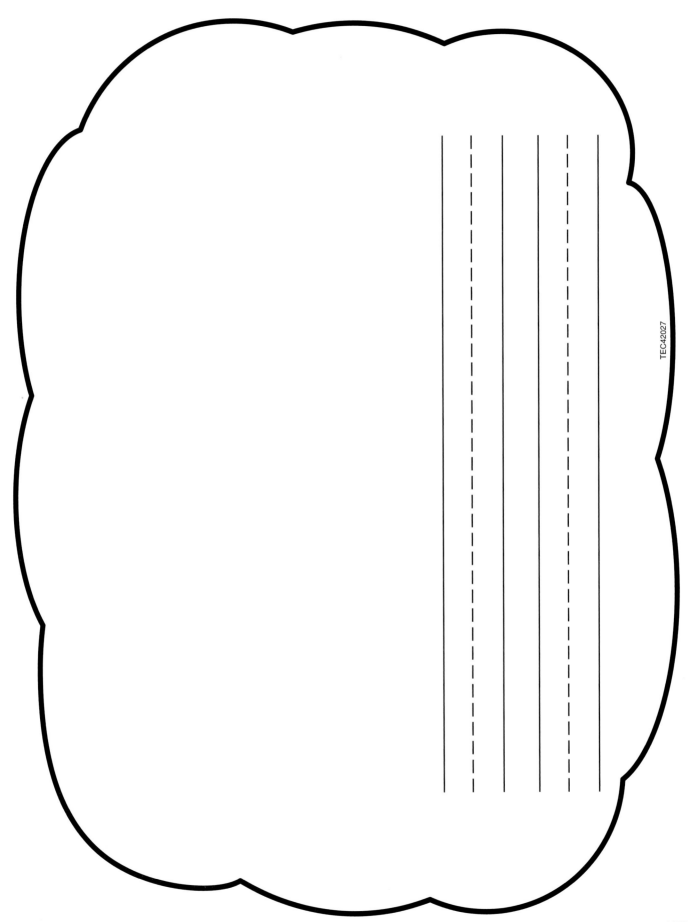

TEC42027

Name _____

October Journal Pal

- acorn
- candy
- fire truck
- pumpkin
- spider
- squirrel

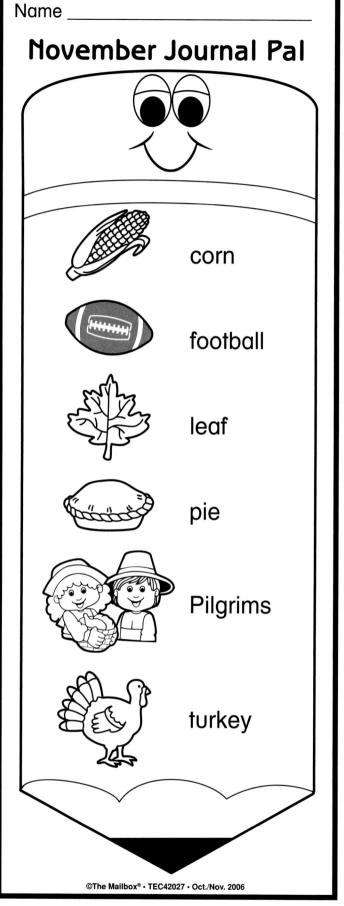

Name _____

November Journal Pal

- corn
- football
- leaf
- pie
- Pilgrims
- turkey

Note to the teacher: This October and November, give each student a copy of the appropriate month's journal pal. Have her write her name on it, color it, and then staple it in her journal.

Name _____

December Journal Pal

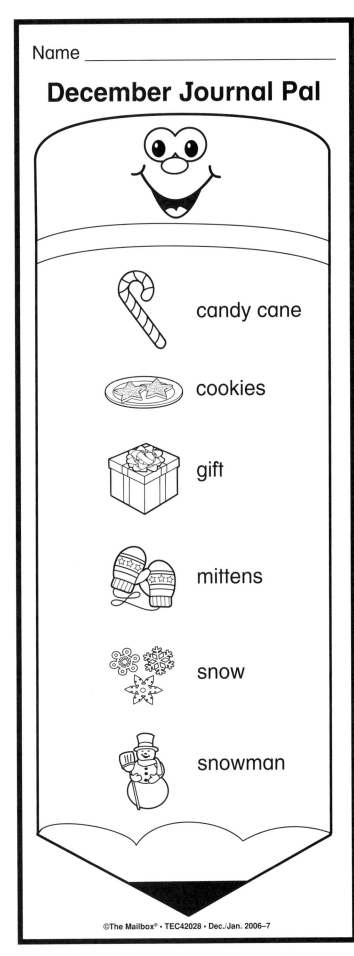

candy cane

cookies

gift

mittens

snow

snowman

Name _____

January Journal Pal

cold

ice skates

penguin

scarf

sled

sweater

Note to the teacher: This December and January, give each student a copy of the appropriate month's journal pal. Have her write her name on it, color it, and then staple it in her journal.

Name _____

February Journal Pal

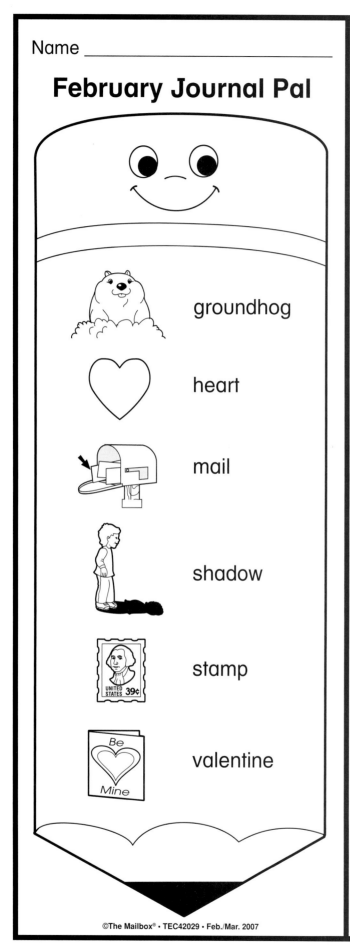

groundhog

heart

mail

shadow

stamp

valentine

Name _____

March Journal Pal

kite

leprechaun

pot of gold

rainbow

shamrock

wind

Note to the teacher: This February and March, give each student a copy of the appropriate month's journal pal. Have him write his name on it, color it, and then staple it in his journal.

Name _____

April Journal Pal

basket

egg

puddle

rabbit

rain

umbrella

Name _____

May Journal Pal

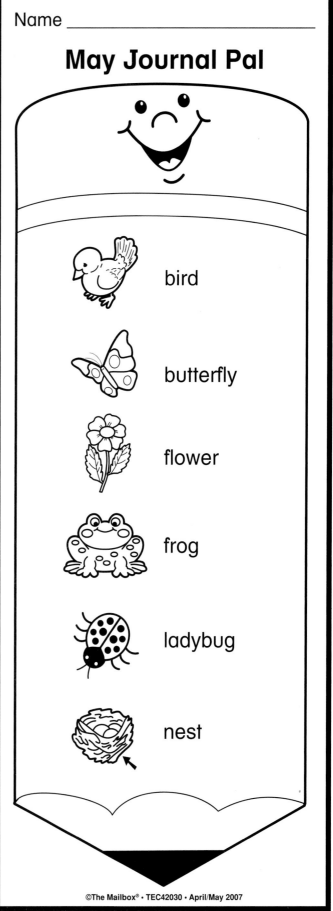

bird

butterfly

flower

frog

ladybug

nest

Note to the teacher: This April and May, give each student a copy of the appropriate month's journal pal. Have her write her name on it, color it, and then staple it in her journal.

Summer Words

Name _____

beach

bike

ice cream

sailboat

swim

swing

©The Mailbox® · TEC42031 · June/July 2007

Picnic Words

Name _____

basket

chips

fruit

grill

sandwich

watermelon

©The Mailbox® · TEC42031 · June/July 2007

Note to the teacher: Give each child a copy of one or both word banks. Ask her to write her name on it, color it, and then refer to it for writing inspiration and spelling help.

LITERACY UNITS

Nuts About Names

Start the school year with this stash of top-notch ideas. They're perfect for boosting students' literacy skills and helping youngsters get acquainted!

Role in a Rhyme
Concepts about print

What's a surefire way to spark students' interest in reading? Why, inviting them to read about someone they know! Write a nursery rhyme on a large sheet of paper, replacing one character's name with a blank each time it appears. Laminate the rhyme and then post it. (Or prepare the rhyme for pocket chart use and have students program blank cards with their names.) Use a wipe-off marker to write a chosen student's name in each blank, and have youngsters identify the name. Then read the rhyme with students. During additional readings, change the featured name and reinforce skills such as tracking print and counting words.

Later, place the rhyme, a pointer, and a wipe-off marker at a center. Arrange for two students at a time to visit the center. Have each student, in turn, write his name in the blanks and then point to each word as he and his partner read the rhyme.

Brooke Beverly, Dudley Elementary, Dudley, MA

Sammy, be nimble.

Sammy, be quick.

Sammy, jump over the candlestick.

A Friendly Game
Identifying names

Here's a winning approach to creating a classroom community. Make one copy of the gameboard on page 166. Write each student's name in a different box and decorate any remaining boxes to designate them as free spaces. (To present fewer names at a time or for larger classes, program more than one gameboard.) Copy the gameboard to make a class supply plus one extra. Cut apart one copy to create name cards. Give each child a supply of Unifix cubes, and have her color her gameboard if desired.

To play one round, take a name card at random. Announce the name, write it on the board, and set the card aside. After each student places a cube on her corresponding box, erase the board. Continue the game as described until each student marks all of the names in a horizontal row and calls out, "Friends!" Since the gameboards are identical, the winners are the students whose names are in the corresponding row.

Kelly MacCall-Carter, Bridge Valley Elementary, Furlong, PA

FRIENDS!

There is a student in our class,
and Kelly is her name-o.
K-E-L-L-Y,
K-E-L-L-Y,
K-E-L-L-Y,
And Kelly is her name-o!

Name-o!
Letter recognition
Give each student a turn in the spotlight with this version of a familiar song. Write the name of a chosen student on the board. Have the youngster come forward; then hand her a pointer. Explain that she needs to point to the letters when the class names them. Then lead the class in singing a version of "Bingo" with the student's name, similar to the verse shown. (For names that do not closely match the rhythm, chant the letters rather than sing them.) **For more advanced students,** repeat the verse and substitute claps for letters as in the traditional version.

Kathie Casale, Small World Day Care Center, Brooklyn, NY

Ready Reference
Literacy skills
This display idea has learning opportunities from *A* to *Z!* Create a word wall with your students' names by posting each name below the corresponding initial letter. Use one or more of the suggestions below, and encourage students to use the display as a spelling reference. **To make the activities easier,** post fewer names at one time.

Phonological awareness: To segment syllables, have students clap, tap, or stomp as they say a name.

Writing: Ask students to write sentences with the names.

Review: Secretly choose a name and give clues about it, such as the beginning sound and the number of letters. Ask the first youngster who correctly guesses the name to point it out.

Carolyn Hoople, Deer Run School, Calgary, Alberta, Canada

Bry-son.

Gathering Letters
Spelling names
Promote teamwork with this partner game. Give each twosome one die, two game markers, one copy of the gameboard on page 167, crayons, and a half sheet of one-inch graph paper cut lengthwise. If desired, have students color their gameboards.

To begin, each player writes his name on the graph paper, writing one letter per box. Then he places his game marker on the starred gameboard space. Player 1 rolls the die and advances his marker the corresponding number of spaces. If the letter he lands on is in either his partner's name or his own name, he colors one corresponding box on the graph paper. If the letter is not in either name, his turn is over. Player 2 takes a turn in the same manner. Alternate play continues until both names are completely colored.

Michele Lasky Anszelowicz, Mandalay Elementary, Wantagh, NY

Furry Friends

Note to the teacher: Use with "A Friendly Game" on page 164.

Teamwork Trail

Note to the teacher: Use with "Gathering Letters" on page 165.

A Splash of Color

This colorful look at words is
guaranteed to brighten skills practice!

Focus on Favorites

Students dress for reading success with this
class book project. On a designated day, have
each youngster wear his favorite color of clothing
to school. Take an individual photograph of each
student. Then mount each photo as desired on a
separate sheet of paper programmed as shown. Help
each youngster write his name in the first blank
and the appropriate color word in the second blank.
Hole-punch students' completed papers and then
place them in a three-ring binder. Title the resulting
book "Colors We Like." Use the book with small
groups to reinforce color words as well as concepts
about print. **For an easier version,** write the color
words in the corresponding colors.

Amy Vogel, Saint Sylvester School, Pittsburgh, PA

Devin likes *blue*

With Flying Colors

With this **pocket chart activity,** students' literacy skills
are sure to take off! Color a copy of page 170, making
each airplane a different color. Cut out the cards and back
them with tagboard for durability. Then choose from the
suggestions below.

Word matching: Write the color word for each airplane
on two separate sentence strips. Underline one word in
each pair with the appropriate color. Display the airplanes
in a pocket chart and have students place each color-coded
word beside the correct airplane. Then ask them to pair
each remaining word with the matching word on display.

Word recognition: Prepare a color word card for each
airplane and display it in a pocket chart. Beside each
card place the correct airplane with the blank side facing
outward. Invite students to read each word and then turn
over the corresponding airplane to check it.

Jackie Wright, Summerhill Children's House, Enid, OK

green

green

yellow

168

Greetings

Add a colorful twist to your morning **group time**! Cut a large square from each of several different colors of construction paper. Write each corresponding color word on a separate blank card. Prepare additional color word cards as needed so that there is either a word card or a colorful square for each student.

To begin, have students stand in a circle. Give each child a word card or a square. Next, invite one student with a square to go to the center of the circle and name her color. Then ask each student with the corresponding word to join her. Have the youngsters in the center of the circle greet one another by name and then return to their places. Continue in the same manner with different colors until each student has been greeted.

Deborah Patrick
Park Forest Elementary
State College, PA

Special Delivery

To prepare this reading and spelling **center,** write a different color word on the front of each of several white envelopes. Then lift the flap of each envelope and color the adhesive side of the flap with the corresponding color. For each letter in the word, program a small blank card. Place the letter cards in the envelope. Close each envelope but do not seal it.

A student takes an envelope, reads the word, and then lifts the flap of the envelope to check it. He arranges the letter cards to spell the word, using the word on the envelope as a model if necessary. After he checks his spelling, he returns the letters to the envelope. He reads and spells each remaining word in the same manner.

Ann-Marie Samaras, Herzl Elementary, Chicago, IL

brown

Write and Read!

Unusual worms are the topic of this simple **booklet** project. To begin, post a list of color words for student reference. Then give each child a copy of the booklet backing and pages on page 171. Have her write a different color word in each blank and color the worm to match. Next, ask her to cut out the backing and pages. Help her staple the pages to the backing as shown. In the space above the pages, ask her to illustrate a bird looking for a worm. After she completes the illustration, encourage her to read her booklet to a classmate.

Rhonda Chiles, South Park Elementary
Shawnee Mission, KS

My bird sees a very big

orange worm.

169

Airplane Cards
Use with "With Flying Colors" on page 168.

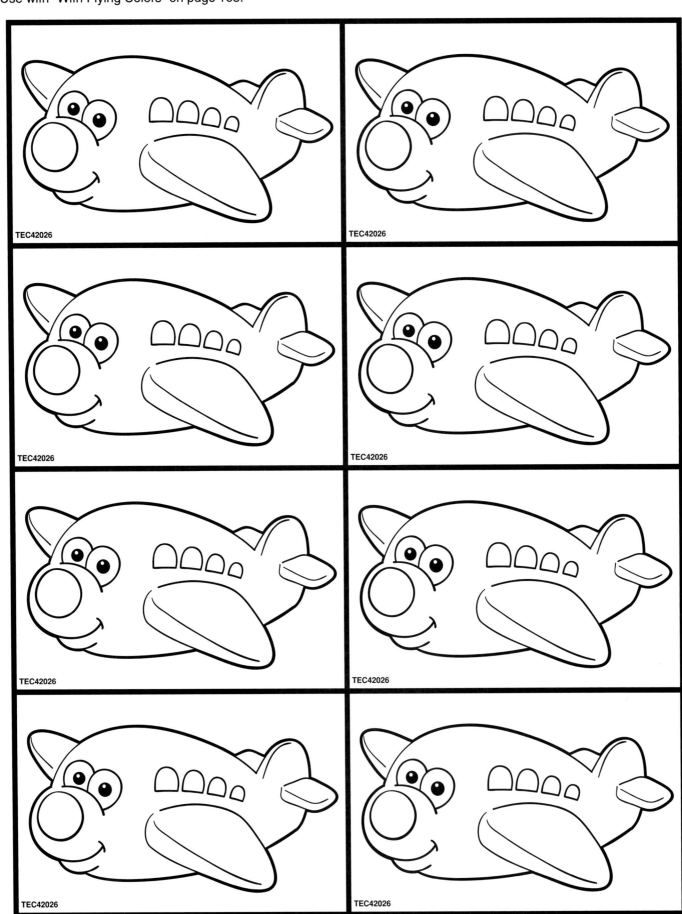

TEC42026

TEC42026

TEC42026

TEC42026

TEC42026

TEC42026

TEC42026

TEC42026

My bird sees a very big

_____

worm.

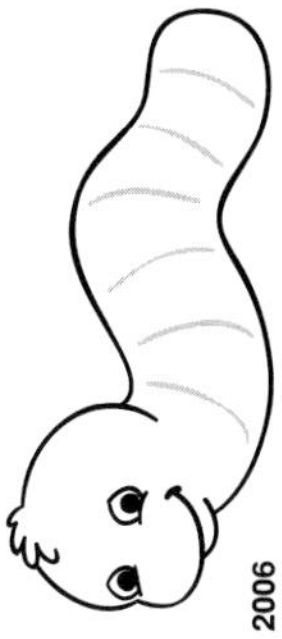

worm.

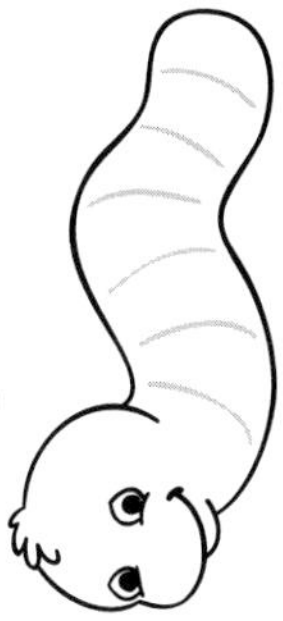

worm.

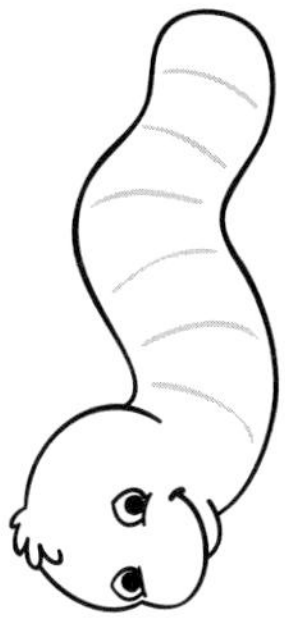

worm.

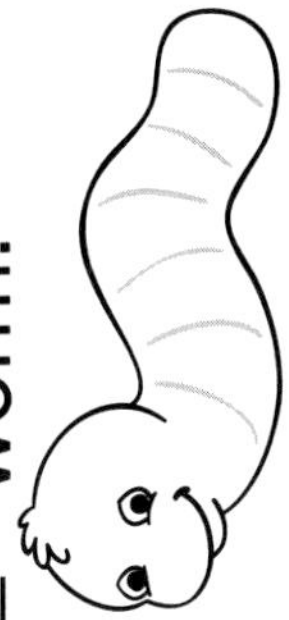

worm.

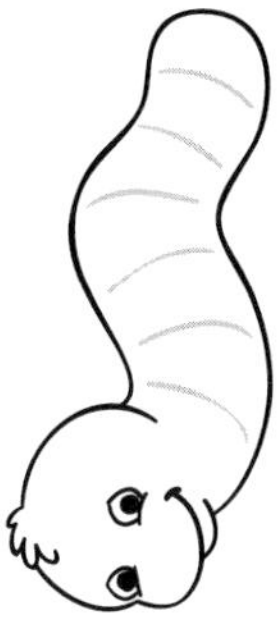

Name _____

Pretty Paint

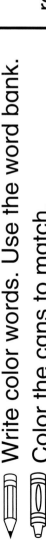 Write color words. Use the word bank.

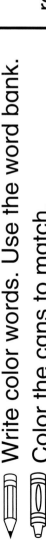 Color the cans to match.

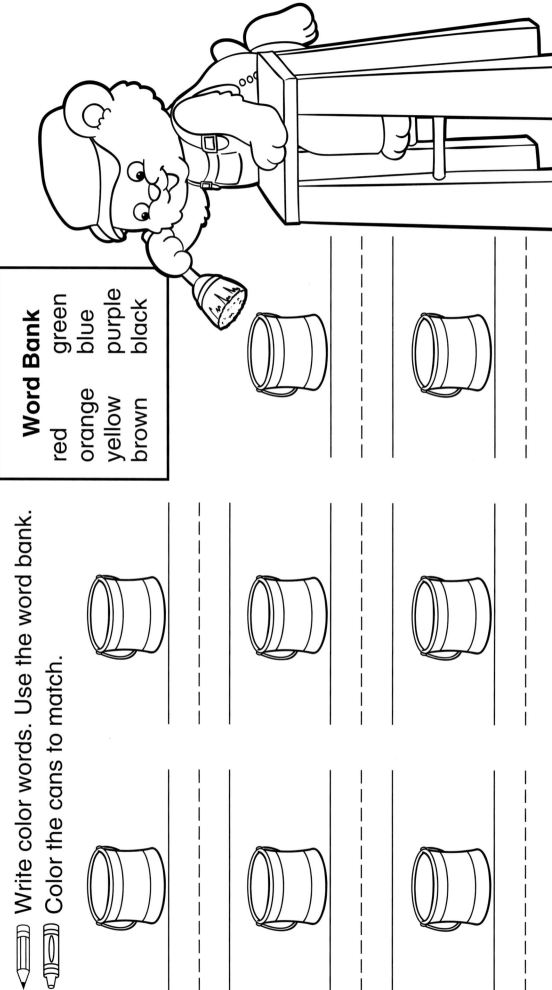

Word Bank

red	green
orange	blue
yellow	purple
brown	black

Alphabet Soup

Serve up a hearty helping of learning fun with these literacy ideas.

Four in a Row
Letter identification

Use this small-group game for winning reinforcement of either lowercase or uppercase letters. Gather the dice from a Boggle game or collect a set of letter manipulatives such as magnetic letters or the tiles from a Scrabble game. Draw a 4 x 4 lotto board with blank space at the top as shown. Make a copy for each group member. Then program the gameboards with chosen letters, writing one letter per space and making each board unique. Invite each youngster to decorate the top of her board with stickers or stamps. Then give students a supply of game markers.

To play one round, Player 1 rolls a Boggle die or takes a letter manipulative at random. Then she names the letter. Each player who has the letter on her board places a game marker on it. The next player designates a letter for players to mark in the same manner. Play continues as described until one player marks four letters in a row and calls out, "Letter lineup!"

Heidi Gross, Avoca Central School, Avoca, NY

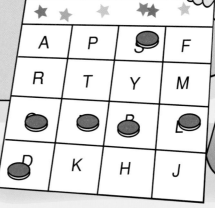

> Letter lineup!

Decorative Door
Letter-sound associations

No doubt youngsters will be eager to contribute to this unique display! Post a large letter cutout on the classroom side of your door. Explain to students that they will help you decorate the door with objects and pictures whose names begin with the letter. Send a note home to parents asking them to help their children collect appropriate items.

To showcase students' finds, have each child, in turn, show the class what he brought. After he names the item, post the item (or a student illustration of it) on the door. If desired, also post the name of the item and encourage students to use the label as a spelling reference. When students line up, they are sure to enjoy studying the display. And when the door is open, the display will let passersby know what your students are learning!

Judith Wrenick
Fraser Valley Elementary
Fraser, CO

Bag Booklet
Letter-sound associations
Here's a creative way to showcase items for a few letters or for the entire alphabet. Gather a supply of resealable plastic sandwich bags. For each student, stack one bag for each letter that you want to reinforce, with the bag openings on the right-hand side. Staple the stack on the left-hand edge for easy handling. Then secure it between two construction paper covers to create a booklet.

To complete his booklet, a youngster writes each designated letter on both sides of a separate 3" x 5" card. Then he inserts the cards in the bags in alphabetical order, placing one card in each bag. Over the next several days, the youngster collects small objects or draws pictures of items whose names begin with the featured letters. He seals each item in the appropriate bag. **For more advanced students,** help youngsters write the name of each item on the appropriate letter card for use as a spelling reference.

Molly Lynch, Arundel School, San Carlos, CA

Ladle a Letter!
Letter-sound associations
To warm up students' literacy skills, place in a soup pot a ladle and class supply of letter manipulatives plus a few extra. Sit with students in a circle and place the pot in front of one youngster. Next, ask the child to scoop out a letter and identify it. Then invite her to ask a volunteer to name a word that begins with the letter. After the volunteer names an appropriate word, have the letter holder set the letter in front of herself and slide the pot to the next youngster. Continue as described until each student has served up some letter-sound practice.

Debbie McColloch
Grace School
Houston, TX

Turtle starts with *t*.

Portable Pockets
Alphabetical order
Students can take this center activity to their seats for skill practice from *A* to *Z!* To prepare, cut out a back pocket from an old pair of jeans, keeping the pocket intact. Or glue a library pocket to the front of a tagboard pocket cutout and title it as shown. Place a scrambled set of alphabet letter cards in the pocket. To complete the activity, a youngster empties the pocket and arranges the cards in alphabetical order.

For a word-building version, place several chosen letter cards in the pocket. Have youngsters form words with the letters and list them on provided paper.

Sharon Vandike, Visitation Inter-Parish School, Vienna, MO

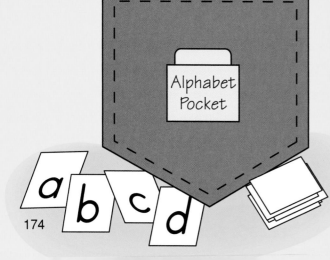

Fill the Bowl!

✏ Write the missing letters.

A B ___ D ___ ___ G ___ ___ J

K ___ ___ N ___ P Q ___ ___ ___

___ T U ___ W ___ ___ ___ Z

Newsworthy Project

Look at what's hot off the presses: an idea guaranteed to promote writing. It's as easy as 1, 2, 3!

ideas by Janet Boyce, Cokato, MN

1. Getting Ready

For each student, fold a 12" x 18" sheet of white paper in half two times (to 6" x 9"). Program one copy of page 177 with the date and your school's city and state. Then copy the page to make a class supply. After each student colors and cuts out his headlines, instruct him to position his paper horizontally with the fold at the bottom. Ask him to glue his "School Times" headline at the top of the paper. Then have him unfold the paper and glue a headline in each remaining section. (He will use both sides of the paper.) **For an easier version,** have each student use a 9" x 12" sheet of paper folded in half, the "School Times" headline, and three other headlines.

2. Writing

Instruct each of your cub reporters to create a self-portrait on an index card cut in half (to 2½" x 3"). Then ask each youngster to glue his artwork to his front page as shown, draw a box around it, and write his name. Over a few days, have him use words and pictures to report on each of the following topics in the appropriate section of his paper.

Class News: a chosen activity or event
Weather: the day's weather
Lunch Menu: the day's lunch choices
Book Corner: a recent read-aloud

Sports: his favorite sport
Playground News: a recent recess
Opinions: his favorite color

3. Publishing

To showcase a student's newspaper, cut away about one inch from the top of a gallon-size plastic bag. Position the bag on a 12" x 18" sheet of paper as shown, with the opening at the top. After you tape the sides of the bag to the paper, have the youngster slide his folded newspaper into the bag. Then invite him to illustrate the construction paper to resemble a newsstand. Post students' newsstands on a hallway wall. It's a great way to share work samples during parent-teacher conferences or anytime of the year!

School Times

_____ date   _____ city, state

©The Mailbox® • TEC42027 • Oct./Nov. 2006

 **Class News**

 **Weather**

 **Lunch Menu**

 **Book Corner**

 **Sports**

Playground News

 **Opinions**

"Pet-acular" Sentences

From group activities to independent practice, this menagerie of ideas is packed with skill-boosting fun!

ideas contributed by Katie Zuehlke
Bendix Elementary
Annandale, MN

Roll, Say, and Write!
Using complete sentences

Success is guaranteed with this group activity. To make two dice, label each pet card on a copy of page 180 with the appropriate animal name. Color and cut out the cards. Then glue one card to each side of a small tissue box. Label each side of another small tissue box with a describing word.

To begin, sit with students in a circle. Next, roll the dice and identify the words rolled. After students agree that the words do not tell a complete thought, guide the group to come up with a complete sentence that uses the two words. Write the sentence on a sheet of chart paper with students' help. To continue, invite a student to roll the dice and identify two words for the group to use in another sentence.

Here is a [dog].

Julia likes this pet.

Its name is Spot.

It can run fast.

This pet is fun.

Filling in the Blanks
Finishing sentences

Here's a no-fail approach to helping students create their own sentences. Cut out a copy of the pet cards on page 180 and label each card with the appropriate animal name. Write the sentences shown on a large sheet of paper, drawing blanks where indicated. Laminate the paper for reuse.

To begin, invite a volunteer to loosely tape a chosen pet card in the first blank and have the group read the sentence. Then ask the volunteer to use a wipe-off marker to write her name in the second blank. After the students read that sentence, instruct the volunteer to use the marker to complete the remaining sentences. Invite students to give her suggestions and spelling help as appropriate. After the group reads all of the completed sentences, remove the pet card and wipe the paper clean to prepare for more sentence-completion practice. **As an extension for more advanced students,** encourage each youngster to write and illustrate sentences in a blank booklet, using the displayed sentences as a model.

Missing!
Capitalizing first words and proper nouns

Where are the uppercase letters? Invite students to put the letters in their proper places with this editing idea. Choose a pet on page 180 and then program several sentence strips with relevant sentences that include proper nouns but no uppercase letters. Laminate the strips for reuse. For each capitalization error, program a copy of the chosen pet card with the appropriate uppercase letter.

To begin, gather a small group of students. Next, invite one youngster to read a sentence. Instruct the students to tell which words need to be capitalized. Have students place a corresponding pet card above each error. Then ask them to use a wipe-off marker to make the corrections. Continue in the same manner with the remaining sentences. When all of the cards are in place, students will know that they have found all of the errors!

I i fed my fish on Friday.

Do you see the bird?

At the End
End marks

Punctuate with play dough? Sure! It's hands-on reinforcement at this center! Color and cut out a copy of the pet cards on page 180. For each pet, write an asking or a telling sentence without end marks. Place the cards, the sentences, and a container of play dough at a center. When a child visits the center, he reads each sentence, uses the play dough to punctuate it, and then sets the corresponding card beside the sentence. **For more advanced students,** include exclamatory sentences.

Pet Parade
Word order, writing sentences

Students can take this center activity to their seats for independent practice. To prepare, compose a sentence about a pet shown on page 180. Write each word in the sentence on a separate copy of the corresponding pet card. (Include the end mark with the last word.) Number the backs of the cards to indicate the correct word order. Program cards for sentences about different pets in the same manner. Then place each set of cards in a separate resealable plastic bag.

A youngster takes one set of cards and arranges them to form a complete sentence. After she checks her work, she writes and illustrates the sentence on a sheet of paper.

That turtle is not fast.

That turtle is not fast.

Pet Cards

Use with "Roll, Say, and Write!" and "Filling in the Blanks" on page 178.
Use with "Missing!" "At the End," and "Pet Parade" on page 179.

TEC42028

TEC42028

TEC42028

TEC42028

TEC42028

TEC42028

Rounding Up High-Frequency Words

Use this rootin'-tootin' collection of ideas with your choice of words.

Wanted: Words

Word recognition or writing words

Here's a fun way to encourage your young buckaroos to be on the lookout for words they know. Title a poster as shown and then laminate it for reuse. Display the poster in your group area. After you read a morning message with students, use a wipe-off marker to write on the poster several high-frequency words that are in the message. Next, designate a student as a deputy reader by giving him a badge to wear (pattern on page 183). Have the group read the first wanted word. Then invite the deputy reader to find the word in the message and circle or highlight it. Continue with the remaining words as described, appointing additional deputy readers if desired.

For more advanced students, draw blanks in place of chosen words in a message. List the words on the poster. Then have deputy readers complete the message by writing the words in the appropriate blanks.

adapted from an idea by Stephanie Affinito
Glens Falls, NY

Deputy Reader

WANTED: WORDS

from

not

we

YEE-HAW!

Reading Rodeo

Reading words, spelling

After your students are familiar with ten or more high-frequency words, try this creative review. Write a different list of three words on each of several large sheets of paper. Post each list in a different area of the classroom. Next, divide students into as many groups as there are lists. Then direct each group to stand near a different list. After the students in each group practice reading their words, have them use a method listed on this page to present their words to the class. Once a group finishes sharing its words in this manner, have the rest of the class cheer, "Yee-haw!" To begin another round, have each group move to a different poster.

- Read the list from top to bottom and then from bottom to top.
- Read each word, in turn, pausing for the class to echo it.
- Clap as you name each letter. Then say the word.
- Pat your leg one time as you name each letter. Then say the word.

Boots Made for Walking
Reading words

This center idea is a perfect fit for both individual students and partners. Make a supply of construction paper boots (pattern on page 183). Label each boot with a different high-frequency word. Then place the boots in a large shoebox at a center. Students who visit the center arrange the boots faceup in a trail on the floor. Then they read the words as they follow the trail from the beginning to the end. The youngsters rearrange the boots in a different order for more boot-scootin' reading fun. **For an easier version,** use fewer words and write each word on more than one boot.

Stephanie Affinito
Glens Falls, NY

Roping Event
Reading and using words

Students will be eager to rope in reading practice with this partner activity! To prepare, tie the ends of a length of yarn together to form a ring (corral). Tie a horseshoe magnet to one end of a shoelace. Make several copies of the cattle cards on page 183 and write a different high-frequency word on each card. Then cut out the cards and slide a paper clip onto each one.

To play, the students arrange the corral on the floor. Then they spread out the cards facedown in the corral. In turn, each student holds the shoelace and uses the magnet to pick up a card. He reads the word, with assistance from his partner if needed, uses it in a sentence, and then sets the card outside the corral. Alternate play continues until all of the cattle are roped as described.

Stephanie Affinito

Hats Off!
Spelling

To prepare this hands-on activity, give each student a sheet of paper and a copy of page 184. After he colors the hat, have him cut out the hat and letter cards. To begin, write on the board a word listed on this page. Instruct students to read the word and spell it aloud. Next, ask each youngster to form the word on his hatband with his letter cards. After each student forms the word, spell it aloud and encourage youngsters to make any needed corrections. Then have each student write the word on his paper and clear his hat. Continue with the remaining words in the same manner.

he	me
her	she
him	the
his	their
is	them
it	this
its	

Badge Pattern
Use with "Wanted: Words" on page 181.

Boot Pattern
Use with "Boots Made for Walking" on page 182.

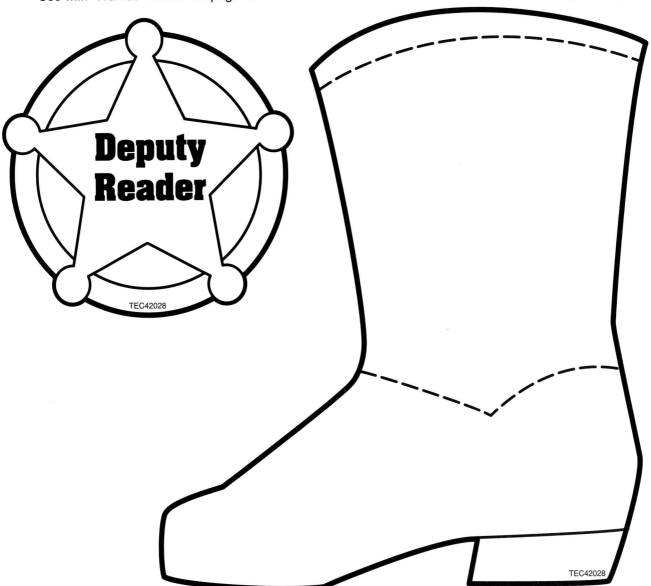

Deputy Reader

TEC42028

Cattle Cards
Use with "Roping Event" on page 182.

TEC42028

TEC42028

Hat Pattern and Letter Cards
Use with "Hats Off!" on page 182.

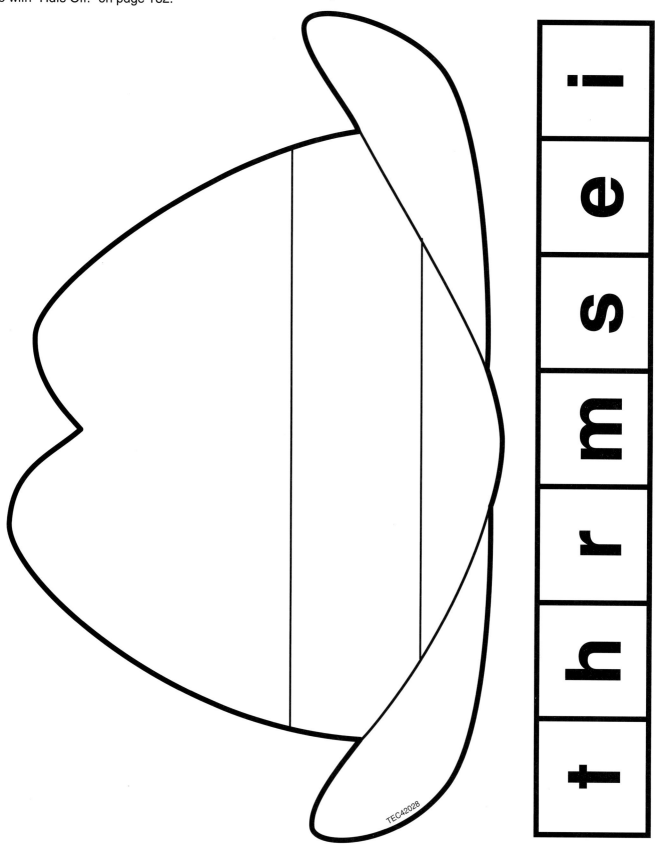

TEC42028

i

e

s

m

r

h

t

Taking Off With Word Families

Send students' literacy skills skyrocketing with these fun-filled activities.

ideas contributed by Ada Goren
Winston-Salem, NC

Reading Rays
Onsets and rimes

Use this small-group activity to warm up students' blending skills. To prepare, write a chosen rime near the edge of a five-inch yellow circle. Cut several 1" x 6" yellow paper strips. Glue the strips to the circle to resemble a sun, gluing one strip directly in front of the rime as shown. Collect several letter manipulatives that can form words with the rime.

To begin, gather several students and set the sun in front of them. Place each letter on a different ray, keeping the ray in front of the rime blank. Next, instruct a child to place a chosen letter in front of the rime to form a word. After she reads the word, invite her to take the letter. Then ask another student to take a turn in the same manner. Continue as described until youngsters have taken all of the letters. For more advanced students, include consonant digraphs or blends by placing corresponding letters on the sun's rays.

Planetary Travels
Sorting by rimes

What words belong on imaginary planets such as Planet *-et* or Planet *-ell?* That's what students determine with this creative activity. Label each of three large construction paper circles with a different rime. Embellish the circles as desired to resemble planets. Post each planet in a different classroom area and suspend a few stars nearby. Make a class supply of word cards with words that include the featured rimes.

To begin, randomly distribute the cards to students. Say, "Get ready for liftoff!" and encourage each youngster to stand beside his chair and silently read the word on his card. Then have each youngster "fly" to the planet with the same rime as his word. After each youngster reaches his destination, ask each group, in turn, to announce the name of its planet and have the group members read their words aloud. To prepare for another round, collect the cards and have students return to their launchpads (chairs).

185

Starry Skies
Sorting by rimes

Here's a learning center idea that's out of this world! Choose two different rimes. Program a supply of die-cut stars with words that have the rimes, writing one word per star. Then select one programmed star for each rime. Glue the chosen stars on separate 12" x 18" sheets of black paper and decorate the paper with several gold or silver adhesive stars. Then place the papers and remaining programmed stars at a center stocked with writing paper. To complete the activity, a student sorts the loose stars by rime onto the decorated papers. She lists each group of words and then reads the lists.

Launching Lists
Writing word families

Invite each of your young astronauts to keep a log of word families with this ongoing project. To begin, each student folds a 9" x 12" sheet of construction paper in half lengthwise. He folds a desired number of 8½" x 11" sheets of white paper in half lengthwise and then staples them inside the construction paper to make a booklet. He cuts a large triangle (top of rocket) and two smaller triangles (wings) from construction paper. He glues the triangles to his booklet as shown and adds desired crayon details. Then he writes a title and his name on the front cover. After you introduce a word family to students, ask each youngster to write the rime at the top of his first blank page. Then dictate words with the rime for students to write.

Load the Rocket!
Writing word families

This skill-boosting activity results in a poster-size word reference. Use colorful markers to draw a simple rocket on a large sheet of chart paper. Label the top of the rocket with a chosen rime and display the poster within student reach. To begin, ask students to read the rime. Then guide youngsters to take turns writing on the rocket words that have the rime. After all of the words you wish to reinforce are written, instruct students to stand. Have them read the list, call out, "Blast off!" and then jump once.

Space Aces

 Cut. Glue.

 Write.

 **f<u>an</u>**

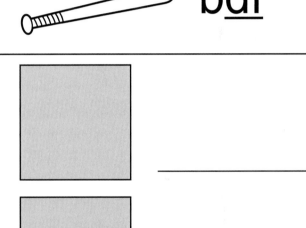 **b<u>at</u>**

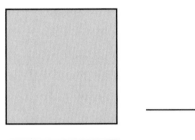

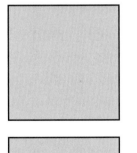

   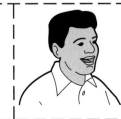  

Shooting Stars

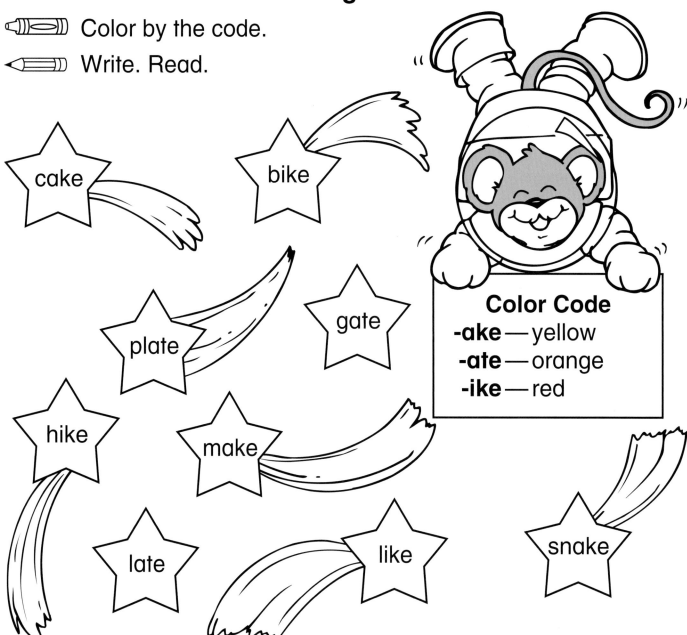

Color by the code.

Write. Read.

Color Code
-ake — yellow
-ate — orange
-ike — red

cake

bike

plate

gate

hike

make

late

like

snake

-ake	-ate	-ike

Oceans of Writing Fun

Your students will be eager to dive into these literacy activities!

ideas contributed by Margie Rogers
Colfax Elementary
Colfax, NC

Friendly Fish

Writing about a personal experience

Friends stick together! That's a lesson your students are sure to learn from *Swimmy* by Leo Lionni. After you read the book aloud, discuss with students how Swimmy shows that he is a good friend to the red fish. Then give each youngster a copy of the fish pattern on page 191. Ask her to write about a summer experience that she had with a friend and remind her to title her work and sign her name. After she completes her writing, instruct her to cut out the fish and glue it on a larger piece of red paper. Then have her trim the paper, leaving a narrow border.

To showcase students' work, back a board with blue paper and title it "Friendly Stories." Display students' fish with a black fish so that they resemble the school of fish led by Swimmy.

The Beach
I wnt to the beach with Livvy. We wnt swming. It was fun.
— Brianna

Sand, Surf, and More!

Using sensory details

Begin this group writing activity with an imaginary trip to the beach. Ask each youngster to close his eyes and picture a beach. Encourage students to imagine certain sensory details and describe their mental images. Then have students open their eyes. Next, display a large starfish that you have drawn on a sheet of chart paper. Title the paper "Beach" and label each arm of the starfish as shown. As you guide students to name sensory details about the topic, write the words or phrases on the appropriate arms of the starfish. Later, revisit the starfish poster with students and incorporate several listed details into a group story.

Beach

see
big waves
lots of people
beach towels
lifeguards

hear
waves crashing
people laughing
seagulls squawking

touch
hot sand
cold ocean
wet seaweed

smell
salty air

taste
salty water
picnic food

Sea Sightings

Contributing to a predictable book

The format of this class book ensures success for young readers and writers. To prepare, title a horizontal 9" x 12" sheet of white paper as shown. Make a crayon rubbing on the top half of the paper with an unwrapped blue crayon. Make wavy cuts along one long edge of a 5" x 12" piece of blue paper to make a cover and then embellish it with desired ocean details. Make a class supply of 4¼" x 11" white pages (half sheets) programmed with writing lines as shown.

To begin, read the book title aloud. Give each child a page and have him use the format shown to write a response to the title. Then instruct him to illustrate his work and sign his name. To complete the book, stack students' completed pages behind the cover and staple the stack to the titled paper as shown. Then open the book to the last page (also the backing of the book) and write "That is what we see under the sea!"

Trish Draper
Millarville Community School
Millarville, Alberta, Canada

What Do You See
Under the Sea?

What Do You See
Under the Sea?

I see pretty shells under the sea.   Diego

Cleo the crab likes to color.
Yellow is her fvrit color.

Clever Crab

Writing a caption

This adorable project is guaranteed to prompt lots of giggles and loads of writing ideas! To make a crab, adhere two white paper reinforcements to a five-inch semicircle as shown and draw a mouth. Then glue to the crab four pairs of legs and two construction paper claws like the ones shown. To begin, introduce the crab to students, giving it a desired name. Explain that it isn't an ordinary crab since it can hold various items and use them as people do. Give several examples, such as a crayon, spatula, and paintbrush.

Next, have each youngster make a crab like yours and a construction paper item for it to hold. Instruct her to glue the crab on the upper half of a sheet of paper, leaving the claws free. Help her bend the claws forward and position them as desired. Then invite her to incorporate the crab into an illustration and write a caption.

Don't miss the graphic organizer on page 192 and the activity for writing how-to sentences on page 193.

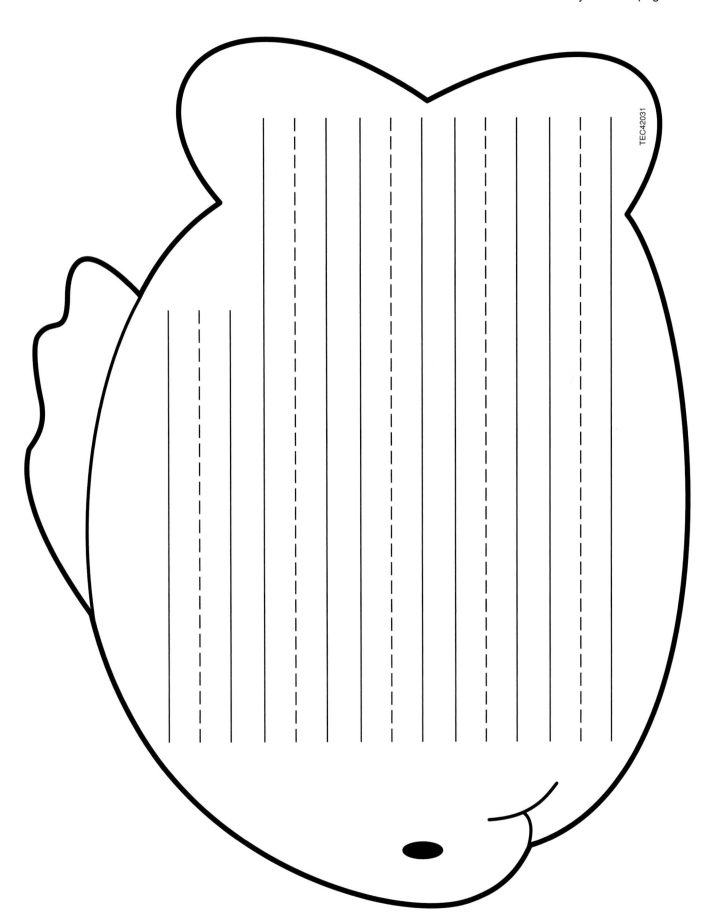

TEC42031

Name _____

Stay With the Topic!

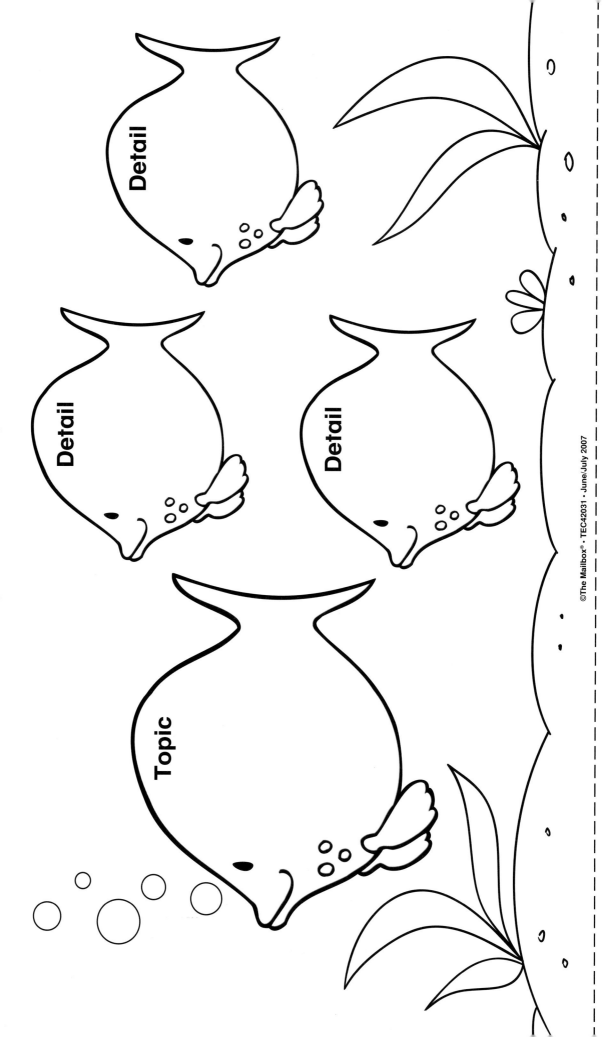

Detail

Detail

Detail

Topic

Note to the teacher: Have each youngster use words or pictures to complete a copy of this page before he writes about a chosen topic.

How to Make a Sand Castle

1.

2.

3.

4.

©The Mailbox® · TEC42031 · June/July 2007

Note to the teacher: Give each student a copy of this page. Have him write how to make a sand castle step-by-step. **For more advanced students,** make one copy and then white-out the numbers before making student copies. Encourage students to use as many copies of the paper as they need and have them number their own steps.

Fine-Feathered Phonics

Send your students' literacy skills soaring with these easy-to-adapt activities.

ideas contributed by Andrea Singleton, Waynesville Elementary, Waynesville, OH

Bird-Watching

Initial consonants or consonant digraphs

Keep this picture-perfect flock on display for quick skill practice. To prepare, make six to ten colorful birds (pattern on page 196). Color and cut out as many consonant picture cards or consonant digraph picture cards on page 197 as you have birds. Glue each card on a different bird. Then arrange the birds on the board.

To begin, write a chosen consonant or consonant digraph on the board. Then have each student pantomime looking through binoculars for a bird with the corresponding picture. After a few moments, invite one or more of your young bird-watchers to point out an appropriate bird and name its picture. Erase the board and write a different letter or letter combination to continue bird-watching.

Home, "Tweet" Home!

Letter-sound associations

Use this versatile lotto game for a variety of topics, such as initial or final consonants and consonant blends. Make three or four copies of the gameboard on page 198. Program each gameboard space with a chosen letter or letter combination so that each board is unique. (You may use each letter or letter combination more than once on a gameboard.) Copy the programmed gameboards so that all together there is a class supply. Make word cards that correspond with the programming. Have each youngster color and cut out a gameboard and a copy of the game markers on page 198.

To play one round, invite each youngster to put his "Free" game marker on a chosen gameboard space. Next, read aloud a word card. Ask a youngster to identify the featured phonics element, such as the initial consonant or consonant blend. Then have each player place a game marker on a matching gameboard space. Continue the game as described until one or more players marks four spaces in a vertical row and calls out, "Tweet! Tweet!"

Which Nest Is Best?

Word families

Here's a Grade A approach to sorting words! Choose two or three word families. For each word family, arrange shredded paper in a disposable bowl or pie pan to make a nest. Then place in the nest a bird (pattern on page 196) that you have labeled with the corresponding rime. Program several egg cutouts with words that have the featured rimes, writing one word per egg. Put the eggs in a resealable plastic bag. Then place the bag and nests at a center.

To complete the activity, a student sorts the eggs into the correct nests and then reads each group of words. **To modify the activity for more advanced students,** arrange for students to sort words into different categories, such as short *i* words and long *i* words.

Flap Those Wings!

Short and long e

For this high-flying activity, place simple illustrations of a nest and a tree in the top row of a pocket chart. Write each word shown in large letters on a separate blank card. To begin, show students a word card and have them read the word aloud. Repeat the word. If the word has a long *e* as in *tree,* each student pantomimes a long-winged bird flying. If the word has a short *e* as in *nest,* each student bends his arms inward and pantomimes a short-winged bird flying. Confirm the correct response and then have a student place the card below the corresponding picture card. After students sort the remaining word cards in the same manner, ask them to read each group of words.

Short *e* Words	Long *e* Words
bed	eat
best	green
hen	he
net	me
wet	see

Songbird Words

Short vowels

To prepare for a small group, color and cut out a copy of the songbird cards on page 196. Make four word cards per vowel and then place them in a small paper bag. To begin, students arrange the songbird cards in a horizontal row. Student 1 takes a word card at random and reads the word aloud without showing it to the group members. After the group members identify the vowel, Student 1 places the word card below the corresponding bird. The players take turns as described with the remaining word cards. **For an easier version,** use only the short *a* and short *i* songbirds.

Bird Pattern

Use with "Bird-Watching" on page 194 and "Which Nest Is Best?" on page 195.

Songbird Cards

Use with "Songbird Words" on page 195.

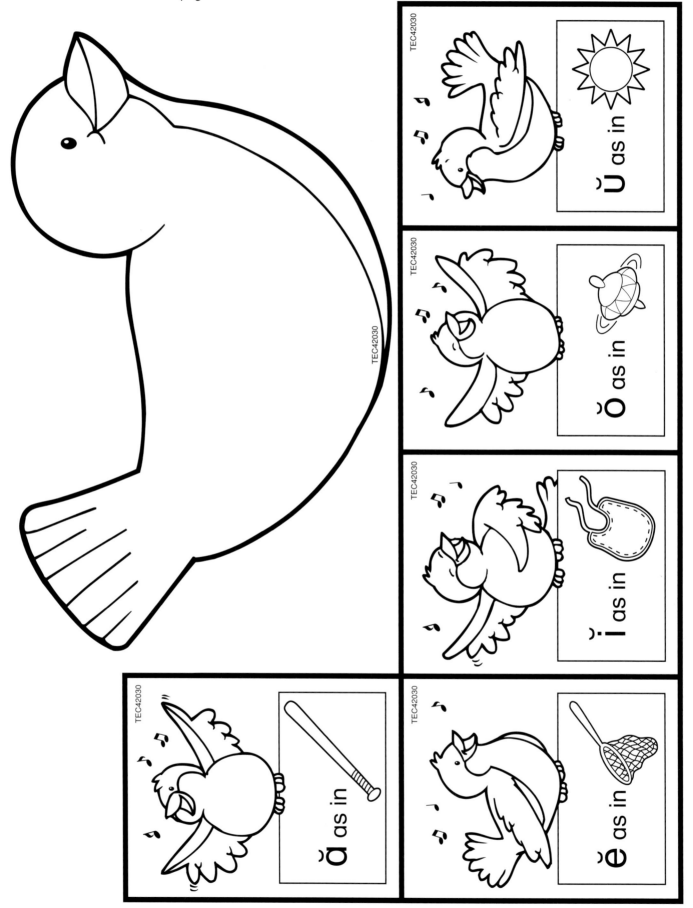

ŭ as in

ŏ as in

ĭ as in

ă as in

ĕ as in

TEC42030

©The Mailbox® • TEC42030 • April/May 2007

Consonant Picture Cards

Use with "Bird-Watching" on page 194.

Consonant Digraph Picture Cards

Use with "Bird-Watching" on page 194.

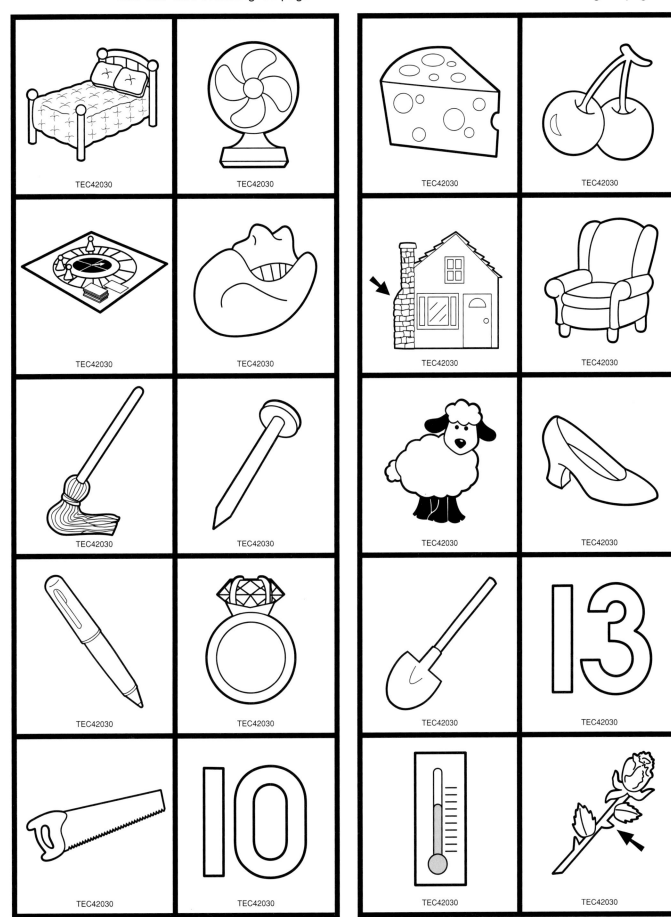

TEC42030

TEC42030

TEC42030

TEC42030

TEC42030

TEC42030

TEC42030

TEC42030

TEC42030

TEC42030

TEC42030

TEC42030

TEC42030

TEC42030

TEC42030

TEC42030

TEC42030

TEC42030

TEC42030

TEC42030

Gameboard and Game Markers
Use with "Home, 'Tweet' Home!" on page 194.

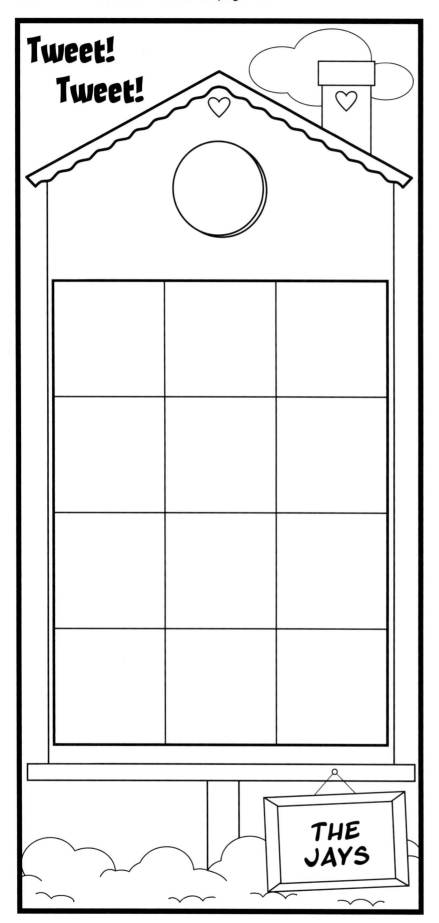

The "Berry" Best
Literacy Games

When it comes to reviewing phonics and word skills, these activities are sure to hit the spot!

ideas by Ada Goren, Winston-Salem, NC

Feed the Bears!
Skill review

Get students up and moving with this "paw-sitively" delightful idea. For every two students, make one bear card (pattern on page 201) and one small strawberry card (pattern on page 202), making half of the bear cards brown and half of them tan. Use an option below to program the cards. To begin, designate two classroom locations as berry patches—one for the brown bears and one for the tan bears. Give each child a card at random. Then have each youngster walk around and look for the classmate who has the card that matches his own card. When he finds him, the two youngsters quickly go to the appropriate berry patch. No doubt students will be eager to see which bears get fed first!

Initial consonants, blends, or digraphs: Write a different letter or letter combination on each bear. Program each strawberry with clip art whose name begins with the corresponding letter(s).
Plurals: Write a simple noun on each bear and the corresponding plural nouns on individual strawberries.

Freshly Picked
Vowel patterns or word families

To prepare this word-sorting game, choose four vowel patterns or word families. Write each chosen phonics element on a separate copy of the berry bucket card on page 201. Color each card and then tape it to the side of a 16-ounce disposable cup to make a berry bucket. For each phonics element, make five copies of a large strawberry card on page 202 and cut them out. Then write a corresponding word on the back of each card. Randomly arrange the cards in a pocket chart with the berry sides facing outward. Divide students into four teams and give each team a berry bucket.

In turn, one player from each team turns over a berry card and reads the word aloud. If the word corresponds with her team's bucket, she puts the card in the bucket. If the word does not match the bucket, she turns the card back over. The teams take turns as described until one team has five cards. **For an easier version,** have a small group play with only two buckets.

Guess Who!

High-frequency words or phonics review

Here's a fresh version of the traditional game Doggy, Doggy, Who's Got Your Bone? Make a class supply of the large strawberry cards on page 202. On each strawberry write a different high-frequency word or a word that has a chosen phonics element, such as an *r*-controlled vowel. Write the same words on individual blank cards.

To play one round, designate a student as Hungry Bear. Give the bear a word card and ask him to cover his eyes. Give each of the other students a strawberry card and have them conceal the words. Next, lead the group in asking the question shown. At this signal, the bear uncovers his eyes. He reads his word aloud and shows it to the group. Then he tries to figure out in three or fewer guesses who has the matching strawberry card. After each guess, the corresponding youngster reveals his word and reads it aloud. Once the bear identifies the correct student or makes three incorrect guesses, each youngster with a berry card reads his word. The student with the matching berry card is the bear for the next round.

Hungry Bear, Hungry Bear, who has your strawberry?

Time for Dessert

Word families

What's the secret to making these pies? Writing words! Cut out a copy of the bear spinner on page 201. Write a different rime on each large berry and color the spinner. Attach a paper clip to the spinner with a brad. Cut apart two copies of the pie pattern on page 202. Place the pie pieces, the spinner, and magnets or reusable adhesive near the board. Divide the board into two columns and write each rime near the top of a different column.

To take a turn, a student spins the spinner. If she spins a rime, she names a word with the rime and writes it below the corresponding column heading. Then she displays one piece of pie in that column. If she spins the berry bonus, she chooses one of the two rimes and then completes her turn in the same manner. Students take turns as described, assembling a pie for each rime. The rime with the first completed pie wins!

-ap
cap
map
clap
nap

-op
hop
mop
stop

Berry Bucket Card
Use with "Freshly Picked" on page 199.

Bear Spinner
Use with "Time for Dessert" on page 200.

Berry Bonus

Small Strawberry Card
Use with "Feed the Bears!" on page 199.

Large Strawberry Cards
Use with "Freshly Picked" on page 199 and "Guess Who!" on page 200.

TEC42031

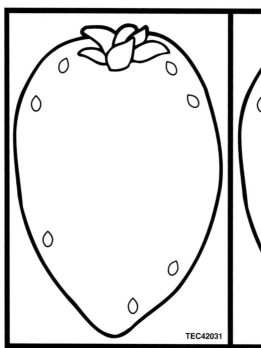

TEC42031

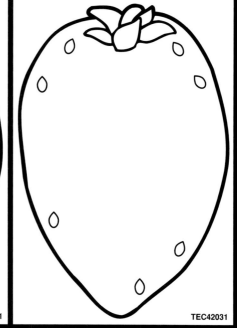

TEC42031

Pie Pattern
Use with "Time for Dessert" on page 200.

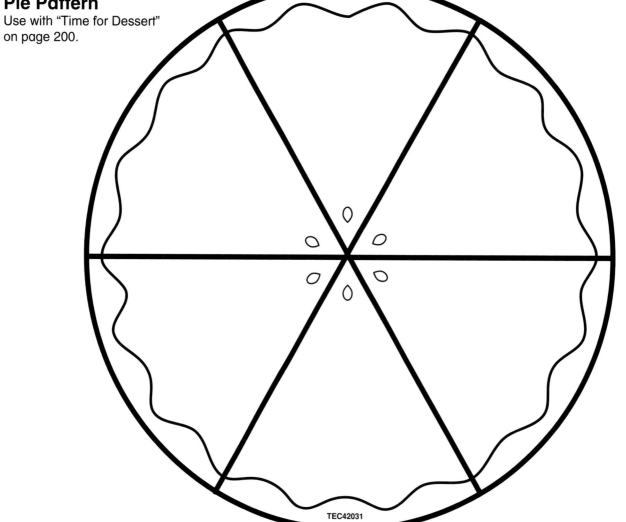

TEC42031

LITERATURE UNITS

Officer Buckle and Gloria

by Peggy Rathmann

No one at Napville School listens to Officer Buckle's safety presentations. That is, until he teams up with a police dog named Gloria. The canine's crowd-pleasing antics steal the show, prompting Officer Buckle to feel that he's not needed. But in the end, both Gloria and Officer Buckle learn that everyone needs a buddy!

ideas contributed by Julie Hays
Maryville, TN

Who Knows the Rules?
Using prior knowledge

Surely your students are more attentive to safety issues than people at Napville School! Find out what they know about the topic with this idea for before, during, and after reading. To begin, draw a star in the center of a sheet of chart paper and label it "Safety." Display the poster in your storytime area. Have students brainstorm school safety rules; write the rules around the star and create a web similar to the one shown. Next, ask students to listen to the story and study the illustrations to learn more about safety. After you read the story aloud, reread the rules that students named earlier. Then invite youngsters to suggest different rules for you to add to the poster.

Leave rocks on the ground.

Walk in the halls.

Keep the floor clean.

Safety

Do not push.

Do not stand on chairs.

Disastrous Consequences
Understanding the need for rules

What happens when a puddle of banana pudding is left on the floor at Napville School? The worst accident ever! Prompt students to think about other cause-effect relationships with this look at safety rules. After a first reading, ask students to imagine that they are Officer Buckle's deputies. Explain that when a deputy sees an unsafe behavior in the story, he should raise his hand. Then revisit the story's illustrations with students, pausing when youngsters raise their hands. At this signal, have a volunteer say, "I spy…" and complete the sentence with his observation. Then draw a sad face on a small sticky note and ask the volunteer to place it near the described illustration. Encourage youngsters to explain why the behavior is dangerous and, if appropriate, have them name a safer alternative.

Later, place the book at a center and invite students to take a closer look at the illustrations. Encourage them to pay particular attention to the banana-related details throughout the story!

Friends can *ride swings.*

Terrific Twosome
Completing a sentence

The theme of friendship takes center stage when Officer Buckle realizes the importance of sticking with his buddy. At the book's conclusion, point out to students that the best safety presentations are the ones that Officer Buckle and Gloria do together. Invite students to name other activities that are fun for friends to do together. Then give each youngster a paper programmed with the sentence starter shown. Have her complete the sentence (or dictate a response for you to write) and then add an illustration.

Valuable Visit
Listening in a group, contributing to a class thank-you note

Who better to reinforce Officer Buckle's safety messages than a police officer? To follow up the story, invite your school's resource officer or a local police officer to visit your classroom. Before the visit, remind your students that when the youngsters at Napville School were poor listeners they missed important information. Then have students describe appropriate listening behavior.

After the visit, discuss with students what they learned from the guest. Then write a class thank-you note for the visitor on a sheet of chart paper, leaving generous margins at the top and bottom. Have each student write his name on a star cutout and glue it near the top or bottom of the letter. Your guest is certain to appreciate hearing from the young listeners just as Officer Buckle does!

Beyond Napville
Naming safety rules

Once your students are familiar with the safety concerns at Napville School, help them tune in to safety issues all around! Lead students in the song below. Then encourage youngsters to name rules that help them stay safe outdoors. After youngsters identify several rules, lead them in verses about different locations—such as at school, on the bus, or at home—and have them name safety rules for each place.

Safety Song
(sung to the tune of "Row, Row, Row Your Boat")

Rules, rules, rules [outdoors]
Keep it safe and fun.
Respecting rules puts safety first,
Protecting everyone.

September 15

Dear Officer Brown,
Thank you for coming to our class. We promise to be safe at school. We will be safe on the bus too.

Sincerely,
Ms. Hays's Class

The Little Red Hen

by Paul Galdone

The little red hen is always busy with household chores, but her friends never want to help her. That all changes, though, after the hen bakes a cake and teaches her lazy friends a lesson!

ideas by Katie Zuehlke
Bendix Elementary
Annandale, MN

Who Will Help?

Story theme, high-frequency words: I, not, said

When you read the story aloud, your students are sure to join in the lazy critters' refrain. Highlight the familiar line with this class book project. To prepare the first page of the class book, write on a sheet of paper, "'Who will help me make a pizza?' asked [your name]." To prepare the last page, write, "I made the pizza all by myself. I will eat it all by myself."

At the story's conclusion, guide students to identify the lesson that the dog, cat, and mouse learn. Show students the first page of the class book. Then give each youngster a paper programmed as shown. Ask him to complete the sentence with the word *said* and his name. Then have him illustrate himself doing something other than making pizza. After volunteers illustrate the pages you prepared, stack students' completed pages between them. Bind the entire stack between two construction paper covers. **For more advanced students,** have each youngster write a second sentence that tells what he is doing in his illustration.

Picture-Perfect Plot

Identifying the beginning and end of a story

The hen's friends change a lot between the beginning of the story and the end! Have students recap the two parts of the story with story placemats. To begin, ask each student to fold a 9" x 12" sheet of white paper in half (to 6" x 9"). Direct her to unfold it and trace the crease. After she colors a border, instruct her to cut out a copy of one pair of labels on page 208 and glue them on her paper as shown. Then ask her to add corresponding illustrations and captions. Laminate students' completed placemats for durability.

Later, invite students to help you prepare a simple snack. When it's time to eat the treat, the placemats will not only be useful, but they will also prompt story-related discussions!

From Wheat to Cake
Sequencing story events

Making a cake is a lot of work for the little red hen! To review the process from start to finish, post a jumbo recipe card titled as shown. During a second reading of the book, encourage students to pay particular attention to the sequence of events. Pause to clarify the meanings of any unfamiliar words, such as *wheat, mill,* and *ground.* At the story's conclusion, guide students to recall how the hen prepares the cake; list each step in order on the recipe card. Then help students read the information step-by-step.

Making the Cake

1. The hen plants some wheat.
2. She waters the wheat.
3. She cuts the wheat.
4. She takes the wheat to the mill to be ground into flour.
5. She mixes the ingredients.
6. She bakes the cake.

Bag of Props
Retelling a story

No doubt your students will be eager to tell others about how the hen teaches her three friends a lesson. To make retelling props, give each youngster a white paper lunch bag and four unlined index cards. Ask him to illustrate the field on one side of the bag and the kitchen on the other side of the bag. Instruct him to illustrate each character on a separate card. Then have him color and cut out a copy of one set of story prop cards on page 208. After he practices using his props to retell the story, encourage him to take his project home for more retelling fun.

Helping Hands
Writing

The dog, cat, and mouse do not like to help, but your students probably do! Use this idea to showcase ways that your students lend a hand. Program the left half of a sheet of paper as shown. Make a copy for each student. Then staple two half sheets of paper to each youngster's copy as shown to make a flip booklet.

After reading the story aloud, ask volunteers to name ways that they help at home and at school. Invite them to tell how they feel after they help someone. Then have each youngster illustrate herself on the left half of her booklet. Ask her to write a different sentence ending on each page of the right half of the booklet. Then instruct her to illustrate her work.

I can help

set the tbl.

Placemat Labels

Use with "Picture-Perfect Plot" on page 206.

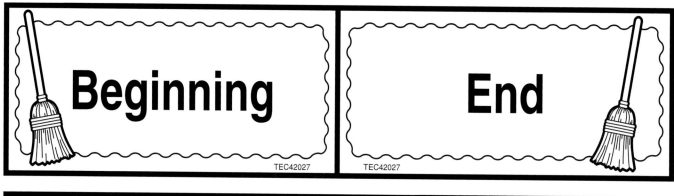

Prop Cards

Use with "Bag of Props" on page 207.

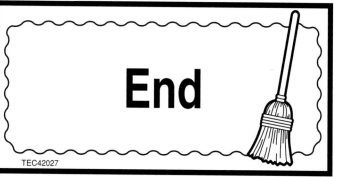

Chicka Chicka Boom Boom

Written by Bill Martin Jr. and John Archambault
Illustrated by Lois Ehlert

A tells B and B tells C to go to the top of the coconut tree. All of the other letters follow suit in a rhythmic race to the top. See what happens after the tree gets so crowded that the letters fall into a heap!

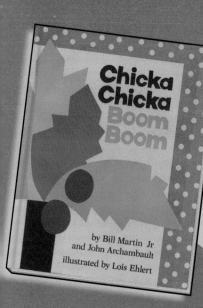

Looking for Letters
Recognizing lowercase letters

No doubt the vivid illustrations will capture your students' interest, so invite them to take a closer look with this group activity. After reading the book aloud, give each child a different lowercase letter card or manipulative. Display any remaining letters or give more than one letter to advanced youngsters. Then revisit selected illustrations with students, including the illustration of when all of the letters fall from the tree. Whenever a child sees her letter pictured, have her stand, hold up her letter, and chant, "Chicka chicka boom boom!" Invite her to name her letter before she sits back down. When students see all of the letters, have the whole group chant in unison!

Zoom! Zoom!
Identifying alphabet letters

This self-contained project is a perfect prop for imitating the story. In advance, cut a class supply of brown and green rectangles (tree trunks and patches of grass) sized to fit paper lunch bags as shown. Program a 26-box grid with the letters of the alphabet, writing one letter per box. Make a copy of the grid and page 211 for each student.

To begin, each youngster colors and cuts out his patterns and directions card. He glues a trunk, his leaves, and his coconuts to a white paper lunch bag as shown. Next, he makes cuts along one long edge of his grass to resemble blades of grass. He glues the grass at the base of the tree, leaving the top edge free to create a pocket. He glues the directions card to the back of the bag. Then he cuts apart his letters. To play, he opens his bag and stands it up. He follows the directions, independently or with a partner, as time allows or until he has put all of his letters in his bag.

adapted from an idea by Elisa Sifuentes
Newman Elementary
Laredo, TX

Coconut Pairs
Matching uppercase and lowercase letters

After the letters tumble from the tree, the corresponding adult letters rush to their sides. Invite students to create similar pairs of letters at this center. To prepare, draw a large palm tree on a piece of tagboard. Program each of several construction paper coconuts with a different uppercase letter. Secure the coconuts to the tagboard with reusable adhesive to allow for later reprogramming. Program additional coconuts with the matching lowercase letters. To complete the activity, a child places each lowercase coconut on the matching uppercase coconut.

Maureen Goodwin
Goshen/Lempster Cooperative Elementary
East Lempster, NH

"Tree-rific" Who's Who
Spelling names

Create a picture-perfect version of the tree with this fun follow-up. Arrange for each youngster, in turn, to spell his name with magnetic letters on a cookie sheet. Then take a photograph of him holding the cookie sheet. After you have a photo of each student, post a large palm tree on a board titled "Chicka Chicka Boom Boom! Look Who Is in Our Room!" Program a separate coconut with the first letter of each student's name, preparing only one coconut for each different letter. Add the coconuts to the display.

To complete the display, have youngsters identify the letter on a chosen coconut. Help each child whose name begins with that letter post his photo near the coconut. Continue in the same manner until each child's photo is displayed. Later, when you're ready to replace the display, set the photos, magnetic letters, and cookie sheet at a center for spelling practice.

Lisa Wilkinson
Benjamin Banneker Elementary
Loveville, MD

From Letters to Words
Using letter-sound associations

What better way to extend this alphabet story than by forming words? Make two copies of the coconut patterns on page 211. Write each of these letters on a different coconut: *a, f, h, m, s,* and *t.* Instruct each student to color and cut out a copy of the programmed coconuts. Have her draw a palm tree on the front of a legal-size envelope as shown and then spread out her coconuts on the treetop. Next, announce a word listed on this page and have students form it with their coconuts. After verifying the correct spelling, guide students to add or change letters to form different words. Then have each youngster tuck her letters in her envelope for safekeeping.

adapted from an idea by Michelle Brown
Watervliet Elementary
Watervliet, NY

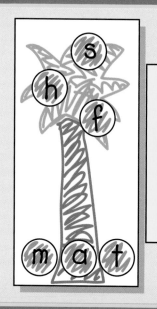

Word List
am
ham
at
sat
fat
hats

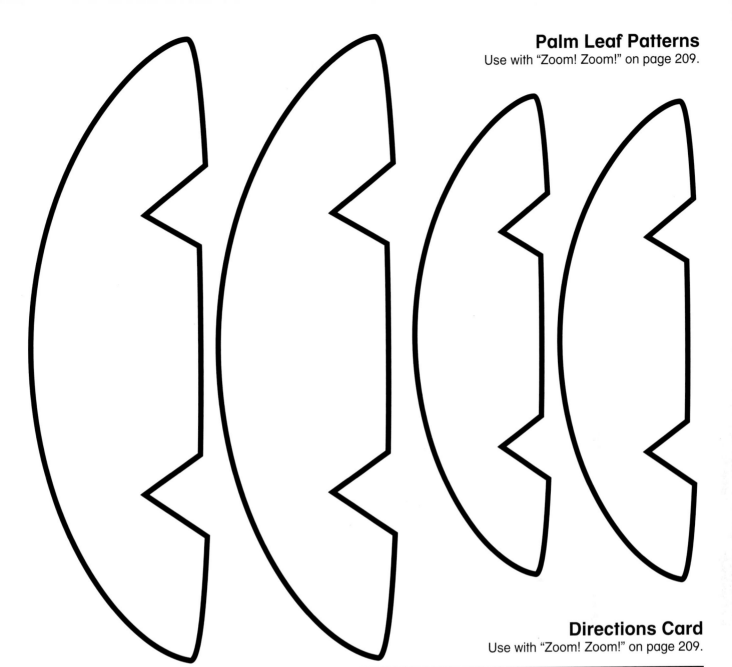

Palm Leaf Patterns
Use with "Zoom! Zoom!" on page 209.

Directions Card
Use with "Zoom! Zoom!" on page 209.

Coconut Patterns
Use with "Zoom! Zoom!" on page 209 and "From Letters to Words" on page 210.

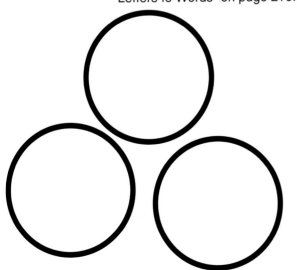

Zoom! Zoom!

1. Put the letters in the grass pocket.

2. Take a letter.

3. Say, "Zoom! Zoom! Letter *[a]*! Zoom! Zoom!" as you move the letter up the tree.

4. Put the letter in the bag.

5. Repeat Steps 2–4.

TEC42026

Three Little Pigs and Two Great Books

Pair the traditional tale with a rib-tickling adaptation for loads of learning fun!

adapted from ideas by Kelly Beach
Astatula Elementary School for the Arts
Astatula, FL

Constructing Comparisons

This version of a Venn diagram is a perfect tool for building comprehension. Gather *The Three Little Pigs* by Paul Galdone or another traditional version of the story and *The True Story of the 3 Little Pigs!* by Jon Scieszka. On a large sheet of paper, draw and title three houses, as shown, to create a poster. After you read both books to students, display the poster. Have students name characteristics that the books share and characteristics that are unique to each book. Write the information on the corresponding houses. After you recap the information, poll students to find out which book they prefer and why. **For more advanced students,** have each youngster complete his own house-themed Venn diagram.

The Three Little Pigs | Both | The True Story of the 3

Centered on the Story

Use these follow-up activities for happily-ever-after skill reinforcement.

Story Center: Color and cut out a copy of the story cards on page 213. Mount the cards on tagboard and then adhere magnetic tape to the back of each card. Place the cards near a magnetic board. To complete the activity, students display the cards on the board as they retell a chosen version of the story.

Science Station: Set out various small building materials such as dominoes, playing cards, cardboard tubes, and craft sticks. Also provide folded-paper fans and a supply of paper. When students visit the center, they build different houses. They determine how well the buildings withstand motion created by blowing on them and waving the fans. Then the youngsters write and illustrate the results.

Writing Center: Set out a class supply of the story cards on page 213, crayons, scissors, glue, and large sheets of story paper. Post a story-related prompt or question. After a student writes a response, he incorporates selected story cards into an illustration.

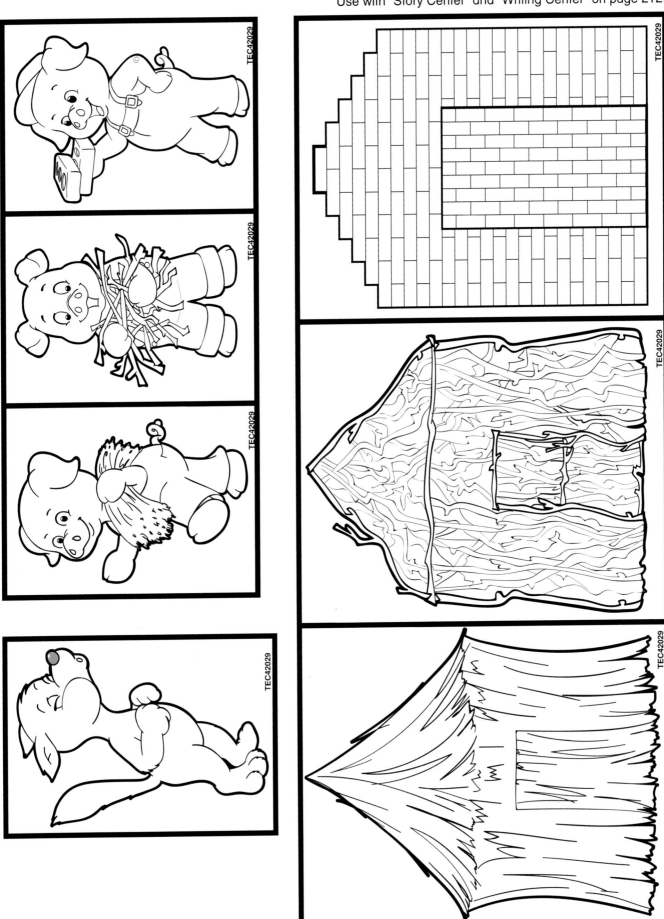

TEC42029

TEC42029

TEC42029

TEC42029

TEC42029

TEC42029

TEC42029

Wonderfully Witty Wood

The playful, predictable text in these two Audrey Wood selections is hard to resist. No doubt your students will want to hear the stories again and again and will eagerly join in the reading.

ideas contributed by Stephanie Affinito
Glens Falls, NY

The Napping House
Written by Audrey Wood
Illustrated by Don Wood
Everyone is sleeping peacefully until a wakeful flea sets off a surprising chain of events.

From Asleep to Awake
Retelling a story

What could be more fun than telling about the transformation from a quiet nap to the tumultuous awakening? To begin this activity, divide students into small groups. Give each group two unlined index cards and three unlined index card halves that you have labeled as shown. Also give each group a small black pom-pom (flea) and a legal-size envelope. Have the students in each group illustrate each card with the corresponding character. Ask them to illustrate a bed on the front of their envelope and sign their names on the back of it.

After students complete their illustrations, ask the youngsters in each group to use their envelope and cards as props as they retell the story to one another. Have them drop the pom-pom on the mouse to represent when the flea joins the story. For take-home practice, arrange for each youngster, in turn, to take his group's project home overnight and use it to share the story with his family.

A Nifty Neighborhood
Using describing words

From the cozy bed to the slumbering mouse, the napping house is packed with descriptive details! Use this display idea to have students create a neighborhood packed with details. To begin, give each youngster a light-colored house cutout. Help him label the roof with a descriptive phrase that includes an adjective and the name of a chosen animal. Then have him add a corresponding illustration below the phrase. Post students' completed houses in a row on a hallway wall, and title the display with a street sign similar to the one shown. **For more advanced students,** feature different describing words. For example, you might have youngsters prepare houses for a display titled "Noisy Road" or "Silly Street."

Colorful Street

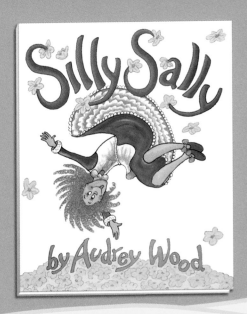

Silly Sally
by Audrey Wood
Silly Sally leads a topsy-turvy procession into town in a very unusual way!

Upside-Down Students
Contributing to a class book

Silly Sally isn't the only one who is head over heels. With this follow-up project, students are too! To prepare, take an individual photograph of each student with his hands raised above his head. (For best results, have him stand in front of a bare wall.) Trim the photo around each child. To begin, give each child a paper programmed as shown. Instruct him to write "Silly" and his name on the blank. Next, have him tear pieces of yellow paper and glue them along the bottom of his paper to resemble flowers. Then ask him to glue his photo upside down on his paper so his hands are on the flowers. Bind students' completed work into a book titled "Silly Students." **For more advanced students,** have each child complete the sentence with an alliterative name for himself.

Karla Barrow
Mt. View Elementary
Brigham City, UT

Silly Justin went to town, walking backwards, upside down.

On the way she met a duck, a silly duck. They drove a truck!

On the Way
Creating a story innovation

Sally's walk to town is full of silly surprises! Ask students to imagine more silly encounters with this rhyming activity. Read the story aloud. Then name the animals that Sally meets and guide youngsters to recall the corresponding rhymes. Next, ask each student to draw a picture of an animal that she would like to meet if she were in the story.

After each youngster completes her illustration, have students sit in a circle with their artwork. Ask one student to stand and show her classmates her illustration. Then lead the group in chanting, "Silly [child's name] went to town, walking backwards, upside down." Help the named student complete the chant by saying a rhyme that is modeled on the story and includes the name of her animal (use a nonsense word if necessary). Then have her sit down. Continue as described until each student has had a turn saying a rhyme.

Make Way for Ducklings

by Robert McCloskey

At first, Mr. and Mrs. Mallard think Boston's Public Garden is a perfect place to live. They quickly realize, though, that the park isn't safe for young ducklings, so they make a nest in a quieter spot. After the ducklings grow, the Mallards cross the highway with the help of friendly police officers and make the park their home.

ideas by Ada Goren
Winston-Salem, NC

HONK! HONK! HONK! HONK! HONK!

Then What Happened?
Sequencing story events

This approach to recapping the story is just ducky! Cut out six yellow copies of the mother duck card and one copy of the picture cards on page 218. Color the picture cards and then glue each card to a different duck. Place the ducks and a supply of sentence strips near a pocket chart. To begin, show students each picture in random order and invite them to tell how it relates to the story. Next, guide students to arrange the ducks in the pocket chart so that the pictures are in story order from top to bottom. Write a student-generated sentence for each picture and display it beside the corresponding duck. Then lead youngsters in reading the sentences to review the story from the beginning to the end!

The Mallards need a safe home.

The Mallards build a nest.

Eight ducks hatch.

Mrs. Mallard teaches the baby ducks.

The police help the ducks cross the street.

The ducks move to the park.

The ducks live near water. I live in an apartment.

Shelter and More
Needs of living things

What do Mr. and Mrs. Mallard look for in a home? Food, water, and shelter! Use this booklet project to help students understand that people have the same needs. For each student, staple three vertical sheets of story paper between two sheets of construction paper. Have each student title his booklet "The Ducks and I" and sign his name. On his first booklet page, instruct him to write about the Mallards' shelter and his own home. After he completes his writing, invite him to illustrate his work. Later, guide him to complete pages about food and water in a similar manner.

Just Hatched
Responding to a story

When a student "cracks open" this unique egg, she reveals her favorite part of the story! Have each student cut out two white copies of the egg pattern on page 219 and a yellow copy of the duckling card on page 218. To begin, each youngster illustrates her duckling with a picture that relates to her favorite part of the story. Next, she positions one egg horizontally. She glues the duckling toward the top of it and writes a caption. Then she cuts her other egg into two pieces with a zigzag cut. She uses brads to attach the pieces to her illustrated egg, as shown, and then writes her name on the front of her project.

I like it when the police stop the cars.

All Together, Now!
Word families

Jack, Kack, Lack, and the other ducklings have something in common: all of their names are in the -ack family! Invite your students to explore other word families at this word-sort center. For each word family that you wish to reinforce, make one copy of the mother duck card and several copies of the duckling card on page 218. Write a different rime on each mother duck and program each duckling with a word that has a featured rime. Place the cards and a paper pond at a center stocked with paper. To complete the activity, a student arranges the mother ducks in a column on the pond. He lines up the ducklings beside the corresponding mother ducks. Then he reads each family of words and lists them on his paper.

From Jack to Quack
Alphabetical order

To begin this follow-up activity, read aloud the page where the ducklings line up behind Mrs. Mallard. Then list on the board the ducklings' names in the same order as they appear in the book. After you guide students to realize that the brood is organized alphabetically, divide youngsters into small groups. Give each group a large plastic egg in which you have placed several word cards that feature the story's vocabulary. Next, ask the students in each group to open their egg, arrange the words in alphabetical order, and then read the words to you. For more "egg-cellent" skills practice, have each group trade its egg and words with another group.

Picture Cards
Use with "Then What Happened?" on page 216.

TEC42030

TEC42030

TEC42030

TEC42030

HONK!
HONK!

TEC42030

TEC42030

Mother Duck Card
Use with "Then What Happened?" on page 216
and "All Together, Now!" on page 217.

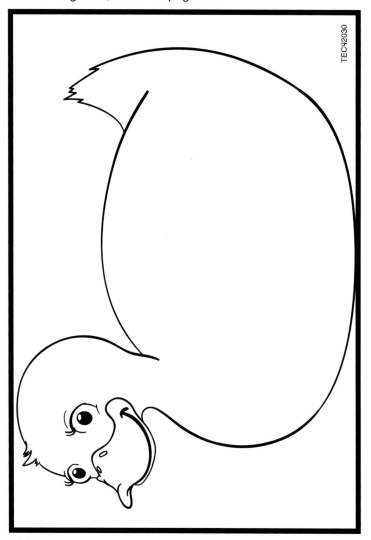

TEC42030

Duckling Card
Use with "Just Hatched" and "All Together, Now!"
on page 217.

TEC42030

218

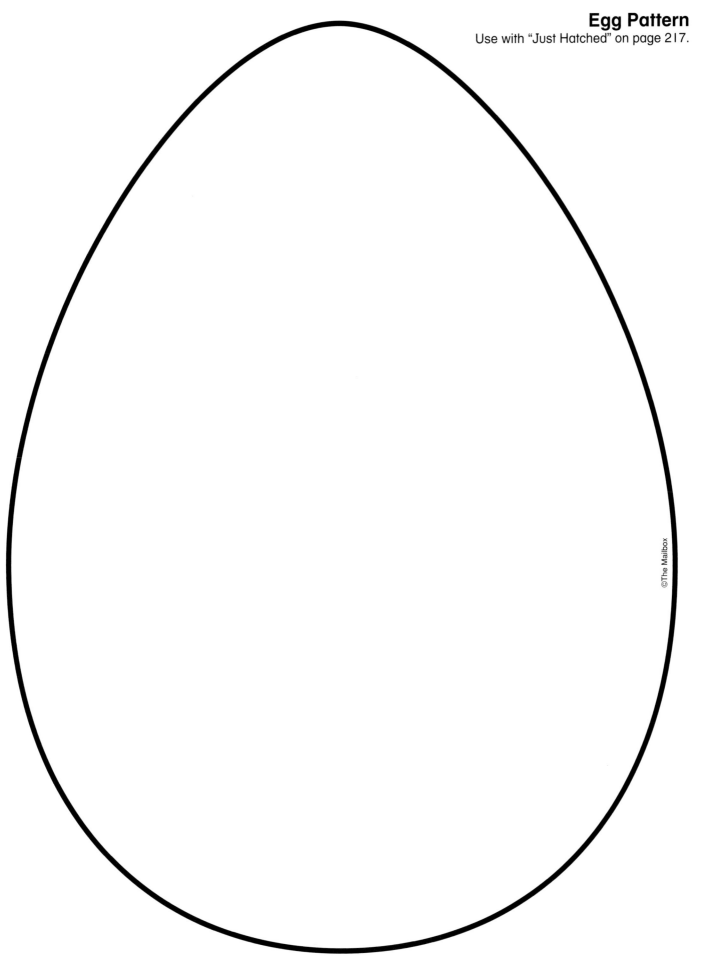

©The Mailbox

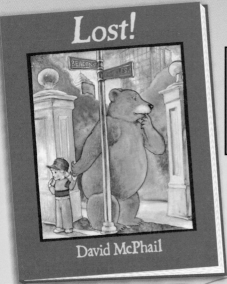

Lost!
by David McPhail

One day a boy discovers a lost bear in the city. He befriends the frightened critter and helps it look for its home in the forest. When they finally find it, the boy realizes that now he is lost!

ideas contributed by Julie Hays
Maryville, TN

Precious Cargo
Making predictions

Set the wheels in motion for a successful storytime with this prereading idea. To prepare, gather a small box and a large box with flaps (not a lid). Place the large box on its side so that the flaps are at one end. Tape the small box to the opposite end as shown to resemble a truck cab. Tape cardboard wheels to the truck and embellish it as desired. Place the book and a toy bear in the truck. Then close the flaps.

To begin, show students the truck and invite them to guess what is inside. Ask volunteers to share their ideas. Then open the truck with great fanfare and remove its contents. Next, show students the book's front cover and read the title. Explain that the cover, bear, and truck give clues about the story. Then invite students to make story-related predictions. After you read the story aloud, have youngsters compare their predictions with the story events. Then place the book, truck, and bear in your classroom library for students to enjoy during independent reading times.

Finding the Forest
Story problem and solution

If one problem-solving strategy doesn't work, try another! That's what the boy does as he helps the bear solve its problem. After you read the story aloud, draw a large truck on the left-hand side of the board. Ask students to identify the main story problem; then write it on the truck. As you guide students to recall in order the ways that the boy tries to solve the problem, write each strategy on a separate sentence strip. Post the strips beside the truck as shown to resemble a road. At the end of the road, draw a tree and label it "Home." Then encourage students to refer to the display as they recap how the boy perseveres in solving the problem.

City and Forest Sights
Comparing and contrasting locations

After sharing the book with students, remind them why the bear mistakes the park for its home. Then guide students to compare and contrast city and forest settings. Next, give each student a copy of sentence starters like the ones shown. Also give him a 12" x 18" sheet of white paper with a line drawn down the center. Instruct him to complete each sentence, glue each to a separate half of his paper, and then add illustrations. For decoration, invite him to draw a bear face on a six-inch brown circle and glue two ears to it. Then have him glue the bear head and two paws to the top of his paper as shown.

In the city, I see lots of crs.

In the forest, I see lots of tres.

Found!
Writing a story

What would your students do if they found a lost animal just as the boy does? Invite them to explore the possibilities with this truck booklet. For each student, fold a 9" x 12" sheet of construction paper in half (to 6" x 9"). With the fold at the top, staple a few sheets of paper inside to make a booklet. To begin, help students brainstorm a list of animals and their homes. Then have each student position her booklet with the fold at the top. To complete her booklet, a youngster uses words and/or pictures to tell about finding a lost animal in a truck. She writes a title and her name on the front cover. Then she glues a four-inch square to her booklet to resemble the cab of the truck. Finally, she glues two wheels in place and adds desired crayon details.

Found!

by Chloe

At the Library
Identifying land and water on maps and globes

When the boy has trouble figuring out where the bear lives, he heads to a place that is sure to have the information: a library. After students are familiar with the story, arrange for a class trip to a library. During the visit, have students look at a globe and various maps. As you help them distinguish between land and water, point out different bodies of water, such as oceans, rivers, and lakes. Guide youngsters to notice that water is blue on maps and globes. To follow up the visit, have each youngster complete a copy of page 222.

Looking for Home

Color the water **blue**.

Color the land **green**.

Cut.

Glue.

ocean	lake	river

Note to the teacher: Use with "At the Library" on page 221. For more advanced students, have each youngster write on the back of his completed paper one way in which a lake and an ocean are different.

FUN FAVORITES by Pat Hutchins

The predictable text and grin-inducing storylines of these books have been delighting children for years! Share the selections with your students and follow up with the accompanying skill-based ideas.

ideas by Katie Zuehlke
Bendix Elementary, Annandale, MN

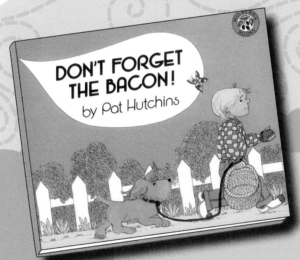

Don't Forget the Bacon!
by Pat Hutchins
When a young boy goes shopping for his mother, he makes a hilarious attempt to remember her requests.

How does the boy confuse his mother's request for a cake with a rake? When you pose this question to students, they're sure to comment on how similar the two words sound. To reinforce the letter-sound relationships, collect a supply of letter cards and gather students near a pocket chart. Use the cards to form the word *cake* in the pocket chart. Then with students' input, change the word to *rake*.

For more practice changing words, display the word *jam* in the pocket chart. After students read the word, say, "Don't forget the [jam]!" Then cover the *j* with an *h*. Prompt the students to ask, "The [ham]?" Reveal the *j* again and say, "No, the [jam]!" and then review how to form the two words. Explore a desired number of different pairs of words in the same manner. (See the suggestions below.) **For more advanced students,** change the final letters of words. ***Changing letters to form words***

Word Pairs

Initial Letters	Final Letters
box, fox	bag, bat
corn, horn	bed, bet
cup, pup	cap, cat
dish, fish	ham, hat
nest, vest	pin, pig

223

The Wind Blew
by Pat Hutchins
In this comical story, a whimsical wind causes mischief throughout one town.

After students are familiar with the story, read it again, pausing at the end of chosen rhyming lines for students to chime in with the appropriate words. Wonder aloud what other things the mischievous wind could sweep up. Then guide students to name pairs of nouns that rhyme. Write the word pairs on the board.

Next, give each student copies of the booklet pages on page 225: three copies of the page with blanks and one copy of the page with the concluding sentence. Have each youngster write rhyming words in the blanks, referring to the words on the board as needed. After he illustrates the pages, sequence them with the conclusion at the end. Then staple the pages between two construction paper covers. Instruct the youngster to title his resulting booklet and sign his name. No doubt he'll be eager to take his rhyming story home and read it to his family! *Rhyming*

The Doorbell Rang
by Pat Hutchins
Ma makes plenty of cookies, or so she thinks until the doorbell rings again and again, signaling the arrival of friends who'd like to share the treats.

Sam and Victoria ensure that each of their guests has an equal share of the cookies. But with this partner activity, one student always has more chocolate chips than the other! To prepare, cut out an even number of construction paper cookies. Draw a different number of chocolate chips on each cookie and then arrange the cookies facedown on a cookie sheet. Place the cookie sheet and a supply of paper at a center.

To begin, one student divides a sheet of paper into two columns and then each youngster writes her name at the top of a different column. Next, each student takes one cookie and writes in the appropriate column the number of chocolate chips on her cookie. The students circle the greater number and then set the two cookies aside. They compare the chocolate chips on the rest of the cookies in the same manner. **For more advanced students,** program the cookies with numbers rather than illustrations of chocolate chips. *Comparing numbers*

The wind took a _____ and a _____.

It blew them high in the sky.

Then the wind took the things it found

and dropped them all to the ground!

A House for Hermit Crab

A House For Hermit Crab

by Eric Carle

After Hermit Crab realizes that his shell is too snug, he moves to a larger shell. Over time, he decorates the new shell and makes it a perfect home. When Hermit Crab outgrows that shell as well, he learns that moving can be both sad and exciting.

Changes!
Making connections

When Hermit Crab outgrows his shell, it's sure to remind students of times when they outgrew things. To explore the connections students make with the story, fold a 9" x 12" sheet of white paper in half lengthwise for each youngster. Then cut the top layer of each folded paper in half as shown. Discuss with students things that people physically outgrow just as Hermit Crab does. Point out that people also emotionally outgrow some things as they mature.

Next, instruct each youngster to place her paper with the fold on the left-hand side. Have her illustrate Hermit Crab on the top flap and herself on the bottom flap. Then ask her to unfold the top flap and write a sentence that tells what Hermit Crab outgrows. In a similar manner, have her unfold the bottom flap and write about something that she has outgrown. It's a simple way to help students relate to the main character!

Ada Goren, Winston-Salem, NC

I don't nede a nite lite any mor.

A Perfect Home

From Plain to Perfect
Listening for information, responding to literature

Everything that Hermit Crab adds to his home has a purpose. After you read the book aloud, ask students to listen carefully for the reason that Hermit Crab adds each item. Then reread the pages about the crab's monthly additions, pausing periodically for students to explain the crab's reasons for choosing the described items.

To extend the activity, display a jumbo hermit crab shell on a large sheet of paper. (Enlarge the shell pattern on page 18 if desired.) Add the title shown. Then have students cut from old magazines pictures of items they think would be good additions to Hermit Crab's home. Ask each student, in turn, to show his picture to the class, explain why he chose it, and then glue it to the shell.

Ada Goren

Shining Examples
Describing words

Beautiful, handsome, and *tidy* are just some of the words that Hermit Crab uses to describe various ocean sights. After students are familiar with the story, guide them to recall several describing words in it. List the words on chart paper. Then give each student a blue paper fish. To decorate the fish to look like a lantern fish, have her make white paint prints with a cotton ball and yellow paint prints with a cotton swab. Showcase students' completed fish with the list. No doubt the display will inspire youngsters to brighten their writing with describing words!

Ada Goren, Winston-Salem, NC

Describing Words
beautiful
handsome
pretty
tidy
fierce
bright

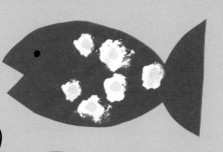

Moving On
Story theme

Hermit Crab's realization that changes can be exciting is a perfect springboard for discussing the next school year. To prepare, make a class supply of the shell pattern on page 18 plus one extra. Write your name on one shell and have each student personalize a shell.

To begin, sit with students in a circle. Spread out all of the shells but yours facedown in the middle of the circle. Hold up your shell and tell students something about the next school year that you wonder about or look forward to. Then take another shell at random and pass it to the corresponding student. After this student takes a turn as described, have him pick up another shell to determine whose turn is next. Continue the activity until each youngster has had a turn. Encourage students to take their shells home as reminders of the exciting new school year ahead!

Seaworthy Neighborhood
Art

This creative project is a fun way to illustrate the story setting. In advance, set out a shallow container of water. Use scissors to scrape flakes of colored chalk on the water. To make one project, place a white construction paper shell (pattern on page 18) facedown on the water. Then remove the shell from the water and let it dry. Sponge-paint the bottom of a sheet of white paper so that it resembles an ocean floor. Draw wavy blue lines to make water and then glue the shell on the ocean floor. Use arts-and-crafts materials to complete the scene with desired details, such as tissue paper sea grass and starfish cut from scrapbook paper.

Jan Lee Wicker
Andrew Jackson Elementary
Halifax, NC

Horton Hatches the Egg

by Dr. Seuss
When a lazy bird named Mayzie tires of sitting on her egg, she persuades Horton the Elephant to take over her duties. While Mayzie enjoys a carefree vacation, Horton faithfully cares for the egg through rain, snow, and other adversities.

ideas contributed by Margie Rogers
Colfax Elementary
Colfax, NC

He was faithful wen it rand. He stad on the nest.

100 Percent Faithful
Vocabulary

When Horton says that an elephant is faithful, he means it! Before reading the book to students, write the word *faithful* on the board. Read the word aloud and ask students to share their ideas about what it means. Then tell students that the elephant in the story is faithful. Ask them to pantomime an elephant swinging its trunk whenever they hear the word *faithful* in the story. Then read the book aloud over one or two sessions, using plenty of expression each time you read Horton's refrain about faithfulness.

At the end of the story, guide students to define *faithful* in their own words. Then have each youngster draw and write about a time when Horton is faithful.

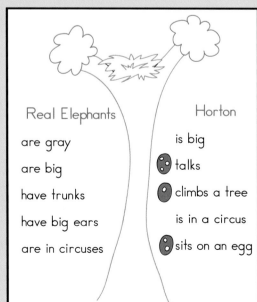

Real Elephants

are gray
are big
have trunks
have big ears
are in circuses

Horton

is big
talks
climbs a tree
is in a circus
sits on an egg

A Fantastic Elephant
Reality and fantasy

Horton is not an ordinary elephant. After all, he climbs a tree, perches delicately on a nest, and sits on an egg for 51 weeks! Invite students to distinguish Horton from real elephants during this follow-up activity. Draw in the center of a large piece of paper a tree with a nest. Then title the two halves of the paper as shown. Post the paper in your group area.

Invite students to tell what they know about real elephants and then have them tell what they know about Horton. Write the information below the corresponding headings. Review the two resulting lists with students and ask them whether the story is a realistic story or fantasy. After students agree that it is a fantasy, have volunteers draw an egg like Mayzie's beside each detail about Horton that is not realistic.

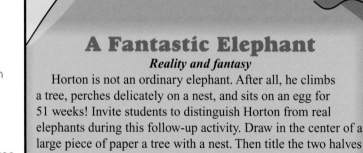

Mayzie and Horton
Comparing characters

Birds and elephants are decidedly different, and Mayzie and Horton are no exception! Write the names of the two characters on separate blank cards and illustrate the cards. Place the cards in a pocket chart to create column headings. Write words that describe the characters on several separate cards.

To begin, give each youngster two blank cards. Instruct him to draw Horton on one card and Mayzie's egg on the other card. Next, take a word card at random and read it aloud. Have each youngster decide which character the word best describes and hold up his corresponding card. After you scan students' responses, announce the correct answer and give any needed explanation. Place the word card below the appropriate heading. Continue as described until all of the words are displayed. Then invite students to tell which character they would prefer to have as a friend and why.

Mayzie	Horton
small	big
bird	elephant
lazy	helpful
selfish	nice
	brave

A New Egg
Rhyming

Is an elephant-bird absurd? Not in the world of Dr. Seuss! Invite students to imagine other unusual creatures with this rhyming activity. After a first reading, reread selected rhyming sentences aloud and have students identify the rhyming words. Next, give each youngster a copy of page 230 and instruct him to complete the rhymes. Then have him color the egg and the rest of the illustration as desired. Finally, ask him to draw on the back of his paper what he imagines is in the egg.

Happy at Last!
Character analysis

Here's a fun way to review the ups and downs of Horton's egg-hatching experience. Divide a large piece of paper into six sections and then label the sections as shown. Place the resulting mat on the floor and have students sit around it. To begin, have one youngster toss a beanbag onto the mat. If the beanbag lands on a section with a word, help the youngster read the word and ask her to name a time when Horton feels that way. If the beanbag lands on the starred section, have the youngster describe how Horton feels at a chosen point in the story and explain why he feels this way. Ask each student to take a turn in the same manner, encouraging youngsters to recall different parts of the story.

happy	sad
★	lonely
surprised	scared

A New Egg

 Write. Use the word bank.

 Color.

    Then draw on the back of this paper.

```
┌─────────────────────────────────────────────┐
│              Word Bank                        │
│   rest     things     see     small           │
└─────────────────────────────────────────────┘
```

What will hatch?

Will it have two wings?

Will it like fun _____?

Will it be big and tall?

Will it be very _____?

Will it fly from the nest?

Will it stay and _____?

What could it be?

I want to _____!

MATH UNITS

That's a Pattern!

Use these movement, color, and shape ideas, and soon your students will notice patterns everywhere!

ideas contributed by Andrea Singleton
Waynesville Elementary
Waynesville, OH

Silly Lineup
Identifying patterns

No advance preparation is needed for this class activity. Have six students stand side by side at the front of the classroom and face the seated students. Ask the seated students to put their heads down and cover their eyes. Then quietly help the standing youngsters position themselves to create a pattern, such as *hands up high, hands on hips, hands up high, hands on hips*. Once the six youngsters are positioned, call out, "Look at the line!" At this signal, the seated students look up and study the pattern. After one of them correctly identifies it, have the youngsters at the front of the room return to their seats. Then help six different students create a pattern for their classmates to identify.

For a fun wrap-up, invite all of the seated students to extend the last pattern created. After each student is in place, have the youngsters read the pattern. To do this, start at the beginning of the line and have each youngster, in turn, describe his position.

Pocket Chart Pleaser
Identifying and extending patterns

Here's a simple way to add a colorful twist to math. Gather two or three colors of 3" x 5" cards. Cut the cards in half. To begin, use several of the cards to create a color pattern in one row of a pocket chart. Set the remaining cards nearby. After students read the pattern, ask a youngster to identify the part that repeats. Then have a volunteer extend the pattern by adding one card. Display a desired number of different patterns for students to identify and extend in the same manner.

For more advanced students, display a pattern as described, leaving out one card. Then have youngsters identify the missing color and set a corresponding card in place.

Pattern maker, pattern maker, what will you do? Show us a pattern and we'll copy you!

Watch and Do!

●▲ *Identifying and copying patterns* ●▲

Students will be eager to clap, tap, and snap during this group activity. Sit with students in a circle. Demonstrate different patterns that you can create while sitting, such as *clap, pat knees, clap, pat knees.* Next, designate one student as a pattern maker. Then lead students in saying the chant shown. At the end of the chant, have the designated youngster demonstrate a pattern of her choice. After students correctly identify the pattern, have them copy it.

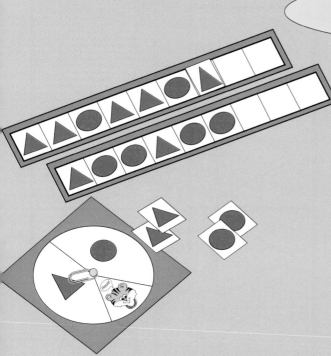

Spinning for Shapes

●▲ *Extending patterns* ●▲

The element of chance makes this partner game a winner. To prepare the game for center use, make one copy of the spinner, shape cards, and pattern strips on page 234. Color the circles one color and the triangles another color. Color the tiger as desired. Cut out the spinner, cards, and strips. Then mount the strips on separate pieces of construction paper for durability. Use a brad to attach a small paper clip to the spinner as shown. Tape the spinner to a larger construction paper square for easy handling.

To play, each player takes one strip. Then Player 1 spins the spinner. If he spins the shape that comes next in his pattern, he takes a corresponding card and sets it in place. If he spins the shape that does not come next, he does nothing. If he spins the tiger, he reads his pattern. Player 2 takes a turn in the same manner. Alternate play continues until one player has added three shapes to his pattern. Then both players take turns as described to complete the second strip together.

Colorful Favorites

●▲ *Creating patterns* ●▲

This quick and easy display idea doubles as an assessment tool. To begin, draw two shapes on the board. Invite students to describe different patterns they can create with the shapes. Next, give each child a 3" x 18" strip of white paper. Have her use her favorite color of crayon to draw a pattern with the shapes. Then ask her to write her name on a construction paper strip that is her favorite color. After she completes her work, invite her to read her pattern to you. Display each student's name with her pattern on a board titled "Read Our Patterns!"

Tasha

233

Spinner, Shape Cards, and Pattern Strips

Use with "Spinning for Shapes" on page 233.

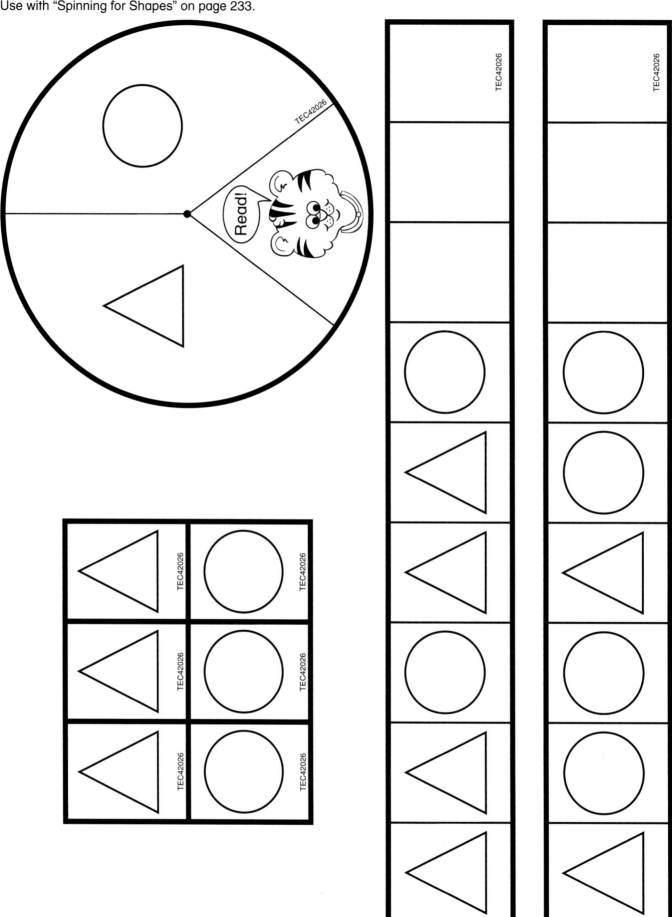

Just "Ripe" Math Ideas

Watch your students' number sense grow with these easy-to-adapt activities!

ideas contributed by Angie Kutzer
Garrett Elementary, Mebane, NC

More Melons?

One-to-one correspondence

Students identify the larger sets at this tempting center. Prepare 12 or more construction paper watermelon slices that are the same size. Divide the slices into two large resealable plastic bags. Place in each bag a different number of small paper plates that is not equal to the number of slices. Cut apart two copies of the center cards on page 237. Set the bags and cards at a center.

To complete the activity, a student empties one bag. She places one watermelon slice on each plate, setting aside any extra slices. She determines whether there are more watermelon slices or more plates and takes the corresponding center card. Then she places the card, watermelon, and plates in the bag for an adult to check. She compares and labels the items in the second bag in the same manner.

Pick of the Crop

Number order

This number mix-up is fresh off the vine! To prepare, cut six whole watermelons from construction paper. Label each watermelon with a different number in a chosen counting sequence. Then embellish the melons with crayon details. Put a star sticker on the melon with the first number in the sequence.

To begin, spread out the melons facedown and ask six students to each take one melon. Explain that the student who has the starred melon will be first in line. Then guide the six students to line up side by side in number order facing the seated students. Have the class read the completed number sequence. Next, secretly choose one number and give a clue about it that includes the word *after* or *before*. After the class correctly identifies the number, collect the melons. Repeat the activity until each student has a turn picking a watermelon. **For an easier version,** instead of giving clues about a number, name the numbers in random order and have the seated students identify the corresponding youngsters.

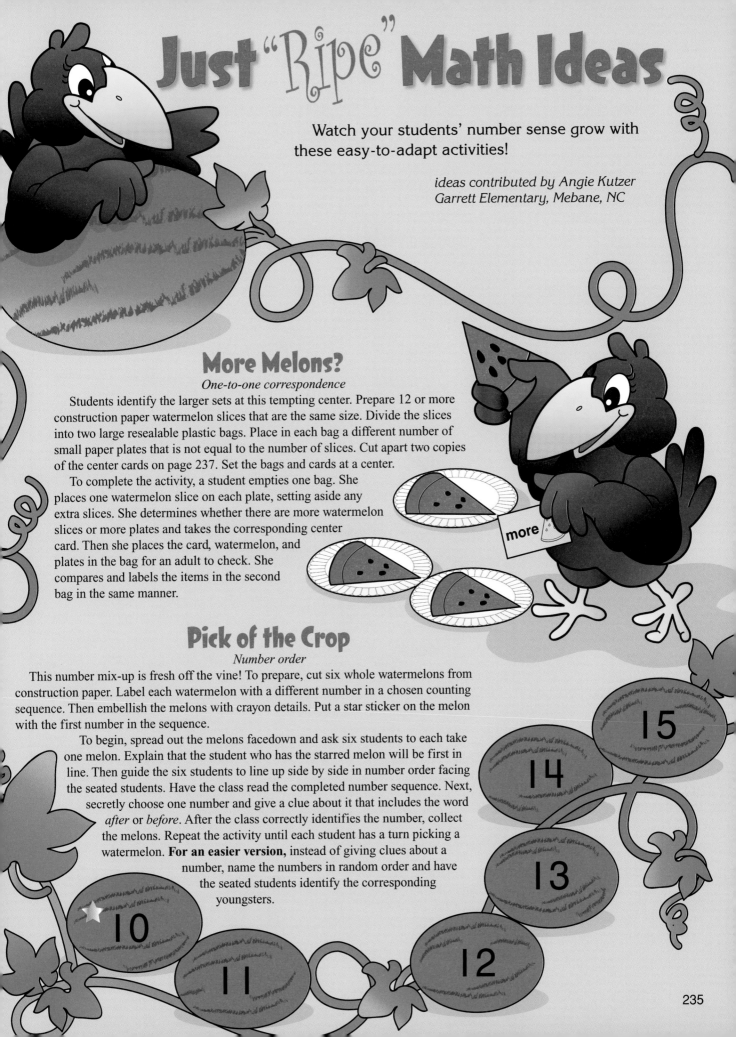

235

Who Will It Be?
Counting

Whet students' appetites for numbers with this catchy chant. Have students sit in a circle. Lead them in clapping a steady rhythm and saying the chant shown. Next, name a target number appropriate for your youngsters' counting abilities. Then have students count around the circle, one number per student, until they reach the designated number. Invite the student who says that number to lead the next round.

> Watermelon, watermelon, juicy and sweet, How many slices can you eat?

Toss and Tell
Comparing sets or numbers

For this group activity, gather two different beanbags. Use bulletin board paper to make a jumbo watermelon slice. Then visually divide it into several sections. Program the sections with different numbers or quantities of seeds. Place the watermelon on the floor and have students sit around it. Next, have two volunteers each toss a beanbag onto the watermelon and name the corresponding number. (If the beanbags land on the same section, instruct the youngsters to toss them again.) Then ask the class to tell who has the greater number. Invite that student to play another round, and have a different youngster take the place of the other volunteer.

Sets of Seeds
Modeling numbers or addition combinations

This hands-on approach to numbers is sliced just right for your students' abilities. Give each youngster a copy of the watermelon seeds on page 237. If desired, have him color his seeds before he cuts them out.

For modeling numbers, instruct each student to color a paper plate half to resemble a watermelon. Write a number from 1 through 12 on the board and have each youngster place that many seeds on his watermelon. After students check their work, ask them to remove a certain number of seeds and count the seeds that are left.

For addition, have each student color two paper plate halves to create watermelon workmats. Ask him to sign his name on a copy of the recording sheet on page 237 and write a number from 6 through 12 on the whole melon. Have him take that many seeds and discard any extra seeds. Next, ask him to place some seeds on one workmat and the rest of the seeds on the other workmat. After he records the corresponding addition combination, have him model and record two different combinations in the same manner.

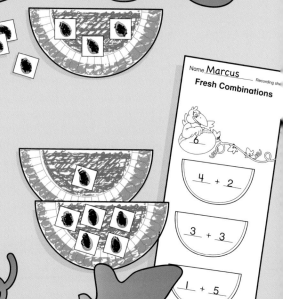

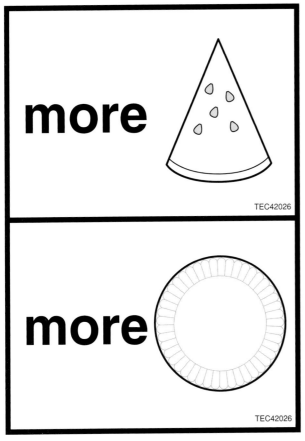

more

more

TEC42026

TEC42026

Watermelon Seed Cards
Use with "Sets of Seeds" on page 236.

TEC42026 TEC42026 TEC42026

TEC42026 TEC42026 TEC42026

TEC42026 TEC42026 TEC42026

TEC42026 TEC42026 TEC42026

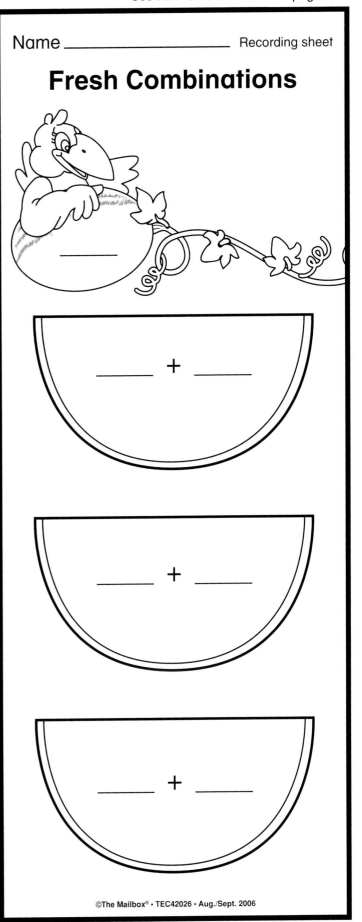

Name _____ Recording sheet

Fresh Combinations

_____

____ + ____

____ + ____

____ + ____

What a Treat!

Count the seeds.

Write how many.

Read.

_____

_ _ _ _ _ _

_____ six

_____

_ _ _ _ _ _

_____ seven

_____

_ _ _ _ _ _

_____ eight

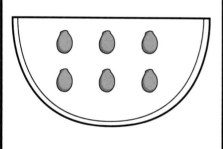 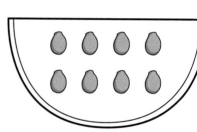

_____

_ _ _ _ _ _

_____ seven

_____

_ _ _ _ _ _

_____ eight

_____

_ _ _ _ _ _

_____ six

Name _____

Sweet Slices

✎ Write the missing numbers.

A.

5 ___ 7 ___ ___ 10 ___

B.

9 ___ 11 ___ 13 ___ 15

C.

12 ___ 14 ___ 16 17 ___ ___

D.

___ 15 16 ___ 18 ___ ___

Bonus Box: Write the numbers from 1 to 20 on the back of this paper.

239

Raking In Math

Put a seasonal spin on a variety of skills with this "tree-rific" collection of ideas!

ideas contributed by Ada Goren
Winston-Salem, NC

Nuts About Geometry
Plane shapes, graphing

This acorn search provides practice with two different skills. Make two copies of the acorn cards on page 242. Program the acorns with different sizes of triangles, squares, and rectangles, drawing one shape per acorn. Copy the programmed cards so that there is one acorn per student. When your students are not present, place the acorns around your classroom in plain sight.

To begin, invite students to imagine that they are squirrels, and ask each youngster to find one acorn and take it to his seat. After students have gathered all of the acorns, ask several volunteers to name the shapes on their acorns. To determine how many triangles, squares, and rectangles there are, help students use their cards to create a graph in a pocket chart. Then ask students questions such as "Are there more rectangles or triangles?" or "How many acorns have shapes with four equal sides?"

triangles

squares

rectangles

I think you're hiding two acorns.

Hide and Peek
Problem solving

Promote number sense with a stash of hidden acorns! To begin, pair students. Give each twosome a large disposable cup and five brown cubes or paper squares (acorns). Partner 1 places the acorns on a work surface. Next, Partner 2 covers her eyes as Partner 1 conceals a chosen number of the acorns by placing the cup upside down over them. Then Partner 2 uncovers her eyes, counts the visible acorns, and tells how many acorns she thinks are hidden. Partner 1 lifts the cup to check. For another round of play, the partners trade roles. **For more advanced students,** give youngsters more acorns.

Leafy Lengths
Using nonstandard units

To prepare this measurement center, cut out several colorful copies of the leaf cards on page 242. Make a class supply of the recording sheet on page 243 and set out the items pictured on it. To complete the activity, a student measures the designated objects' lengths with the leaves and records the measurements to the nearest whole unit. Then he colors the illustration of the shortest object yellow and the illustration of the longest object orange.

How many leaves long is it?

In the Treetop
Comparing sets or subtraction

For this versatile center, illustrate a large tree with a green treetop. Write a number from 6 to 10 on the trunk. Place ten orange and ten yellow Unifix cubes (leaves) in a paper lunch bag. Place the bag and illustration at a center stocked with paper. When a student visits the center, have her take the designated number of leaves at random and place them on the treetop.

For comparing sets, the student writes how many leaves there are of each color. If the numbers are equal, she draws a happy face. If the numbers are not equal, she circles the greater number.

For subtraction, the youngster models one color of leaves falling off the tree and then writes the corresponding subtraction sentence.

Piles of Leaves
Comparing numbers

An autumn wind adds an element of chance to this partner game. Make one copy of the leaf and wind cards on page 242. Number the leaf cards with a desired range of numbers, writing one number per card. Have each youngster color and cut out a copy of the programmed cards and the wind card. Then ask him to write his initials on the back of them.

To play one round, the students in each pair sit across from one another. Each player shuffles his cards and then stacks them facedown. Next, he sets his top card faceup on the playing surface. If the players' cards have different numbers, the player with the greater number "rakes up" both cards and sets them aside. If the cards are the same, each player sets aside his own card. If a player sets down a wind card, he imitates the sound of wind and pushes both cards to the other player. After the players compare the rest of their cards in this manner, the player with more cards is declared the winner.

241

Acorn Cards

Use with "Nuts About Geometry" on page 240.

Leaf and Wind Cards

Use with "Leafy Lengths" and "Piles of Leaves" on page 241.

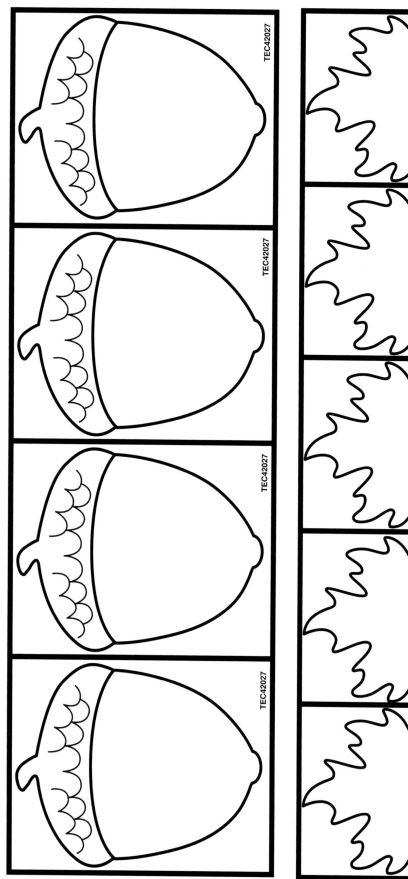

Leafy Lengths

Measure.
🖊 Write.
🖍 Color.

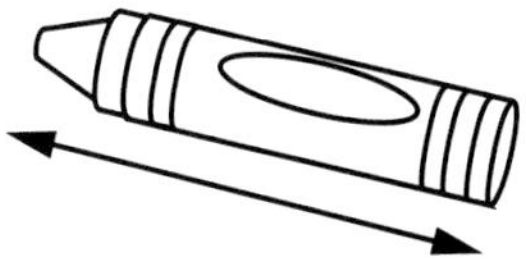 crayon	about ____ leaves
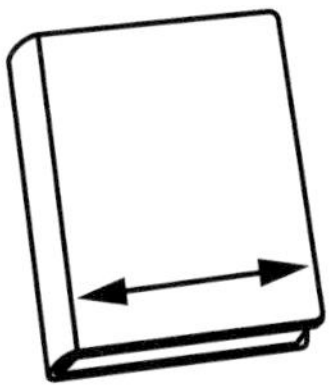 book	about ____ leaves
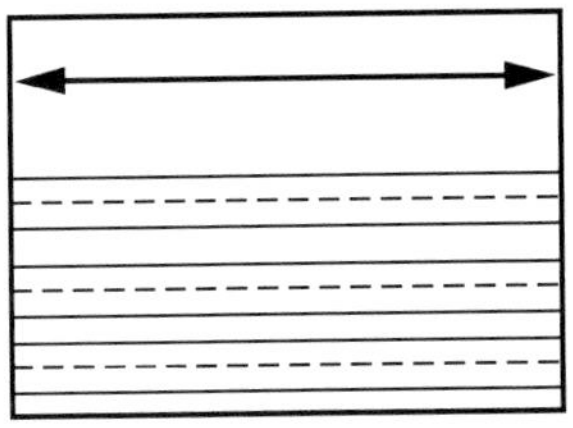 paper	about ____ leaves
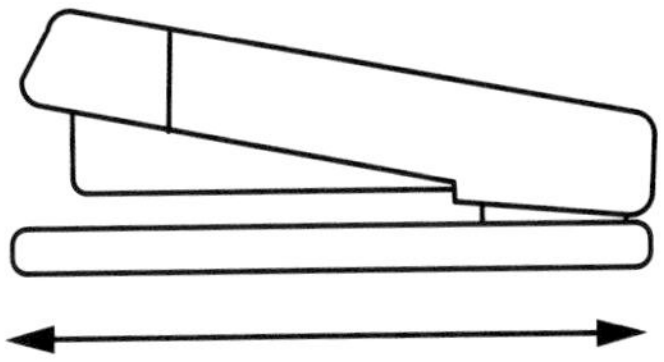 stapler	about ____ leaves
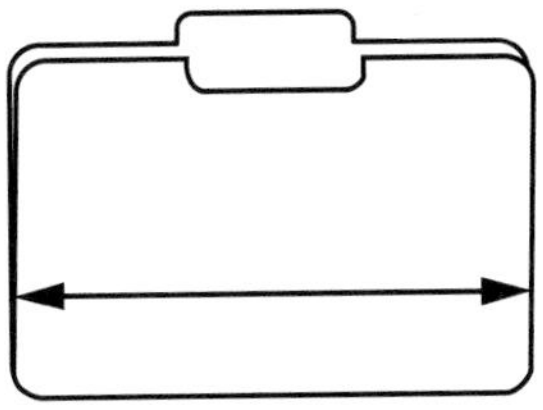 folder	about ____ leaves

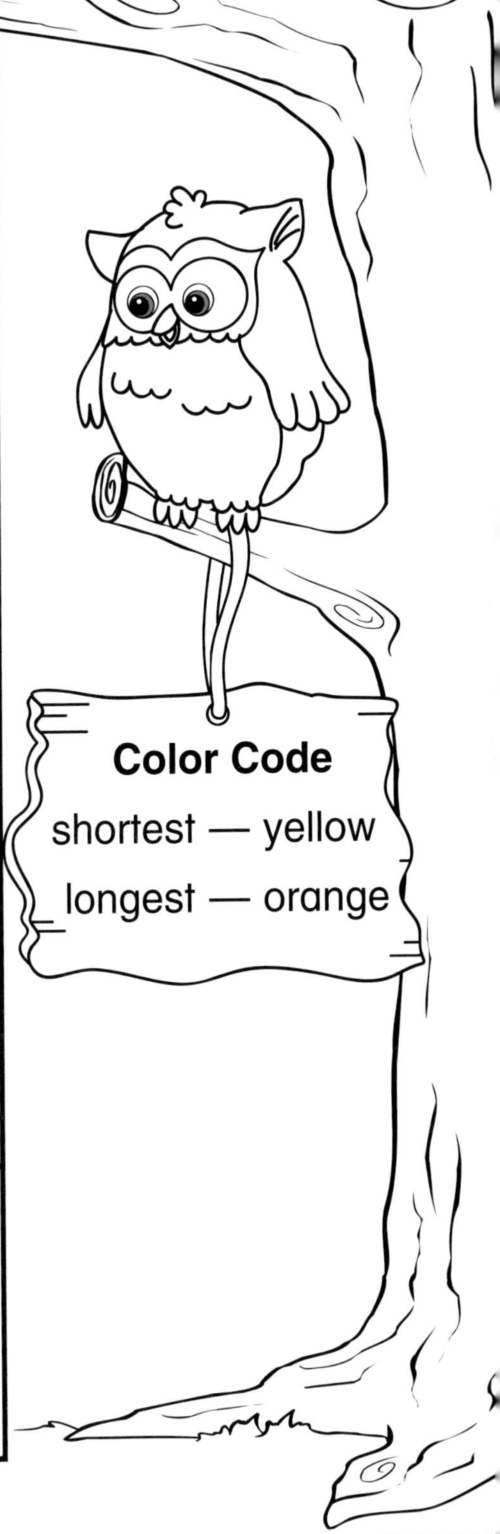

Color Code

shortest — yellow

longest — orange

Note to the teacher: Use with "Leafy Lengths" on page 241.

Counting on Coins

This treasure trove of ideas holds valuable skills practice!

Pocket Change
Coin recognition

For this song activity, have each student color and cut out a copy of the coin cards on page 246. Then instruct students to stand with their cards. Next, lead students in the first verse of the song below, prompting each child to put his penny card in his pocket during the last two lines. (If he doesn't have a pocket, have him pantomime the action.) Then confirm that each youngster put the appropriate card in his pocket. Repeat the verse three more times as described, substituting the appropriate lyrics for each remaining coin.

Sapna Datta
English Estates Elementary
Fern Park, FL

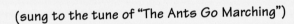

(sung to the tune of "The Ants Go Marching")

[The penny is small and brown, you see]. Hurrah! Hurrah!
[The penny is small and brown, you see]. Hurrah! Hurrah!
[The penny is small and brown, you see].
[It's worth one cent; that's enough for me!]
And it jingle-jangles down in my pocket
With the rest of the coins. Clink! Clink! Clink!

Lines for additional verses:
The nickel is silver and smooth all around.
It's worth five cents, heads up or down.

The dime is tiny and silver too.
It's worth ten cents; I know it's true.

The quarter is the biggest one.
It's worth 25 cents, and now we're done.

Unbeatable Bargains
Modeling money amounts

Here's a fun variation of a typical shopping activity. Cut out several pictures of familiar items from newspaper flyers. Glue the pictures on separate blank cards and label them with grade-appropriate prices. Place the cards, a class supply of blank booklets with three white pages, an ink pad, and a set of coin stamps at a center. To purchase an item, a child chooses a card. She writes the name of the item and its price on her first booklet page and then stamps a corresponding set of coins. After she records a different purchase on each remaining page in the same manner, she titles her booklet and decorates the cover as desired.

adapted from an idea by Pam Johnson
DeSoto Trail Elementary
Tallahassee, FL

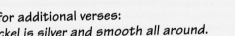

Visual Values
Coin values

Whenever a student needs to know how much a certain type of coin is worth, a number line can help! Use a number line on display or post a length of adding machine tape numbered from 1 to 25. Color and cut out enlarged copies of the coin patterns on page 246. Then post each coin above the number on the number line that corresponds with its value.

Hillary Whaley
R. D. Head Elementary
Lilburn, GA

Money With a Twist
Coin recognition or values

This partner version of the Twister game is sure to get rave reviews! Write each of these phrases on a separate blank card: "right hand," "left hand," "right foot," and "left foot." Then place the cards in a container. Use a brad to secure a paper clip to a copy of the spinner pattern on page 246. To prepare a floor mat, color and cut out four enlarged copies of each coin pattern on page 246. Then glue them on a large piece of paper as shown. Laminate the mat for durability if desired.

To begin, Player 1 takes a card at random and reads it aloud. Then he spins the spinner and names the coin (or value). Next, Player 2 places his corresponding hand or foot on an appropriate coin on the mat. After Player 1 returns the card to the container, he directs Player 2 to make several additional moves as described. Then the players switch roles.

Robin Melancon
East Petersburg Elementary
East Petersburg, PA

What a Find!
Determining money amounts

To prepare this small-group activity, decorate a container to resemble a treasure chest. Then place a supply of imitation coins in the chest. To begin, show a small group of students the treasure chest and reveal the contents with great excitement. Then give each student a copy of the recording sheet on page 247 and two or more coins. Have her illustrate the coins on the first treasure chest on her recording sheet and label each coin illustration with the corresponding value. Instruct her to write the value of the set where indicated. After you check her work, collect her coins and give her different coins. Continue in the same manner until each youngster completes her paper.

adapted from an idea by Kristin Bynum
Vivian Fowler Elementary
Mt. Pleasant, TX

Coin Cards

Use with "Pocket Change" on page 244.

Spinner Pattern

Use with "Money With a Twist" on page 245.

Coin Patterns

Use with "Visual Values" and "Money With a Twist" on page 245.

Name _____

What a Find!

Draw each set.
Write each money amount.

In All

_____ ¢

In All

_____ ¢

In All

_____ ¢

In All

_____ ¢

Note to the teacher: Use with "What a Find!" on page 245.

100ᵗʰ Day Circus Celebration

Use these creative ideas to make the much-anticipated school milestone a day to remember. They're just the ticket for fun-filled math practice!

ideas contributed by Laura Wanke, Luther Academy at Gloria Dei, Rockford, IL

Tickets, Please!
Counting sets to 100

What's the price of admission to this math circus? Why, 100 items, of course! In advance, ask each child to bring to school on the designated day 100 small items in a nonbreakable container. Plan to have a few extra containers of items available for children who do not bring any. You might gather die-cut balloons, pink or blue cotton balls (cotton candy), and pom-poms (costume decorations), for example. To designate a display table, tape the ends of streamers to the edges of a tabletop, allowing the streamers to hang down.

When students arrive on the designated day, instruct each child to adhere a personalized sticky note to his container and place it on the table. Later, after each child shows his 100 items to the class, prompt students to share their strategies for counting large quantities, such as making sets of ten and moving items aside as they are counted. Then have students count their items.

> Now, in the center ring, students will jump up and down. The audience will count by tens!

Perfect Performances
Counting by ones, fives, and tens

To prepare this entertaining activity, cut out a copy of the clown spinner card on page 250 and use a brad to attach a paper clip to each spinner. To begin, have students sit in a large circle. Invite two or three volunteers to stand in the center of the circle. Tell students that the volunteers (performers) will do an action as you and the rest of the students (audience) count to 100. To determine what the action is and how the audience will count, ask a volunteer to spin both spinners. Then announce with great fanfare what both groups will do. After the volunteers complete their act, invite them to take a bow as you and the audience give them a round of applause. Continue in the same manner until each youngster has had a turn performing.

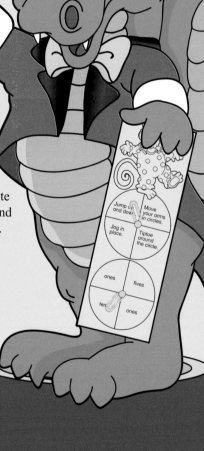

Tightrope Act
Counting by tens

Students take a step-by-step approach to skip-counting at this center. Write the numbers from 10 to 100 by tens on a vertical length of adding machine tape, leaving a few inches between the numbers. Place the resulting number line on the floor. To complete the activity, a student reads the numbers as she walks beside the number line with her arms outstretched. For added fun, she may tiptoe or walk with one foot in front of the other. **For more advanced students,** prepare number lines for counting by tens and by fives, writing on the backs of sentence strips instead of on adding machine tape. Students arrange each set of sentence strips end to end in number order to assemble the number lines. Then they walk along them as described.

Bunches of Balloons
Problem solving, modeling 100

Creating this high-flying display takes teamwork. Make a supply of the balloon cards on page 250. Help students decide how they will work together to color exactly 100 balloons for a poster. After students color the balloons, guide them to determine how to arrange the cards on a length of bulletin board paper so that the balloons can be easily counted. For example, they might arrange the cards in rows or in groups of fives. Have the youngsters glue the cards in place; then number the balloons as desired. Display the resulting poster to celebrate teamwork as well as the 100th day of school!

Circus Tales
Using a hundred chart

For this story problem idea, give each student a Unifix cube and a hundred chart. Next, ask a student to name a type of circus animal or performer. Tell students a corresponding story problem similar to the one shown that they can solve with their charts. Write the numbers you name on the board. Then instruct each youngster to place his cube on his chart to mark the first number you named. Ask him to solve the problem and put a finger on the answer. After volunteers tell how they determined the correct answer, have each youngster clear his chart to prepare for another problem.

An elephant eats 20 peanuts. Then it eats 10 more. How many does it eat in all?

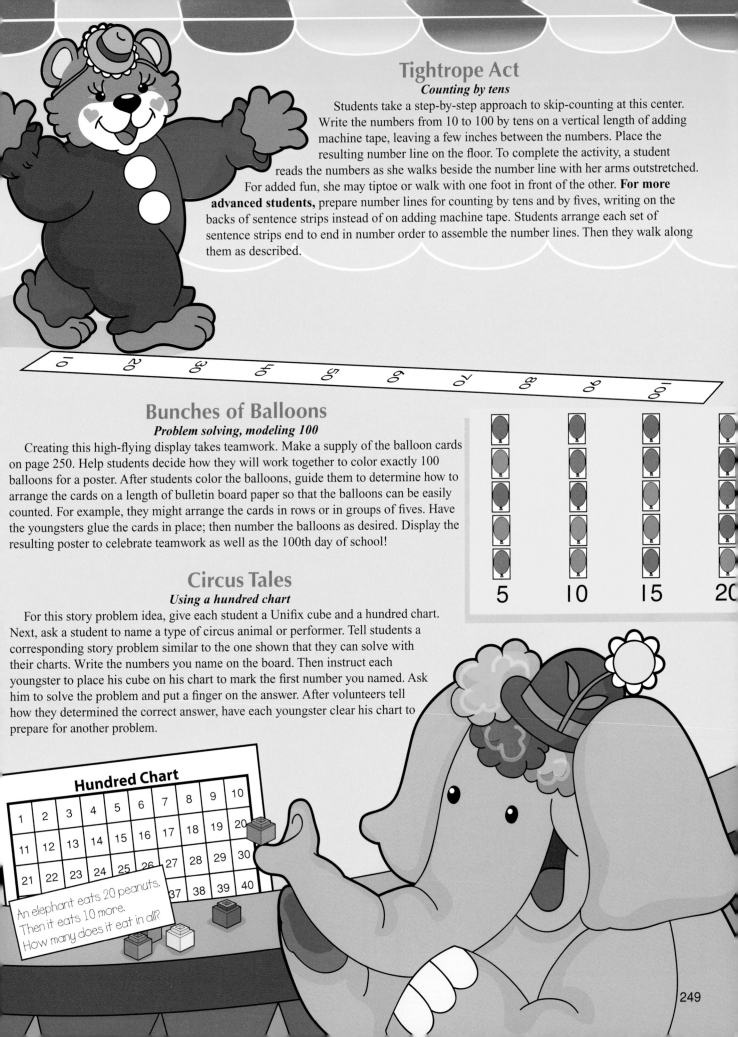

249

Clown Spinner Card
Use with "Perfect Performances" on page 248.

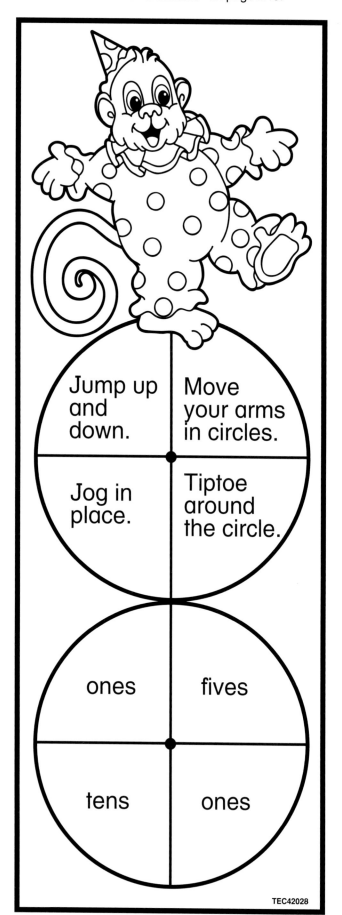

Jump up and down.

Move your arms in circles.

Jog in place.

Tiptoe around the circle.

ones

fives

tens

ones

TEC42028

Balloon Cards
Use with "Bunches of Balloons" on page 249.

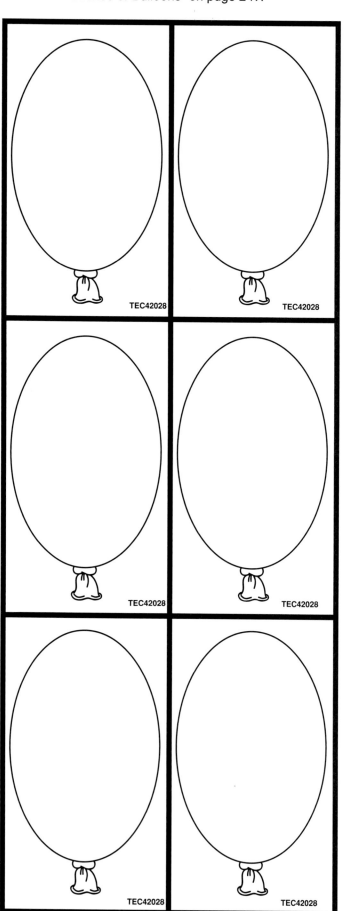

TEC42028

TEC42028

TEC42028

TEC42028

TEC42028

TEC42028

BRIGHT IDEAS FOR TELLING TIME

Your students' math skills are sure to shine when you use these timely ideas.

Minute, Hour, and Day
Estimating time

Help students develop concepts of time with this booklet project. To begin, have youngsters name various activities. Guide them to tell whether each activity takes about one minute, one hour, or one day to complete.

Next, give each student a copy of page 253. Instruct him to write his name where indicated and answer each question. After he cuts apart his labels, give him four half sheets of white paper (5½" x 8½"). Ask him to glue the titled label in the center of one piece of paper and each numbered label at the top of another piece of paper. Have him stack the numbered papers in order and place the titled paper on top. Staple the stack to make a booklet and then invite the youngster to illustrate each page.

Four o'clock!

Clock Walk
Reading analog clocks

For this upbeat game, cut out a class supply of the clock cards on page 254. Draw clock hands on each clock to show various times. (Two cards may have the same time.) Arrange the cards faceup in random order in a circle on the floor.

To begin, play some cheerful music and invite youngsters to walk around the circle. After a few moments, stop the music and have each youngster stand beside a different card. Announce a featured time. Each youngster who is beside a corresponding card picks it up and shows the clock to the group. After the group reads the clock(s), have each cardholder return her card. Resume the music to continue.

Sheila Criqui-Kelley, Lebo Elementary, Lebo, KS

On the Schedule
Relating time to events

Add this activity to your daily routine to give students real-life math practice. Glue a clockface (without clock hands) on a poster programmed as shown. Laminate the poster for reuse and then display it within student reach. Each morning, tell students when a certain event will occur that day. For example, you might announce the time for a special class or a guest reader. Help students use wipe-off markers to complete the poster with the corresponding information and draw clock hands to show the time. As youngsters anticipate the event, they're sure to keep track of the time!

Betsy Ruggiano, Victor Mravlag School #21, Elizabeth, NJ

Kid Clock
Modeling time

Every student has a role in creating this jumbo demonstration clock. Number 12 blank cards from 1 to 12. Give each card to a different student. Then ask the cardholders to sit in a large circle in numerical order to represent a clockface. Have two different students stand in the center of the circle. Instruct one of them to lie down to represent the minute hand and ask the other student to sit with his legs out in front of him to represent the hour hand.

Next, announce a chosen time. Invite a student to tell the clock hands how to show the time. After the clock hands are in place, review their positions and the corresponding time with students. Then ask youngsters to switch roles and announce a different time for students to model as described.

Jennifer Waters, Stratford, CT

Read, Draw, and Check!
Modeling time

Wipe-off markers make this center activity a student favorite. Make one or two copies of page 254. Laminate the clock cards and cut them out. Gather an equal number of blank cards and write a different digital time on each card. On the back of each time card, stamp a clockface and draw clock hands to show the corresponding time. Place all of the cards at a center stocked with wipe-off markers and tissues.

A youngster stacks the time cards faceup. She reads the time on the top card, draws hands on a clock card to show that time, and then sets the pair of cards aside. She continues with the remaining cards in the same manner. Then she turns over the time cards and checks her work. She wipes off the clock cards to prepare the center for the next visitor.

Karen L. Wise, St. Thomas Elementary, St. Thomas, PA

All About Time

by _____

©The Mailbox® • TEC42029 • Feb./Mar. 2007

What takes about **one minute** to do?

_____

1

What takes about **one hour** to do?

_____

2

What takes about **one day** to do?

_____

3

Clock Cards

Use with "Clock Walk" on page 251 and "Read, Draw, and Check!" on page 252.

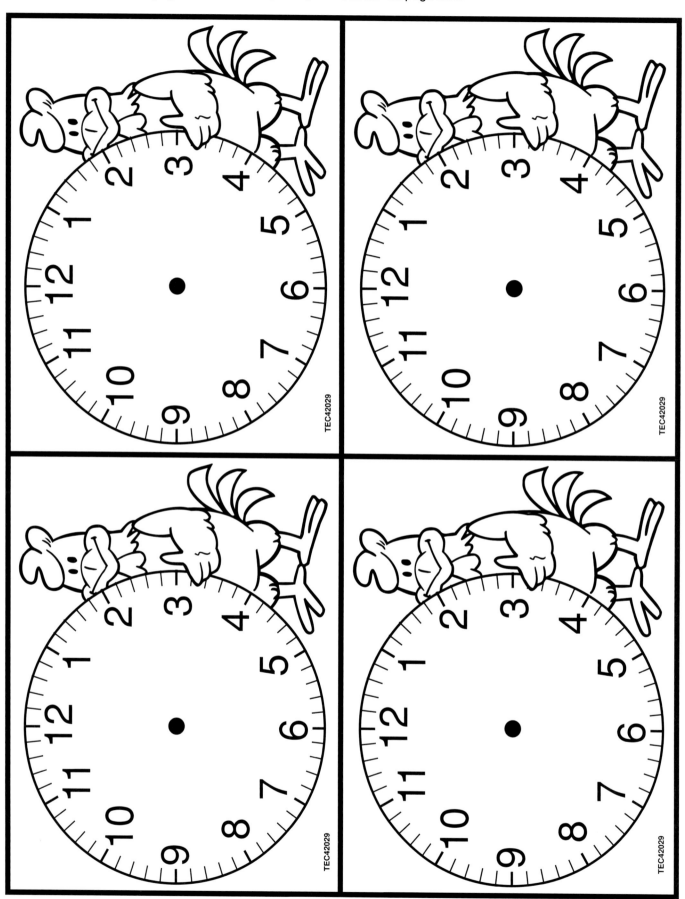

TEC42029

TEC42029

TEC42029

TEC42029

Early Bird

YAWN!

Cut.

Glue.

A.

B.

C.

D.

E.

F.

G.

H.

| 4:00 | 10:00 | 6:00 | 9:00 |
| 7:00 | 2:00 | 3:00 | 12:00 |

Dynamite Domino Math

Looking for creative ways to increase students' number sense? Try these playful ideas!

Roll and Decide!
Matching sets

Chance and strategic thinking are at play with this partner game. Place ten dominoes and one die at a center. To play, each youngster takes five dominoes at random. Then Partner 1 rolls the die. Partner 2 announces the number and looks for a matching set on one of his dominoes. For example, if the die shows three dots, he looks for a domino that has exactly three dots on one half. If he has a matching set, he places that domino aside. (If he has more than one match, he chooses one of the corresponding dominoes to set aside.) If he does not have a match, his turn is over. Then the partners trade roles. Alternate play continues as described until one partner sets aside all of his dominoes and is declared the winner.

Number Sentence Savvy
Adding or fact families

Use this idea with a small group or the entire class. To begin, give each youngster a domino that has a different number of dots on each half. Then choose an option below.

For addition, each child needs a recording sheet similar to the yellow paper below. She labels the first illustration to show how many dots are on each half of her domino and then completes the corresponding addition sentence. After she rotates the domino, she labels the next illustration and completes the addition sentence. Then she trades her domino with a different domino and completes the rest of her paper in the same manner.

For fact families, each child draws a blank domino at the top of a sheet of paper. She labels the drawing to show how many dots are on each half of her domino and writes the total number of dots beside the drawing. Then she writes the corresponding fact family.

adapted from an idea by Lisa Lumley
Bowman Elementary
Bowman, GA

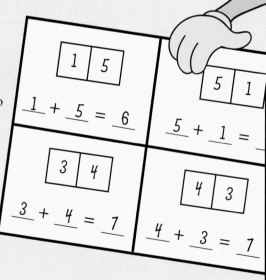

1	5

$1 + 5 = 6$

5	1

$5 + 1 = \_$

3	4

$3 + 4 = 7$

4	3

$4 + 3 = 7$

| 4 | 6 | 10
|---|---|

$4 + 6 = 10$

$6 + 4 = 10$

$10 - 6 = 4$

$10 - 4 = 6$

Terrific Trains
Adding

This activity helps students realize that different addition combinations may have the same sum. Arrange for three students to play at one time. Have the players spread out 24 dominoes facedown.

To play one round, each player takes one domino and announces the sum of the two sets of dots. If each player has a different sum, the player with the greatest sum takes the three dominoes and makes a train with them as shown. If two players have the same sum, they make a group train with their two dominoes and the third player begins building his own train with his domino. (If all three players have the same sum, they all make a group train.) The students play additional rounds as described, adding dominoes to the group train or their own trains, until all of the dominoes have been played. No doubt students will be eager to find out which trains grow the longest!

adapted from an idea by Angie Kutzer
Garrett Elementary
Mebane, NC

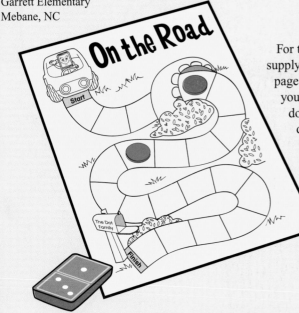

On the Road
Subtracting

For this partner trail game, each twosome needs two game markers, a supply of dominoes (doubles removed), and a copy of the gameboard on page 258. Each player sets his game marker at Start. To take a turn, a youngster takes a domino at random and holds it with the larger set of dots on the left. She announces the number of dots on each half and determines the difference with help from her partner as needed. Then she advances her game marker that many spaces. Players take turns as described until one player reaches Finish. **For an addition version,** each player adds the sets of dots on her domino and then rolls a die to determine how many spaces to advance.

Angie Kutzer

Digit Switcheroo
Comparing numbers

Here's a supersimple activity for two-digit numbers. Remove the doubles from a set of dominoes and place the remaining dominoes in a container. To begin, ask a volunteer to take a domino from the container and then hold it horizontally. Have him tell first how many dots are on the left half and then how many are on the right half. Write the two numbers on the board to create a two-digit number. Then instruct the volunteer to rotate the domino; write the corresponding two-digit number. After students read the numbers, have the volunteer circle the greater two-digit number. Then erase the board to prepare for another number comparison.

Angie Kutzer

On the Road

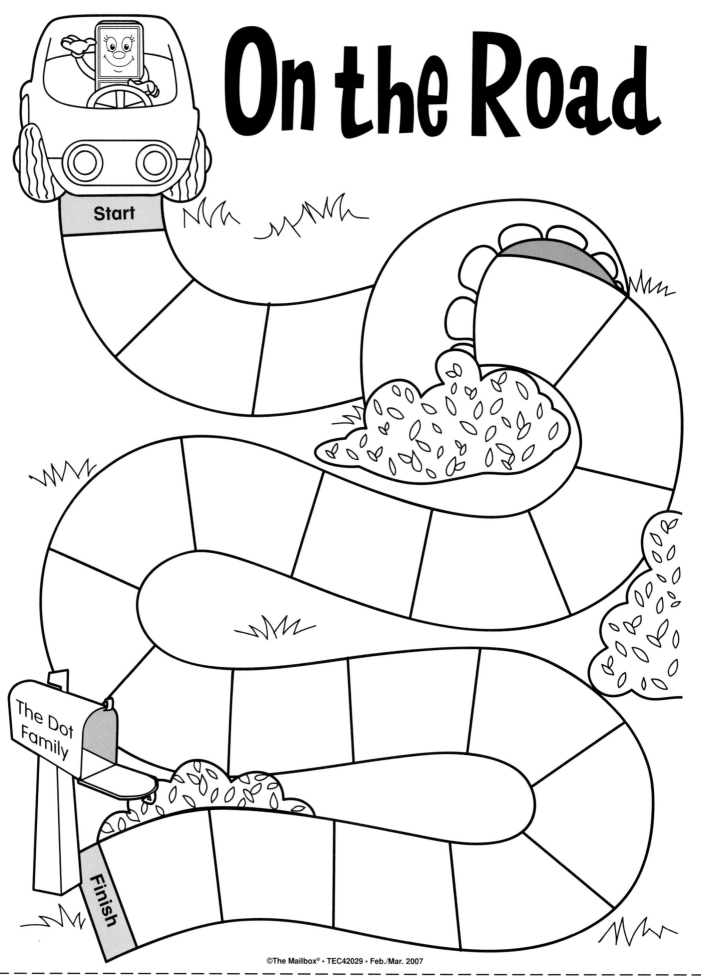

Start

The Dot Family

Finish

©The Mailbox® • TEC42029 • Feb./Mar. 2007

Note to the teacher: Use with "On the Road" on page 257.

"Scent-sational" Addition and Subtraction

No doubt your students will experience the sweet smell of success with these freshly picked math ideas!

"Bee-utiful" Problems
Beginning addition

What's the buzz? It's a hands-on approach to combining sets! Draw two flowers side by side at the top of a sheet of paper and one flower below them. Then draw an arrow from each flower at the top of the paper to the flower at the bottom of the paper. Give each student a copy of the resulting workmat. Instruct him to color each flower a designated color. Also have him cut out one or more copies of the bee cards on page 261 to use as manipulatives.

Next, tell students story problems about the bees and flowers, such as "Two bees buzz around the red flower. Three bees land on the blue flower. Then all the bees fly to the purple flower. How many bees are there in all?" As students model the story on their workmats, their understanding of addition is sure to blossom!

Michelle Saville
Beall Elementary
Frostburg, MD

Seven Tall Tulips
Beginning subtraction

Add a poetic twist to math! Display seven construction paper tulips, one of each color shown below. Then recite the first verse of the poem and remove the described tulip at the appropriate time. After students determine how many flowers are left, write the corresponding subtraction sentence on the board or a sheet of chart paper. Continue in a similar manner with the remaining verses, inviting youngsters to pick the tulips as described. For reinforcement, help students prepare a class book version of the poem or individual booklets that they can take home. It's a great way to cultivate both their math and reading skills!

Samantha Moyer
Webster Elementary
Oskaloosa, IA

[Seven] tall tulips planted in a row.
[Mother] picked the [yellow] one, leaving [six] to grow.

Use the words below to continue with verses 2–6. Then conclude the poem with verse 7.
Verse 2: Six, Father, blue, five
Verse 3: Five, Grandma, purple, four
Verse 4: Four, Grandpa, green, three
Verse 5: Three, Brother, red, two
Verse 6: Two, Sister, pink, one
Verse 7: One tall tulip planted in a row.
I picked the orange one, leaving none to grow.

Picking Posies
Creating and solving problems

To prepare this center activity, cut out one copy of the flower and operation cards on page 261 per student. Make a recording sheet like the one shown and copy it to make a class supply. Place the flower cards and operation cards in separate containers at a center.

When a student visits the center, she takes two flower cards and one operation card. Then she arranges the cards on her recording sheet to create a math problem. After she is satisfied with her work, she glues the cards in place and writes the answer. She completes the rest of the paper in the same manner. **For an easier version,** use just the addition cards and the flower cards for the lower numbers.

Angie Kutzer
Garrett Elementary
Mebane, NC

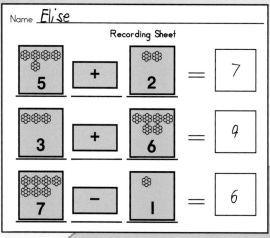

Name *Elise*

Recording Sheet

$5 + 2 = 7$

$3 + 6 = 9$

$7 - 1 = 6$

Flower Power
Addition or subtraction

Cultivate students' basic fact skills with this small-group game. Prepare a supply of construction paper blossoms about three inches in diameter. Glue a skunk card (see page 261) on each of three blossoms. Write a different addition or subtraction problem on each remaining blossom. Scramble the flowers and place them in a flowerpot.

To take a turn, a child takes a flower at random. If the flower has a problem, he reads it aloud and solves it. If he is correct as verified by the group members, he sets the flower aside. If he is not correct, he returns the flower to the flowerpot. If the flower has a skunk card, he returns to the flowerpot any flowers he set aside and places the skunk flower in a discard pile. The players take turns as described until all the flowers are picked.

Angie Kutzer

Pretty Petals
Fact families

This math activity doubles as a display idea. Give each student a colorful circle that you have labeled with the three numbers in a chosen fact family. Next, ask her to glue four construction paper petals to the circle to make a flower. Instruct her to write each number sentence in the corresponding fact family on a different petal. Then have her glue a stem and two leaves to the flower and write her name on a leaf. Showcase students' completed fact family flowers on a bulletin board to create a garden of math magnificence!

Kristine Ardizone
Johnston Street Elementary
New Iberia, LA

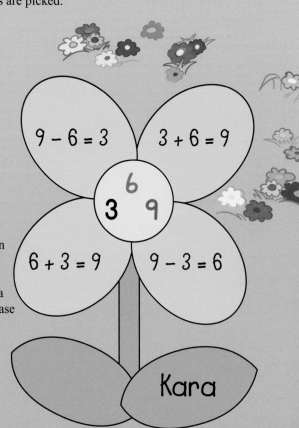

$9 - 6 = 3$　$3 + 6 = 9$

3　6　9

$6 + 3 = 9$　$9 - 3 = 6$

Kara

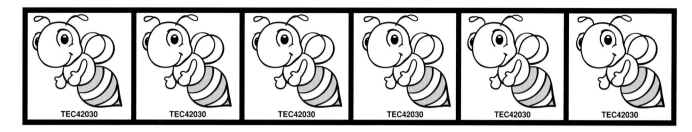

Flower and Operation Cards
Use with "Picking Posies" on page 260.

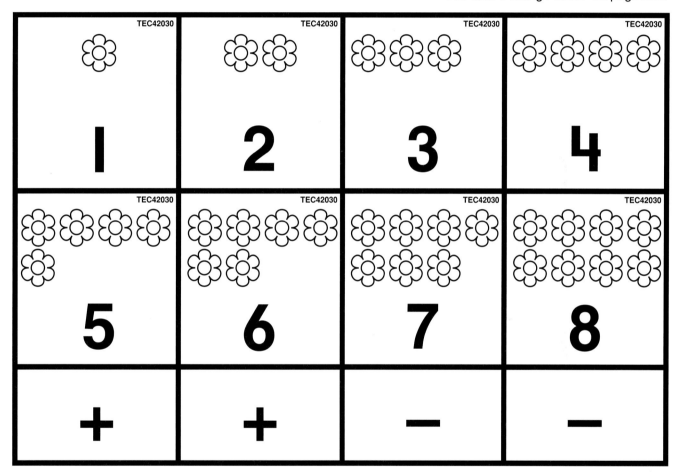

Skunk Cards
Use with "Flower Power" on page 260.

Terrific Tulips

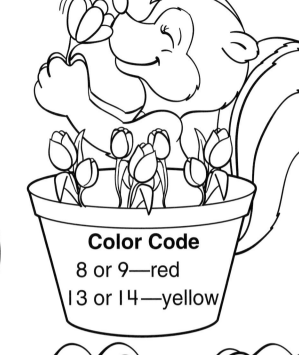

Add or subtract.

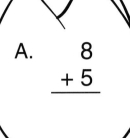 Color by the code.

Color Code
8 or 9—red
13 or 14—yellow

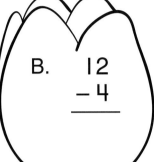

A.   8
    + 5

B.   12
   − 4

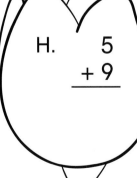

C.   6
    + 8

D.   14
   − 5

E.   9
    + 4

F.   13
   − 5

G.   14
   − 6

H.   5
    + 9

I.   7
    + 7

J.   12
   − 3

For Good Measure

Keep your students' math skills growing with these linear measurement ideas!

Useful Inchworms
Nonstandard units

What better way to introduce a measurement activity than by reading aloud *Inch by Inch* by Leo Lionni? After you share the book with students, give each youngster copies of the inchworm ruler patterns on pages 264 and 265. Have her cut out the patterns and glue them together where indicated. Guide students to name various classroom objects that they can measure with their inchworm rulers. Then pair students. Give each youngster crayons and a recording sheet similar to the one shown.

Each twosome chooses one object to measure. Each partner illustrates it on the first half of her paper and labels it. Then she estimates the length of the object and writes her estimate with a crayon. After the partners measure the object to the nearest whole inchworm and agree on its length, each student writes the measurement on her paper. Then the partners choose a different object to illustrate and measure in the same manner.

Kristin McLaughlin
Boyertown, PA

Name _Jada_

Recording Sheet

glue

Estimate. _10_ inchworms
Measure. _6_ inchworms

journal

Estimate. _12_ inchworms
Measure. _11_ inchworms

Fresh From the Garden
Customary units, comparing lengths

Harvest both math and reading practice with this booklet project! Give each youngster copies of the booklet pages on pages 264 and 265. Confirm that each student can identify the featured vegetables. Instruct each youngster to measure the vegetables and write the measurements in the provided spaces. Then have him color the pages and cut them out.

Next, ask each student to sequence his pages from the smallest vegetable to the largest. Place the sequenced pages between two 4" x 8" construction paper covers and staple the stack at the top. Then invite the youngster to complete his resulting booklet with a title and cover illustration. After he practices reading his measurable story, no doubt he'll be eager to take it home and share it with his family!

See the orange carrot, so big I can share it!

_5_ inches

adapted from an idea by Anna Marie Conaway
Davis Elementary
Malone, NY

Inchworm Ruler Pattern
Use with "Useful Inchworms" on page 263.

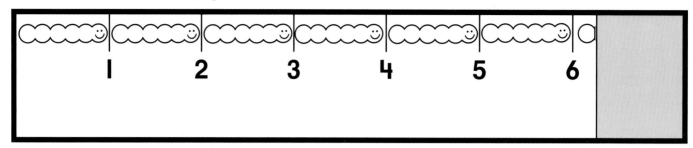

Booklet Pages
Use with "Fresh From the Garden" on page 263.

See the purple beet,
Round and sweet.

_____ inches

See the green peas,
Small as you please.

_____ inches

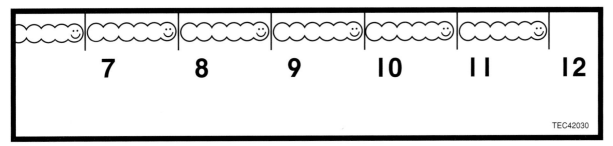

TEC42030

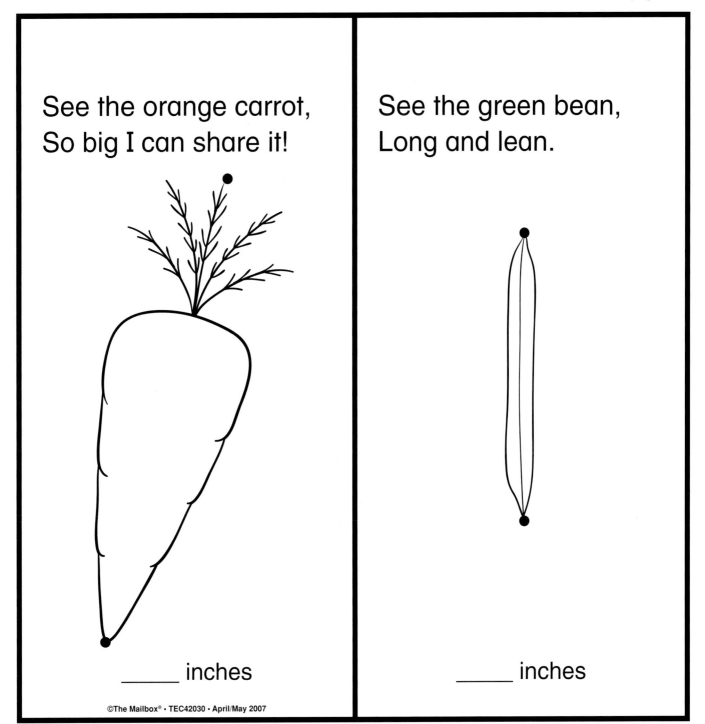

See the orange carrot,
So big I can share it!

_____ inches

See the green bean,
Long and lean.

_____ inches

All Abuzz About Math

Get your hive humming with these "bee-dazzling" ideas for skills such as addition, subtraction, and fractions.

Super Stripes
Subtracting 1 or story problems

It's easy to make this math prop! Draw a bee without stripes at the top of a sheet of paper. Give each child a yellow copy of the paper and several narrow black construction paper strips (stripes). Then choose an option below.

Subtracting 1: Instruct each student to arrange the stripes on his bee. Then have him remove the stripes one at a time and write each corresponding subtraction sentence. He's sure to recognize the resulting math pattern!

Story problems: Have each student model an addition or a subtraction story problem, such as "The bee has five stripes. Then it gets two more. How many stripes does it have in all?" After the youngster determines the answer, ask him to write the corresponding number sentence below the bee.

adapted from an idea by Donna Battista
Parkview Elementary, Valparaiso, IN

$$6 - 1 = 5$$
$$5 - 1 = 4$$
$$4 - 1 = 3$$

Beehive Buzz
Addition

Shaking up a beehive is usually unwise, but with this idea it results in hands-on math practice. To prepare, stick together a yellow and a black sheet of self-adhesive craft foam back-to-back. (Or glue together a yellow and a black sheet of paper.) Cut the foam into small squares to make bee counters. Choose a number of counters based on your students' addition skills and then place the counters in a large disposable cup (hive). Have students complete the activity individually at a center stocked with paper. Or arrange for several students to work together.

To begin, a child shakes the hive and then pours out the bees. She counts how many sides of each color are showing. After she writes a corresponding addition sentence, she returns the bees to the hive. She models and writes several more number sentences in the same manner. **For more advanced students,** also have youngsters write the related subtraction sentences.

Angie Kutzer, Garrett Elementary, Mebane, NC

$$6 + 6 = 12$$
$$8 + 4 = 12$$
$$5 + 7 = 12$$

Fly to the Hive!
Skill review
During this versatile small-group game, players make a beeline for the hive! To prepare for three students, color a copy of the gameboard on page 268. Gather three yellow pom-poms (bees) and a supply of blank cards. Write "Super Buzz!" on several of the cards. Program the remaining cards to reinforce a chosen skill, such as telling time, addition, or counting sets of coins.

To begin, one player stacks the cards facedown. Each player places a bee at the start of a different path. To take a turn, a player takes the top card. If he draws a "Super Buzz!" card, he advances two flowers. If he draws a card with a math skill, he responds as appropriate. If he is correct as verified by the other players, he advances one flower. If he is incorrect, his turn is over. The players take turns as described until each bee reaches the hive!

Angie Kutzer, Garrett Elementary, Mebane, NC

Card Combinations
Addition
Here's an "un-bee-lievably" fun way to create number sentences. Instruct each student to color a copy of page 269 and then cut out the number cards. Help her staple three randomly chosen cards to the first box and the three remaining cards to the second box as shown. Then have her flip the cards to create four different pairs of numbers and write an addition sentence with each number pair.

Angie Kutzer

Ten minus two equals eight.

Mmmm...Honey!
Strategic thinking, subtraction
Youngsters will be eager to play several rounds of this brain-teasing partner game! Give each pair of students 18 pieces of Honeycomb cereal. Have the partners arrange their cereal to make a hive. Explain that the goal of the game is to be the player who does not remove the last piece of cereal.

In turn, each partner removes either one or two pieces of cereal from the hive and says the corresponding subtraction sentence. The players continue taking turns in this manner until they take all of the cereal. The player who does *not* remove the last piece of cereal wins. **For an easier version,** use fewer pieces of cereal and do not have students identify the subtraction sentences.

Angie Kutzer

Fly to the Hive!

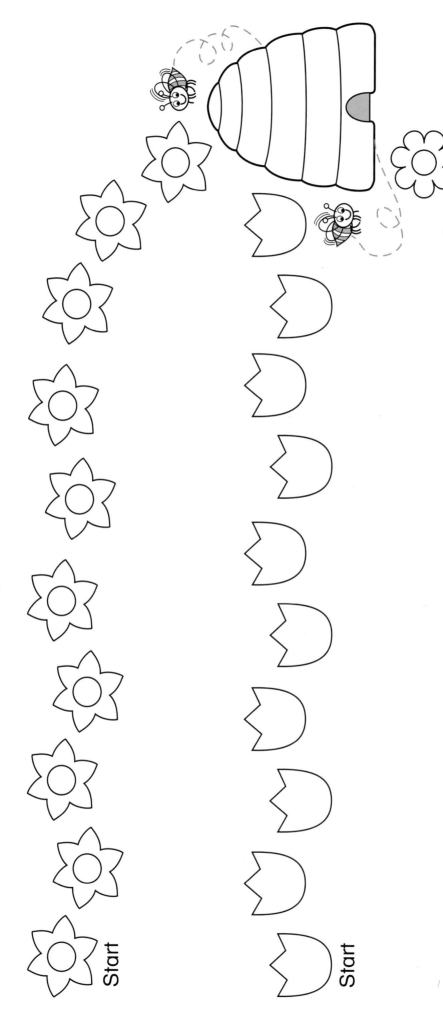

Start

Start

Start

Note to the teacher: Use with "Fly to the Hive!" on page 267.

Buzz! Buzz!

Listen for directions.

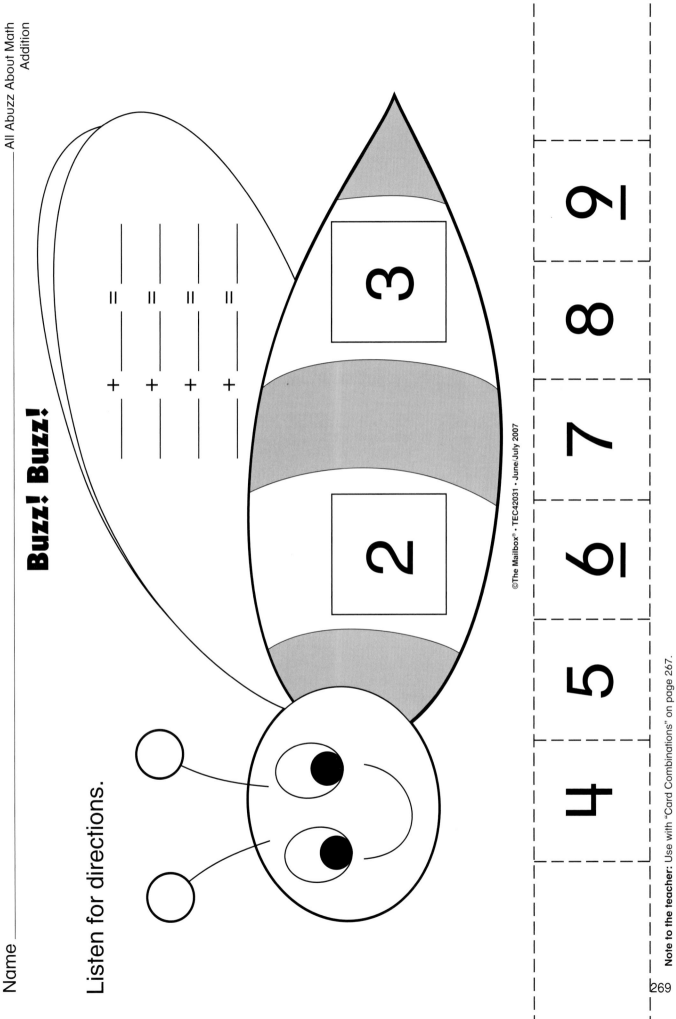

+ ___ | ___ = ___

+ ___ | ___ = ___

+ ___ | ___ = ___

+ ___ | ___ = ___

3

2

4   5   6   7   8   9

©The Mailbox® • TEC42031 • June/July 2007

Note to the teacher: Use with "Card Combinations" on page 267.

Name —————————————————————

All Abuzz About Math
Fractions

Hive, Sweet Hive!

✂ Cut.

🧴 Glue.

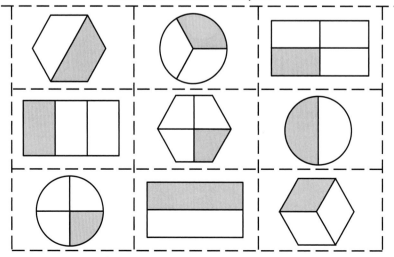

270

SCIENCE AND
SOCIAL STUDIES UNITS

Martin Luther King Jr.

Commemorate Dr. King's legendary dream with these simple activities.

Introducing Dr. King

Launch a discussion about the heroic leader by reading aloud *Happy Birthday, Martin Luther King* by Jean Marzollo. It's a perfect way to familiarize students with concepts such as peace and justice.

Hand in Hand

When Dr. King was a young boy, he and his white friends could not go to the same school. After you share this information with students, tell them that Dr. King dreamed that all children could study together. Explain that he helped change laws so that this could happen.

Next, have each student illustrate a copy of the friendship card on page 273 to resemble herself and a friend. After each student cuts out her card, have her fold it in half with the illustration to the outside. Ask her to imagine how she would feel if she were apart from her friend just as young Martin was. Then invite her to represent Dr. King's vision of unity by unfolding the card. To check students' understanding, have each youngster glue her open card at the top of a large sheet of paper and write about Dr. King's dream.

Poetic Promise

To begin this display idea, invite youngsters to tell what they will do to keep Dr. King's dream alive. Then have each young-ster draw a self-portrait and glue it to a slightly larger piece of construction paper. Showcase students' artwork around the poem shown to promote the goal of peace, love, and harmony.

Jessica Hines
Clarksville Elementary
Clarksville, TX

Dr. King once had a dream
That we'd all get along.
Today we pledge to live in peace
And keep his dream strong.

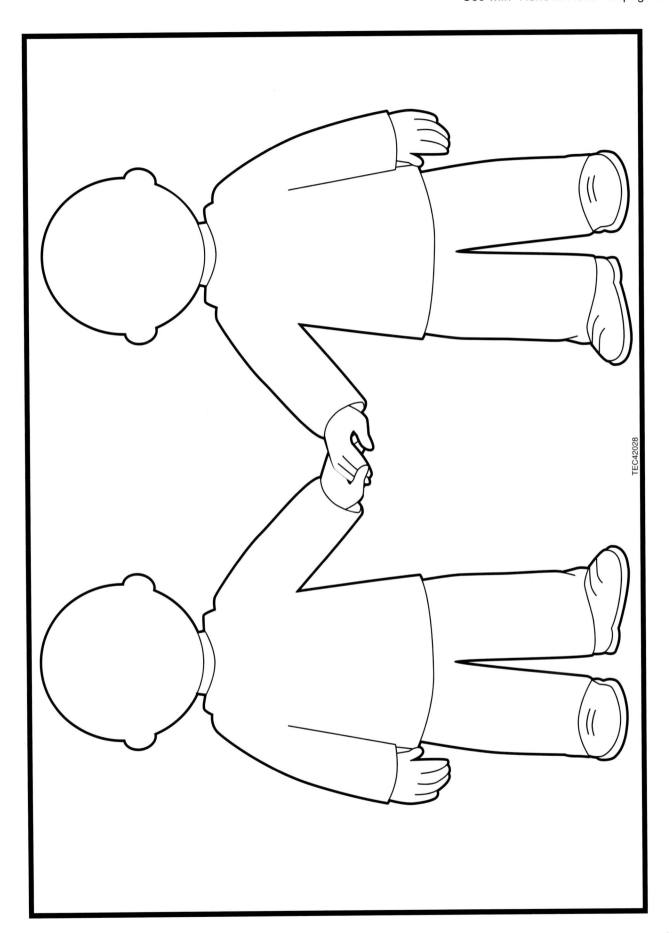

Hip Hip Hooray for EARTH DAY!

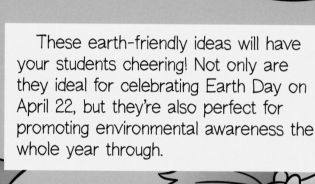

These earth-friendly ideas will have your students cheering! Not only are they ideal for celebrating Earth Day on April 22, but they're also perfect for promoting environmental awareness the whole year through.

Totally "Tee-rific"
Arts and crafts

Get students in the spirit of Earth Day with this T-shirt decorating idea. To begin, help each child use brown fabric paint to illustrate a leafless tree on the front of a plain white T-shirt. Have him use green fabric paint to make handprints on his shirt that resemble leaves. Then have him use craft sponges, brushes, and various colors of paint to embellish his artwork. Allow the paint to dry.

On the back of each child's T-shirt, use a fabric marker to write a desired Earth Day slogan, the child's name, and the date. Encourage students to wear their completed shirts on a schoolwide cleanup day or whenever they do their part to clean up the earth!

Krista Shifflett, McGaheysville Elementary, McVille, VA

(sung to the tune of "This Land Is Your Land")

This land is our land.
Let's lend a helping hand.
Reduce the garbage.
Put litter in the trash can.
Reuse your bottles; recycle plastics.
Let's keep our whole earth litter free!

Litter-Free Land
Song

Use this catchy tune to show students that the three Rs—reduce, reuse, and recycle—work in harmony. After youngsters are familiar with the song, have them suggest motions to incorporate during later repetitions. For a literacy-boosting extension, make a student-illustrated class book, with each line of the song on a separate page.

Bridget Morgan
Sevierville, TN

Team Spirit

Community service project

Have your students team up with buddies in an older grade for this partner project. In advance, ask the manager of a local grocery store to give you paper grocery bags that students may decorate for store customers. Work with an upper-grade teacher to pair each of her students with one of your students. Have the partners decorate the bags with Earth Day slogans and illustrations. Then return the decorated bags to the store. It's a great way to promote environmental awareness!

Cindy Casillas, Lindbergh Elementary, Little Falls, MN

Thank You, Earth!

Classroom display

With this idea, it's clear why students are fans of Mother Earth! Read aloud a book about Earth Day, such as *3 Pandas Planting* by Megan Halsey. Next, give each student a copy of the writing form on page 276. Have her color the earth and illustrate a favorite outdoor activity. Then instruct her to write her name on the first blank and complete the caption. Showcase students' completed work around a large earth on a bulletin board, and title the display "What on Earth Do You Enjoy?"

Suzanne Moore, Irving, TX

All Around the Earth

Learning centers

Pay tribute to our planet and its resources with this winning lineup of centers. In the middle of the classroom or center area, display a globe or an enlarged copy of the earth pattern on page 276. Set up the centers described below around the model earth. After all youngsters have completed the activities, bring students together to discuss their work. Then give each child a colorful copy of the award ribbon on page 276.

Edible Earths: Each student needs a rice cake and whipped cream cheese that you have divided and tinted blue and green. She spreads the cream cheese on a rice cake to make a model of Earth.

Hooray for Trees! A student cuts from child-friendly magazines pictures of things made from wood. Then she glues them on a construction paper tree.

Treasured Class Book: Each child needs a circular page programmed with the sentence starter "The earth gives us…" She finishes the sentence and illustrates it. Later, bind the completed pages behind an enlarged copy of the earth pattern on page 276 and title the resulting book "Earth's Treasures."

Kelley Russell, Rogersville City School, Rogersville, TN

Writing Form

Use with "Thank You, Earth!" on page 275.

_____ likes to _____

_____

Award Ribbon and Earth Patterns

Use with "All Around the Earth" on page 275.

TEC42030

_____

is a friend of the earth!

TEC42030

Teacher Resource Units

WELCOME TO OPEN HOUSE!

Looking for ways to make your back-to-school event memorable? Try these creative ideas. A good time will be had by all!

Come In!

No doubt your guests will feel right at home when they spot this **hallway display.** To make a house, cut a triangle (roof) from bulletin board paper to fit above your classroom door. Then cut a rectangle to fit along each side of the door. Mount the pieces around your door to assemble the house. Use desired arts-and-crafts supplies to add details, such as windows, flowers, and a mailbox. Then set a welcome mat in front of the door.

Randi Austin, Gasconade Elementary, Falcon, MO

The Star Attractions in Our Classroom
1. Class Pet
2. Computer
3. Library
4. Blocks
5. Listening Center

Walk of the Stars

Students show their parents the star attractions with this **classroom tour** idea. A few days before open house, poll students to determine the five most popular classroom items or areas. Prepare a numbered list of the top vote getters and copy it to make a class supply. If desired, make the list on a copy of page 280. Label each featured attraction in the classroom with a numbered star. Before the event, set copies of the list near the classroom door. Have each student refer to a list as she gives her parent(s) a tour.

Kristin Webber, Eagle Heights Academy, Youngstown, OH

MUSIC
1:00 Tuesdays

Super Slide Show

Not only will this **presentation** impress parents, but it will also make open house easier for you. To prepare, use presentation software to create several slides on topics relevant to your classroom. For example, you might include photographs of different classroom areas and daily activities. You might also include slides with helpful information.

Play the show at a scheduled time on a television screen or computer monitor. Or play it in a continuous loop for open house guests to view at their convenience. You'll be free to greet parents and answer any questions they might have!

Staci Royer, North Harlem Elementary, Harlem, GA

A Great Visit

What's the key to a successful open house? Making your guests feel at ease as you share **information.** In advance, prepare for each family a packet of information such as your classroom schedule and policies. Conclude the packet with a thank-you note for attending the open house. Also, have each student make a greeting card to welcome his family.

On the night of the event, place each youngster's card at his workspace. Set out refreshments and post sign-up sheets for classroom volunteers, guest readers, or similar classroom needs. As guests arrive, play soft music. Invite each family to look around the room and find their child's workspace. While the guests enjoy the cards and refreshments, give each family an information packet. It's sure to be a handy resource throughout the year!

Nancy Aquino, Steele School, Baldwin, NY

"Hand-some" Wall

Create a feeling of community with this **schoolwide display.** Post the title shown near your school's main entrance. Nearby place on a table a supply of markers, scissors, and various colors of construction paper. Before open house, encourage each staff member to trace his hand. Then have him cut out the tracing, label it with his name, and post it below the display title. Post a sign encouraging open house guests to add their hand tracings to the display. For large schools, arrange for one display per grade level near the corresponding classrooms.

Kathy Balzer, Remington Elementary, Potwin, KS

Everyone Has a HAND in Education!

Hannah's School Work

Magnetic Memory Holders

These student-made **gifts** make it easy for parents to display their children's work. A few days before the event, gather a class supply of wooden rulers and two wooden spring-type clothespins per child. For each child, program a paper strip similar to the one shown. To begin, a child paints two clothespins and allows the paint to dry. Next, she adheres strips of magnetic tape to the back of a ruler. She glues her programmed strip to the front of it. Then she uses craft glue to attach the clothespins to the ruler as shown.

Before open house, have each student leave her completed project at her workspace for her parent(s) to find. Encourage each recipient to post the ruler on his refrigerator at home and use it to showcase samples of his child's work.

Nikki Buwalda, Randolph Elementary, Randolph, WI

Star Attractions in Our Classroom!

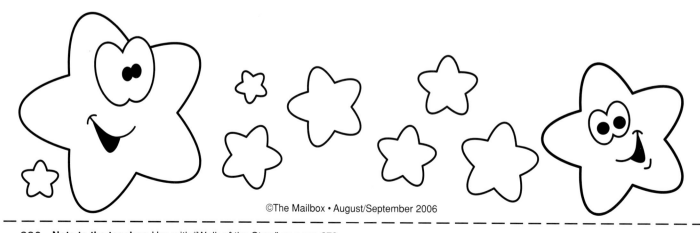

Note to the teacher: Use with "Walk of the Stars" on page 278.

What a Memorable Year!

Use these creative ideas from our readers
to end the school year in a big way.

Letter by Letter
Display

Piece together school memories with this quilt project. List the letters of the alphabet on chart paper, leaving writing space after each letter. Then post the list. Next, guide students to recall various activities and details from the school year. Write the information beside the corresponding initial letters with student input. For example, after students recall a field trip to an apple orchard, they might suggest that you write "apple orchard" beside the letter *a*.

After the list is complete, write each letter near the top of a separate paper square. Assign each square to a student. Then have the youngster illustrate and write the corresponding listed word or phrase. Ask her to glue the illustrated square to a larger colorful square and then draw black stitch marks along the border. To make corner squares for the quilt, attach photos of classroom activities to four colorful squares. Arrange all the squares on a hallway wall to create a quilt from *A* to *Z!*

Beth Marquardt, St. Paul's School of Early Learning, Muskego, WI

a
apple orchard

r
reading

The Top Ten
Group Project

What are some of the best things about this past school year? That's what students explore with this fun look back! Help students brainstorm a list of the ten things that they like most about their current grade. Then, with student input, rank the listings from 1 to 10, with 1 being the favorite listing. Next, divide students into ten groups and assign each group a different number from 1 to 10. Have the students in each group create a poster featuring their number and the corresponding listing. After students complete the posters, ask the groups to stand with their posters in descending order. Have each group, in turn, present its work to the class. Then take a photo of each group with its poster. The photos are perfect for an end-of-the-year display. You can also incorporate them into a display or presentation for next year's open house!

Jackie Baker, Hagerstown Elementary, Hagerstown, IN

We took turns feeding our pet fish.

Poetic Keepsake
Writing

Try this creative twist on yearbooks. Help each youngster use the format below to write a poem about himself. Or help the class write one poem about each student over several days. Invite each youngster to illustrate the poem about himself with a self-portrait or photo. Then, for each youngster, bind a copy of each classmate's paper, along with his own, between two covers. The resulting yearbooks are sure to be treasured mementos!

Title: Child's name
Line 1: Two words or phrases that describe the child
Line 2: Phrase telling what the child likes about school
Line 3: Phrase telling what the child is good at
Line 4: Child's name

Jackie Baker, Hagerstown Elementary, Hagerstown, IN

Michael

Nice, funny
Likes centers and recess
Good at drawing cars
Michael

A Cool Year
Individual Project

This mouthwatering idea is great for the last week of school. Give each child a construction paper ice-cream scoop and cone or a colorful frozen ice-pop cutout and a craft stick. Have the youngster write on her frozen treat what she enjoyed about school this past year. Instruct her to write her name on the project and then use glue or tape to assemble her treat. If desired, serve real frozen treats for students to enjoy while youngsters show their work to the class. **For an easier version,** have students illustrate and label their favorite school memories on the treats.

Stacy Roman, Sacramento Elementary, Alamogordo, NM

Moving On
Song

After you and your students share fond memories of the past school year, use this catchy tune to encourage youngsters to look ahead. If desired, modify the lyrics by substituting a different month or replacing the school year phrase with *we'll be going to [first] grade.*

adapted from an idea by Sandra Kuball
Holy Cross School
New York, NY

(sung to the tune of "She'll Be Comin' Round the Mountain")

In [August], [we will start a new school year]. Hooray!
In [August], [we will start a new school year]. Hooray!
We had lots of fun this year.
All the memories we'll hold dear.
In [August], [we will start a new school year]. Hooray!

THEMATIC UNITS

Sailing Into a New Year

Launch the school year with these seafaring ideas!

ideas contributed by Pam Ballingall
Manchester, NH

Meet the Crew!
Class display

Welcome your students aboard with this get-acquainted activity. Make a class supply of page 286. On each boat, write a different student's name on the left sail. Give each student her boat. Read the sentence starter and invite students to name some of their favorite things. Then ask each youngster to draw on her blank sail something she likes. As students work, help each youngster complete her sentence or dictate a sentence ending for you to write. After students complete their illustrations, invite them to color their boats as desired. Post students' completed papers on a board titled "Meet the Crew!" Cover the bottom edge of each paper with a construction paper wave and then staple the ends of each wave in place.

All Hands on Deck
Job chart

When it comes to creating a classroom community, this idea charts a smooth course. To prepare, cut blue 4" x 6" index cards lengthwise into wavelike strips so that there is one strip per classroom job. Label each strip with the name of a job. To make a display title, make wavelike cuts along the top edge of a blue sentence strip. Write the title shown on the side of the strip that has only a baseline. Display the title in the top row of a pocket chart and the job names below it. Make a class supply of the ship card on page 287.

To begin, explain to students that you need their help to take care of the classroom and to do routine tasks. Then direct their attention to the job display and review the expectations for each job. Next, give each youngster a ship card. Have him write his name on the bottom part of the ship. Then ask him to glue his ship onto a piece of construction paper for durability. To assign the jobs, tuck a ship behind each job label. Explain that any students who are not assigned a job have the special responsibility of keeping the classroom shipshape!

A Fine Fleet
Math or literacy

Use this easy-to-adapt activity to launch practice with shapes, letters, or words. Copy the sailboat cards on page 287 so that there is one for every two students. Use one of the options below to program the cards. Then cut each card into two pieces, cutting along the mast. Give each youngster one part of a card. Then call out, "Set sail!"

At this signal, each student looks for the student who has the other part of her card. When she finds her, the two youngsters sit together and position their cards to form a boat. After each student is seated, have each twosome tell the group what is on its boat.

Shapes: Draw an identical shape on each sail. Vary the colors of the shapes among the different pairs of cards.

Letters: Write an uppercase letter on one sail and the corresponding lowercase letter on the other sail.

Words: Draw colorful stripes on one sail and write the corresponding color word on the other sail.

All Aboard!
Literacy

Find out what your students know about letters with this small-group activity. Draw a large boat on a magnetic whiteboard. Display several magnetic letters beside it. Then ask, "Who can put the letter [M] aboard?" Invite a volunteer to find the named letter and put it on the boat. Continue the activity in the same manner until all of the letters are aboard. **For more advanced students,** ask questions such as "Who can put the letter for *mouse* aboard?"

Book Launch
Literature

What's the best way to interest students in your classroom library? Share a story that's guaranteed to hook them! Show students the front cover of *Who Sank the Boat?* by Pamela Allen. Read aloud the title and invite students to predict the answer. Then read the story, pausing at each question for students to respond. At the book's conclusion, ask students who sinks the boat. To guide their thinking, wonder aloud what would happen if the mouse got on the boat first. Lead students to realize that all of the animals play a role in the boat capsizing. Then set the book in your classroom library along with a toy boat and small plastic animals that represent the characters. Encourage students to revisit the book and act out the story.

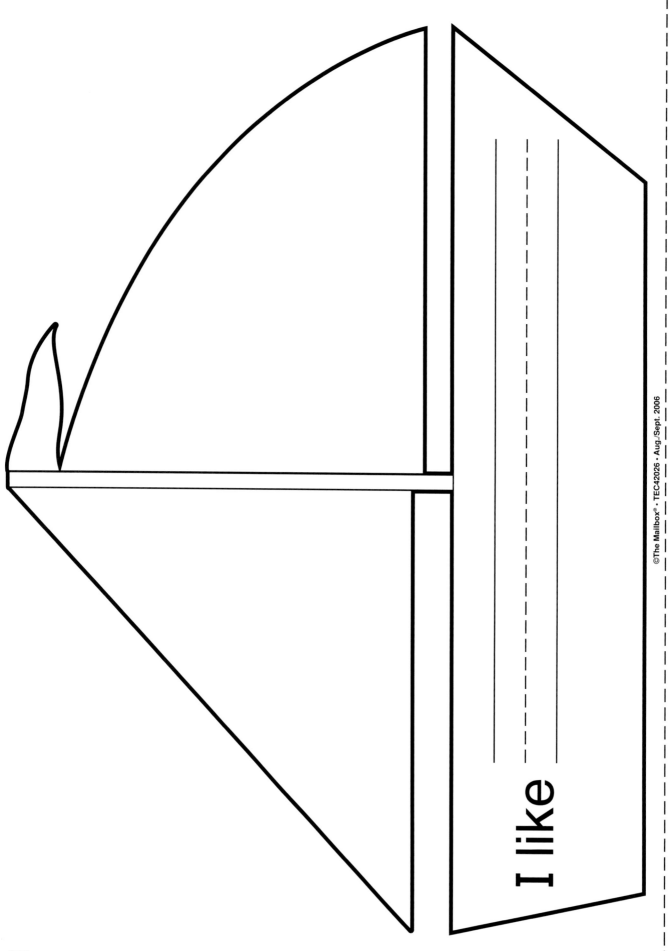

I like

Note to the teacher: Use with "Meet the Crew!" on page 284.

Ship Card

Use with "All Hands on Deck" on page 284.

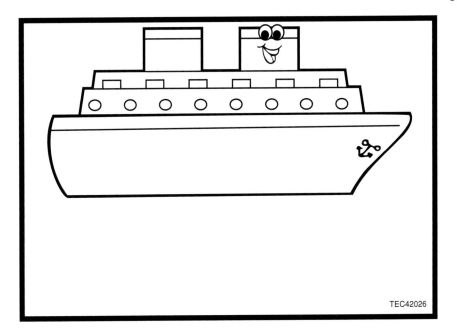

TEC42026

Sailboat Cards

Use with "A Fine Fleet" on page 285.

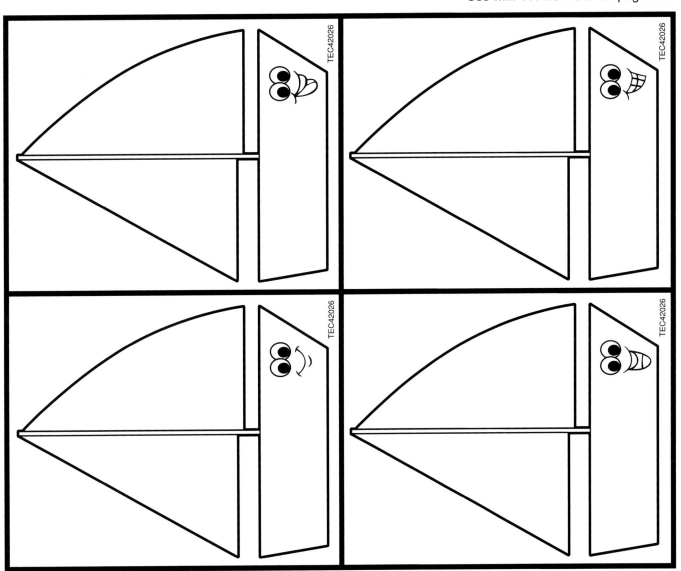

Barnyard Bonanza

What's on the farm? A bumper crop of learning fun!

Sensational Sing-Along

Modeling numbers, ordinal numbers

Tune up students' math skills with this toe-tapping introduction to the farm. Lead students in the song shown. Then assign each student or student pair a different set of items that the farmhand gives in the song. Have the students use provided arts-and-crafts materials to illustrate their sets on large sheets of paper. If desired, help them label their resulting posters with the appropriate lines of the song.

Next, instruct students to sit with their posters. As you lead the class in the song, have students stand and hold up their posters at the appropriate times. At the end of the song, help the students display the posters in order from the fewest to the most items. Then ask students several questions with ordinal numbers, such as "What did the farmhand give on the second day of farming?"

April Arnold, Alum Creek Elementary, Lewis Center, OH

Eight cows a-mooing.

The 12 Days of Farming

(sung to the tune of "The 12 Days of Christmas")

On the first day of farming, my farmhand gave to me
A rooster on the barn roof.

On the second day of farming, my farmhand gave to me
Two pecking hens,
And a rooster on the barn roof.

Use the phrases listed below to continue with verses 3–12, repeating each previous line in descending order.

Third day: three bales of hay
Fourth day: four baaing sheep
Fifth day: five golden eggs
Sixth day: six crops a-growing
Seventh day: seven scarecrows waving
Eighth day: eight cows a-mooing
Ninth day: nine ducks a-quacking
Tenth day: ten tractors plowing
Eleventh day: 11 pigs oinking
Twelfth day: 12 horses neighing

8 cows a-mooing

Friendly Farmers
Art, writing

To prepare this display idea, ask each youngster to use a construction paper circle and arts-and-crafts materials to make a self-portrait. Or take an individual close-up photo of each student, enlarge each photo, and then trim it. Make tagboard shirt and overalls patterns for students to share. (Use the patterns on page 291 if desired.)

To make a farmer, have each youngster trace a shirt and an overalls pattern on construction paper and then cut out the tracings. Ask her to cut a hat, two boots, and two hands from construction paper. Then instruct her to assemble her project as shown and glue it together. Invite her to add details, such as a pipe cleaner pitchfork and a pom-pom chick. After she finishes her project, have her complete the sentence starter shown. Display each student's artwork with her sentence on a hallway wall.

Nikki Buwalda, Randolph Elementary, Randolph, WI

Abby

If I were a farmer,

I wd hv pigs.

Life on the Farm
Living and nonliving

To begin this classification activity, read aloud a nonfiction farm book, such as *Farming* by Gail Gibbons. Then write a student-generated list of farm sights on the board. Add to the list as needed so that both living and nonliving things are included. After you remind students of the characteristics of living things, assign each student a listed sight. Have him draw it on provided paper and then help him label his illustration and trim around it. After each youngster completes his work, post a large sheet of paper that you have divided into two columns titled as shown. Then have each student post his artwork in the correct column.

Living / Nonliving

pig / tractor
sheep / barn
tree / scarecrow

Locations
rooster: on the roof
cat: in the barn
pig: left of the hay
dog: right of the hay
sheep: next to the fence
duck: in front of the fence

Everything in Its Place
Positional words

Following directions is the key to completing this barnyard scene! If desired, introduce the activity by reading aloud *Rosie's Walk* by Pat Hutchins. To begin, have each student color a copy of page 292 and a copy of the animal cards on page 293. Ask her to cut out the animals. Then use the locations listed on this page to direct students where to place their animals. When all of the animals are correctly positioned, ask students to glue them in place. **For more advanced students,** have each youngster use positional words in sentences about the scene.

Critter Clues
Comprehension

This interactive class book is as much fun to create as it is to read! Have each student illustrate and label a secretly chosen farm animal on an unlined 4" x 6" card. Help him describe his animal on a copy of the envelope label on page 293. After he glues his label on the front of a legal-size envelope, ask him to write his name on the envelope and card and place the card in the envelope. Hole-punch students' envelopes as shown. (Be careful not to punch their cards.) Then use metal rings to secure the envelopes between two barn-shaped covers. Read aloud the resulting book, pausing after each set of clues for youngsters to guess the animal before you reveal the illustration.

Judy Dorsey, Lorraine Elementary, Stockbridge, GA

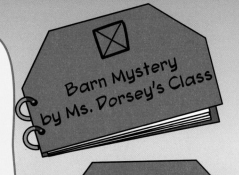

Barn Building
High-frequency words

Put a fun spin on reviewing words! To prepare this small-group activity, gather a supply of high-frequency word cards. Draw a barn and a haystack on the board. Draw four blanks for the word *barn* as shown. Color a tagboard copy of the spinner pattern on page 293 and attach a paper clip to it with a brad.

To begin, hold up a word card and ask a student to read it. After she correctly identifies the word, invite her to spin the spinner. Then write the corresponding letter in the appropriate blank (if the letter is already on the barn, randomly write it on the haystack). Have students take turns reading and spinning as described until the word *barn* is formed. No doubt students will be eager to play again and see how quickly they can "build" the barn!

Math in the Cornfield
Spatial reasoning

A scarecrow takes shape at this pattern block center. Place crayons, copies of the workmat on page 294, recording sheets similar to the one shown, and a supply of pattern blocks at a center.

A child places pattern blocks on a workmat as indicated. Then she removes the blocks one at a time and colors the shapes to match the blocks. When she finishes coloring the workmat, she sorts the blocks she used and completes a recording sheet. **For more advanced students,** make one copy of page 294 and white-out the inner lines. Then make copies. Have each student fill in the outline with pattern blocks as desired.

Jennie Jensen, Bennett Elementary, Bennett, IA

290

©The Mailbox

©The Mailbox

©The Mailbox

Busy Barnyard

Listen and do.

©The Mailbox® • TEC42027 • Oct./Nov. 2006

Note to the teacher: Use with "Everything in Its Place" on page 289.

Animal Cards
Use with "Everything in Its Place" on page 289.

TEC42027

Envelope Label
Use with "Critter Clues" on page 290.

Animal Clues

I am _____.

I have _____ legs.

I say, "_____."

What am I?

Silly Scarecrow

Follow your teacher's directions.

Note to the teacher: Use with "Math in the Cornfield" on page 290.

Marvelous Mittens

Warm up students' math and literacy skills with this cozy collection of seasonal ideas.

ideas contributed by Ada Goren
Winston-Salem, NC

Handy Poll
Graphing

Are your students smitten with mittens, or do they love gloves? To find out, post the two sentences shown. Make two hand tracings, one with your fingers apart to resemble a glove and one with your fingers together to resemble a mitten. Cut out each tracing and display it to the left of the corresponding sentence.

Prompt a class discussion about how mittens and gloves are alike and how they are different. Then ask each student to write her name on a sticky note. Instruct her to post it beside the sentence she agrees with more to create a graph as shown. After the graph is complete, help youngsters compare the number of names in the two rows, using words such as *more, fewer,* and *equal.* **For more advanced students,** have each student write two sentences about the graph.

Mittens are marvelous. — Tasha, Mark, Kayla, Owen, D.J.

Gloves are great. — Nigel, Rosine, Luis, Suna

It is very cold today.

On the Line
Literacy

For this easy-to-adapt center, choose an option below. Prepare a supply of mittens (pattern on page 297) as described. String a clothesline in your classroom within student reach. Place the mittens and a supply of clothespins nearby.

Onsets and Rimes: Make several mittens. Program half of them with a chosen rime. On each remaining mitten, write an onset that can be used to form a word with the rime. A student clips each onset and rime to the clothesline to form a word. Then he reads the entire mitten lineup.

Word Order: Write each word in a chosen sentence on a separate identical mitten (include the end mark with the last word). Prepare mittens for additional sentences in a similar manner, using a different color for each sentence. Place each set of mittens in a separate resealable bag. A student arranges a set of mittens on the clothesline to form a sentence and then reads the sentence.

Pair by Pair
Counting by twos

Here's a visual way to increase students' number sense. To prepare, draw on the board a large number line from 1 to 10 and circle the even numbers. Make five different colors of pairs of mittens (pattern on page 297). Then post the mittens above the number line in pairs, placing each mitten above a different number.

To begin, have students study the number line and describe the mitten and number patterns. Suggest that the patterns can help students count quickly. Then lead students in counting the mittens by twos. After sufficient skip-counting practice, divide students into small groups and give each group a handful of manipulatives. Ask each group to randomly pair its manipulatives, arrange the pairs in a row, and then count the manipulatives by twos.

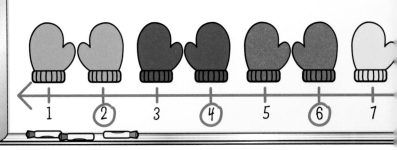

One-of-a-Kind Mittens
Describing words

This display idea pairs creativity and language skills. Have each student make two construction paper mittens (pattern on page 297). Invite her to decorate her mittens with arts-and-crafts materials, such as crayons, cotton, glitter glue, and rickrack. After she is satisfied with her creations, have her tape one end of a length of yarn to the back of each cuff. Next, ask her to complete a copy of the mitten poem on page 297 with words that describe her mittens. Instruct her to sign her name and glue the completed poem to a larger piece of colorful paper. To showcase students' work, display the mittens with the corresponding descriptions on a board titled "Warm, Woolly, Wonderful Mittens!"

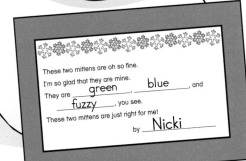

These two mittens are oh so fine.
I'm so glad that they are mine.
They are ___green___, ___blue___, and
___fuzzy___, you see.
These two mittens are just right for me!
by ___Nicki___

Cool Comparison
Literature

Give a Venn diagram a wintry twist! Make two poster-size mittens and then glue a large snowball between them as shown. Label each mitten with a different version of the traditional story *The Mitten*. Title the snowball "Both." Then display the resulting poster. After sharing the two versions of the story with students, guide them to compare and contrast the books. Write features unique to each book on the corresponding mittens and write features they have in common on the snowball. Then ask students to tell which book they prefer and why.

Jan Brett's Book

Alvin Tresselt's Book

Both

Mire Kabashi, P. S. 88, Ridgewood, NY

Mitten Pattern
Use with "On the Line" on page 295 and "Pair by
Pair" and "One-of-a-Kind Mittens" on page 296.

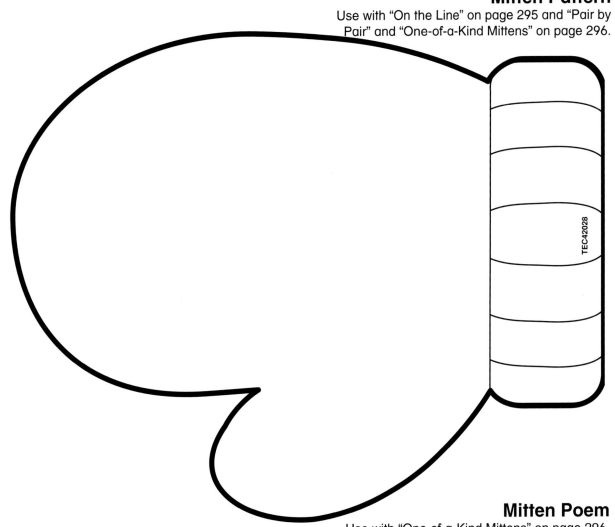

TEC42028

Mitten Poem
Use with "One-of-a-Kind Mittens" on page 296.

These two mittens are oh so fine.

I'm so glad that they are mine.

They are _____, _____, and

_____, you see.

These two mittens are just right for me!

by _____

TEC42028

At the End of the Rainbow

What's at the rainbow's end? It's a colorful collection of ideas with golden opportunities to reinforce science, math, and literacy skills.

Wonder and Learn
Graphic organizer

Spark students' curiosity with this eye-catching version of a KWL chart. On a length of white bulletin board paper, draw a rainbow extending from a cloud to a pot of gold. Title the three parts of the illustration as shown and then display the resulting poster. To begin, invite youngsters to tell what they know about rainbows. Note the information on the cloud. Next, guide students to ask questions about the topic. Write the questions on or around the rainbow. Over a few days, share relevant nonfiction books, such as *All the Colors of the Rainbow* by Allan Fowler. Then prompt students to recall what they have learned and complete the poster with the information.

adapted from an idea by Andrea Singleton
Waynesville Elementary, Waynesville, OH

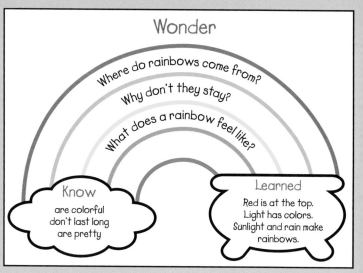

Wonder

Where do rainbows come from?
Why don't they stay?
What does a rainbow feel like?

Know
are colorful
don't last long
are pretty

Learned
Red is at the top.
Light has colors.
Sunlight and rain make rainbows.

Look!
Science

Your students are sure to be surprised to learn that a CD contains a rainbow! Gather an old CD and a flashlight. Give each student a sheet of paper and have her draw a line down the center of it. Next, remind students that scientists are careful observers. Show them the CD and ask each youngster to draw and describe it on the first half of her paper. After each student completes her work, dim the lights and shine the flashlight on the CD at an angle so that rainbow colors appear on a wall. Invite students to describe what they see. Then turn the lights on and have each student record her observations on the second half of her paper. Afterward, tell students that light is made of different colors. Explain that the CD helps make the colors visible much like rain sometimes makes the colors in sunlight visible.

Emile Blake, Sherrills Ford Elementary, Sherrills Ford, NC

In the Clouds
Phonics

What words have the long *a* sound as in *rain* and *rainbow?* That's the question students explore with this pocket chart activity. To prepare, illustrate and label a strip of paper to make a heading similar to the one shown. (If appropriate for your students, label the second cloud "Short *a.*") Display the heading in the top row of a pocket chart. Color and cut out the picture cards on page 301. Back the cards with tagboard for durability. Shuffle the cards and then stack them facedown.

To complete the activity, have a volunteer take the top card and name the picture. If the word has a long *a* sound, his classmates give a thumbs-up. If it does not have a long *a* sound, they give a thumbs-down. The volunteer places the card below the correct cloud. Students sort the remaining cards in the same manner and then name the pictures in each group. **For more advanced students,** have youngsters match word cards to the sorted pictures and then study the vowel patterns.

Golden Coin Toss
Math or reading

For this easy-to-adapt activity, cover two cardboard circles with gold foil to make coins. To make a floor mat, divide a large piece of paper into 12 sections and color them as shown. Choose an option below and program 12 blank cards as described. Then attach a different card to each section. (Use reusable adhesive to allow for later reprogramming.) Place the mat on the floor and have students take turns as described below.

Addition: Program the cards with various numbers, writing one number per card. To play, a youngster tosses both coins onto the mat. She reads the numbers in the sections where the coins landed and then announces their sum.

High-frequency words: Write a different word on each card. To play, a youngster tosses a coin onto the mat. She spells the corresponding word and then the group names it.

Andrea Singleton, Waynesville Elementary
Waynesville, OH

Teamwork Brightens the Day!

Stacy Wingen, Howard Elementary, Howard, SD

Lots of Links
Math

Teamwork and estimating go hand-in-hand with this display idea. Cut a supply of 1" x 9" construction paper strips in the colors shown to represent a rainbow. Divide students into six groups. Give each group strips in one of the colors and clear tape. Have the students in each group use the supplies to begin making a paper chain.

After each group makes a fairly long chain, have one group stand and hold its chain outstretched. Invite students to estimate how many links long the chain is. Then lead students in counting the links by twos to determine the actual number. Have students estimate and determine the lengths of the rest of the chains in the same manner. Then, depending on the desired size of the display, ask students to add more links to their chains. Arrange the completed chains on a large bulletin board to resemble a rainbow. Complete the display with a title, sun, and pot of gold.

Orderly Colors
Writing sentences

This booklet project not only gives students practice writing sentences but also reminds them of the order of the colors in a rainbow. For each student, stack three sheets of white paper and position them vertically. Slide the top two sheets upward about one inch and then slide the top sheet up one more inch. Fold the papers forward to create six graduated pages. Staple along the fold.

Beginning with red and the top page of his booklet, each youngster colors the bottom edges of his pages, as shown, to represent the colors in a rainbow. He uses the format shown to write a sentence on each page. Then he illustrates his work.

adapted from an idea by Andrea Singleton
Waynesville, Elementary, Waynesville, OH

Red is an apple.

Follow the Rainbow!
Writing prompt

Here's a ready-to-use prompt that's perfect for a March display. Give each student a copy of page 302. Have her sign her name and write a response to the prompt. After she colors the rainbow, ask her to cut along the bold lines and glue her work on a sheet of blue paper. Showcase students' completed work on a board or hallway wall as desired.

TEC42029

TEC42029

TEC42029

TEC42029

TEC42029

TEC42029

TEC42029

TEC42029

TEC42029

TEC42029

TEC42029

TEC42029

Rainbow Pattern

Use with "Follow the Rainbow!" on page 300.

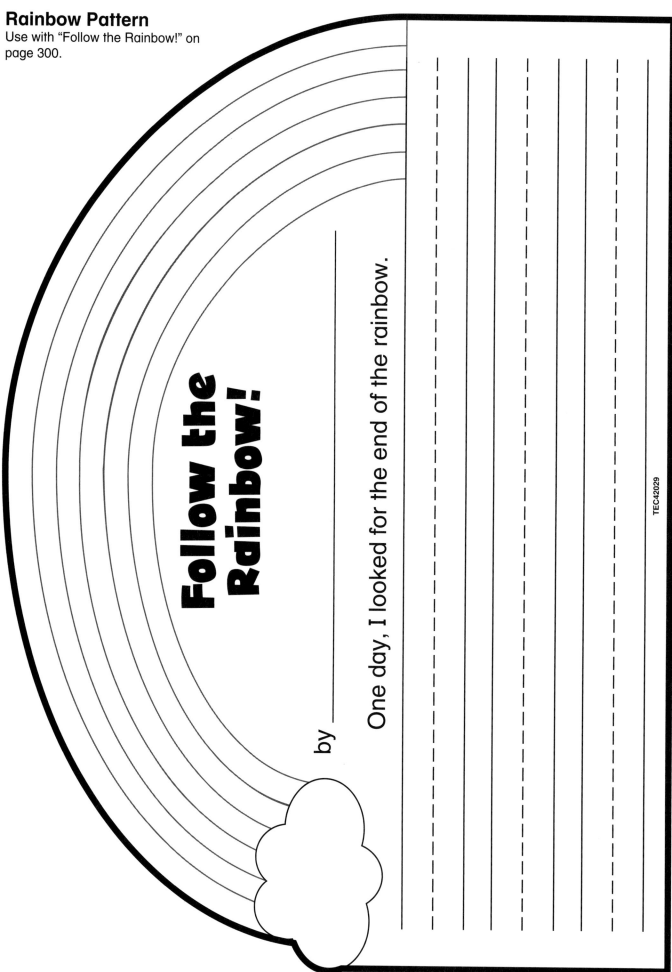

Follow the Rainbow!

by _____

One day, I looked for the end of the rainbow.

TEC42029

Butterflies!

These colorful ideas are just what you need to brighten literacy, science, and math skills!

ideas by Laurie K. Gibbons
Huntsville, AL

Wonderful Words

Phonological awareness, vocabulary

What's handy about this introduction to butterflies? It doubles as a syllable segmenting activity! Write on the board one of the word pairs shown, writing one word below the other. Read aloud the two words. Then have students clap once for each syllable as they repeat the words. Say and clap the words again to help youngsters determine how many syllables are in each word. Next, guide students to compare how long the words sound and look. After you share the relevant information shown, erase the board and present a different word pair in the same manner. **For more advanced students,** later post the words and a large butterfly to create an eye-catching word bank.

Butterfly Words

eggs: A female butterfly lays eggs.
caterpillar: A caterpillar hatches from an egg.

legs: A butterfly has six legs.
insects: Butterflies are insects.

antennae: A butterfly has two feelers.
wings: Most butterflies have colorful wings.

fly: Unlike moths, most butterflies fly during the day.
flowers: Most butterflies eat nectar from flowers.

Beautiful Book

Describing words

Butterflies are certainly pretty, but what other adjectives can be used to tell about them? Invite students to use a variety of describing words with this class book. In advance, make a class supply of large white butterfly-shaped pages and the prompt shown.

To begin, help students brainstorm a list of words that describe butterflies. Next, give each child a page and have him create a butterfly illustration on the upper portion of it. Help him complete a prompt to tell about his butterfly and then glue it below his artwork. Bind students' completed pages behind a colorful butterfly shape; then glue a butterfly body and two antennae to the front cover. Title the book and decorate the front cover as desired.

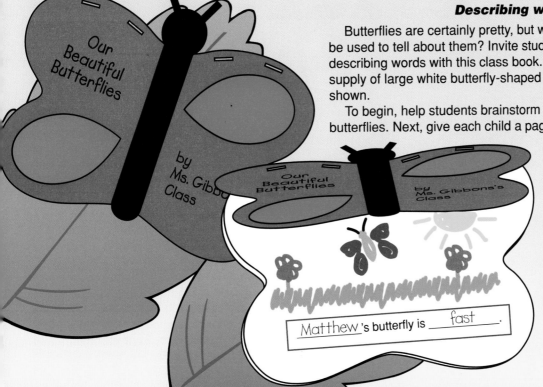

Our Beautiful Butterflies
by Ms. Gibbons's Class

Matthew's butterfly is ___fast___.

303

Begin With an Egg!

Life cycle

The wings on this cute project show the transformation from an egg to a butterfly. For each student, trace the butterfly wing pattern on page 306 on a folded piece of construction paper and then cut out the tracing. Each child also needs four white circles, one black butterfly body, black paper scraps, and a set of life cycle labels (patterns and labels on page 306). To begin, read aloud *Waiting for Wings* by Lois Ehlert or *The Very Hungry Caterpillar* by Eric Carle. Discuss the butterfly life cycle with students. Then use the steps below to help each child make a creative reminder of the four stages.

Steps:

1. Glue the body to the butterfly wings as shown.
2. Cut out the labels. Glue each label at the top of a different circle.
3. Illustrate each circle.
4. Glue the circles on the butterfly's wings in order clockwise, beginning at the top left wing. Draw arrows as shown.
5. Cut two antennae from black paper and then glue them to the butterfly.

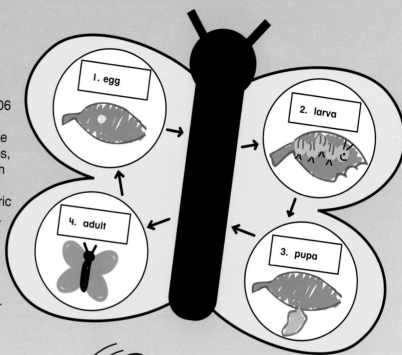

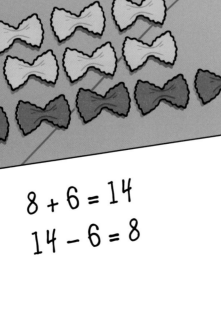

$$8 + 6 = 14$$
$$14 - 6 = 8$$

"Pasta-bilities"

Math

What better manipulatives for spring than butterfly pasta? Use food coloring to dye a supply of pasta. (Add a drop or two of rubbing alcohol to the food coloring for more vibrant colors.) Then choose from the center ideas below.

Estimating: Place a supply of pasta in a clear, unbreakable container and label the container with the number of pieces inside. Place different quantities of pasta in two other clear containers. Each student estimates the two quantities, using the labeled container as a guide. Then she writes her estimates on provided paper. After each child completes the activity, help students compare the actual quantities with their estimates.

Measuring: Students use the pasta to measure the lengths of items, such as a pencil, shoelace, and ruler.

Number sentences: Place two colors of pasta in each of several small bags. (Vary the amounts.) For each bag, a student writes a corresponding addition sentence. **For more advanced students,** have youngsters also write a related subtraction sentence.

Winged Wonders
Symmetry

Your students might be surprised to learn that there is math on the wings of a butterfly! Show students a few photo illustrations of butterflies. Point out that the designs on the wings are symmetrical. Next, give each child a white butterfly cutout. Instruct him to use a black crayon to trace the line of symmetry on his butterfly. Then invite him to color half his butterfly as desired and write his name on the back of it.

After each child completes his coloring, have him trade butterflies with a classmate. Ask him to illustrate the blank half of the butterfly he receives to create symmetrical wings. Display students' completed work on a board titled "High-Flying Symmetry" to remind youngsters that math is everywhere!

> There are two tens and five ones. That makes 25.

Bunches of Butterflies
Place value

Catching butterflies in this flower garden gives students practice counting tens and ones. To prepare this small-group activity, gather a supply of five-ounce disposable cups. Put a different amount of butterfly pasta (10–50 pieces) in each of several resealable plastic bags. Give each student in the group a bag of pasta (butterflies) and a copy of the workmat on page 307.

Next, each child places one butterfly on each flower on her workmat. Then she puts the ten butterflies in a cup (net) and places the cup in the box at the top of her mat. She continues with her remaining butterflies in the same manner until she cannot make another set of ten. Then she tells you how many tens and ones are represented on her mat and how many butterflies there are in all.

Butterflies	Both	Moths
usually fly during the day	are insects	usually fly at night
are usually colorful	have wings	are not usually colorful
are usually bigger than moths	have six legs	are usually smaller than butterflies

Same but Different
Graphic organizer

Use this adorable version of a Venn diagram to help students compare moths and butterflies or two different butterfly books. Draw a large butterfly similar to the one shown. Title each wing with a chosen topic and label the body "Both." As students brainstorm relevant details, write the information in the appropriate sections. It will be easy for youngsters to see how the topics are alike and different!

Butterfly Patterns and Labels
Use with "Begin With an Egg!" on page 304.

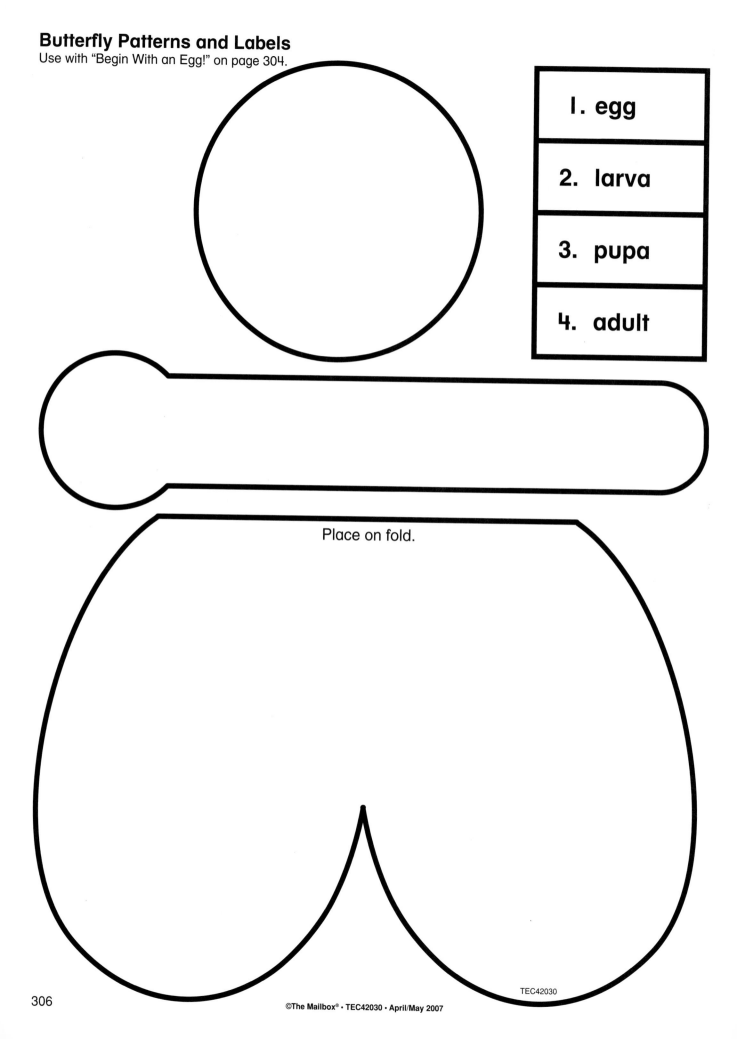

| 1. egg |
| 2. larva |
| 3. pupa |
| 4. adult |

Place on fold.

TEC42030

Name _____

Catching Butterflies

Note to the teacher: Use with "Bunches of Butterflies" on page 305.

New at the Zoo

This menagerie of ideas is packed with literacy, math, and science fun!

ideas by Laurie K. Gibbons
Huntsville, AL

Tiger
black   long tail
orange   runs
stripes   growls

Look!
Characteristics of animals

An imaginary trip to the zoo is just the ticket for prompting students' prior knowledge. To begin, read aloud *Going to the Zoo* by Tom Paxton or another grade-appropriate zoo book. Then invite students to stand and imagine that they are at a zoo. Instruct them to walk in place as you "lead" them to an exhibit. When you arrive at the exhibit, announce a type of animal and write its name on a sheet of chart paper. Next, encourage youngsters to close their eyes and visualize the animal. Guide students to tell about the animal's appearance and behavior and then have them open their eyes. "Visit" several different animal exhibits with students in the same manner.

For more advanced students, list the observations about each animal on a separate poster-size paper and have students illustrate the posters. The posters will be great discussion starters or writing references!

one lion   two lions

One or Two?
Plural nouns

Students see double with this booklet! For each student, stack four sheets of white paper on one sheet of gray paper. Place a gray copy of page 310 on the stack. Staple the stack along both sides of the cover. Cut along the outline through all thicknesses. Then carefully cut along the line in the center of the front cover, cutting through the white pages as well. (Leave the back cover intact.)

To begin, post a list of four or more zoo animals whose names are simple nouns. (Or use the picture cards on page 311 to make an illustrated list and give each child a copy.) Next, have each youngster open his booklet to the first set of pages. On the left-hand page, instruct him to write "one" and the name of a listed animal. On the right-hand page, ask him to write "two" and the plural form of the animal's name. Then invite him to illustrate his work. Have him complete the remaining pages in the same manner.

Fill the Zoo!
Literacy or math

This small-group game is so easy to adapt, you'll use it again and again! Program a supply of blank cards to reinforce a chosen skill, such as letter knowledge, contractions, or telling time. Gather a small group of students and stack the skill cards facedown. Have each student color and cut out a copy of the game mat and animal cards on page 311. Then put all of the animal cards in an open box.

To take a turn, a student takes the top skill card and responds as appropriate. (Provide help as needed.) Then she takes an animal card at random and puts it on the corresponding section of her game mat. (If that section already has two animals, she returns the card.) The players take turns as time allows or until one player has two animals in each section of her game mat. Then the players compare how many animals they have in their zoos.

Animal Antics
Story problems

To prepare for this math activity, enlarge the animal cards on page 311 for pocket chart use. Color and cut out a few copies of the enlarged cards. Then set the cards near a pocket chart. Give each child an individual whiteboard and writing supplies. To begin, tell an animal-related addition or subtraction story. As you repeat the story, have a volunteer use the cards to model the problem in the pocket chart. Then instruct each of the other students to write the corresponding number sentence on his whiteboard and hold it up for you to see. After you confirm the correct response, clear the pocket chart to prepare for another problem.

Zookeeper, zookeeper, it's time for us to guess. Tell us if we're right—no or yes!

Safari Sort
Animal similarities and differences

Here's an intriguing way to stretch students' thinking. Collect a supply of small plastic zoo animals. Sit with students in a circle and place several animals in the center of the circle. Designate a student as the zookeeper and have her sort the animals by a secretly chosen characteristic, such as color, number of legs, or type of covering. Then lead the group in saying the chant shown. After students identify how the animals are sorted, invite a different youngster to be the zookeeper for the next round.

Booklet Cover

Use with "One or Two?" on page 308.

2

at the Zoo

One or Two

1

Animal Cards

Use with "One or Two?" on page 308 and "Fill the Zoo!" and "Animal Antics" on page 309.

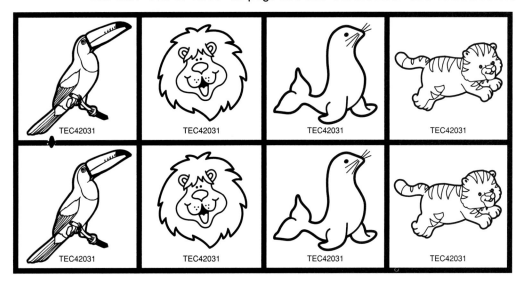

Zoo Game Mat

Use with "Fill the Zoo!" on page 309.

Bird Hut

Lion Lookout

Seal Pool

Tiger House

©The Mailbox® • TEC42031 • June/July 2007

The Zoo Crew

Circle the correct words.

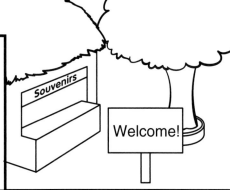

 bear bears	 lion lions	
 seal seals	hippo hippos	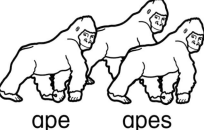 ape apes
snake snakes	zebra zebras	tiger tigers

Look at the words above.

 Write each circled word on the correct list.

One	**More Than One**
_____	_____
_____	_____
_____	_____
_____	_____

INDEX